Labour and the Money Power

Labour and the Money Power

Australian Labour Populism 1890–1950

Peter Love

MELBOURNE UNIVERSITY PRESS
1984

First published 1984
Printed in Australia by
The Dominion Press-Hedges & Bell, Victoria, Australia, for
Melbourne University Press, Carlton, Victoria 3053
U.S.A. and Canada: International Scholarly Book Services, Inc.,
P.O. Box 1632, Beaverton, OR 97075
United Kingdom, Europe, Middle East, Africa:
HB Sales
Enterprise House, Ashford Road, Ashford, Middlesex,
England TW15 1XB

National Library of Australia Cataloguing-in-Publication entry

Love, Peter, 1946–
Labour and the money power.
Bibliography,
Includes index.
ISBN 0 522 84266 6.

1. Populism—Australia—History. 2. Labor and labouring classes—Australia—History. I. Title.

335′.00994

To Sue

For many expressions of a generous spirit

Contents

Illustrations

Acknowledgements

This book is a revised version of a master's thesis submitted to La Trobe University in 1980. In preparing it I incurred many debts. Staff members of the La Trobe, National and Mitchell libraries provided efficient and friendly assistance beyond the call of duty. Friends in the History Department at La Trobe University offered valuable criticism and many kindnesses. In the course of the research and writing I was helped financially by a Commonwealth Scholarship and the Humanities Research Committee at La Trobe. I am grateful to all concerned for their support. My greatest debts, however, are to my wife Sue, who provided encouragement and most of the money, and to my supervisor Dr Peter Cook, whose scholarly advice and comradely criticism I value more than he supposes.

In the transition from thesis to book many others have lent a hand. Professor Robin Gollan, whose earlier work suggested some of the themes explored here, was a particularly helpful examiner. Dr Eric Fry and Mr Les Louis have offered perceptive observations of the original thesis. Drs John Merritt, Andrew Moore, Stephen Niblo and Michael Schneider read sections of the manuscript with sympathetically critical eyes. All these generous people, however, may be reassured to know that I accept full responsibility for what follows.

The illustrations are taken from the newspaper collections at the La Trobe and National libraries where Graeme Johanson and Bill Tully made photographs at ridiculously short notice. I am grateful also to George Finey for permission to reproduce one of his cartoons.

In accordance with contemporary publishing practice, I have reduced the notes and references to an absolute minimum. Fellow workers in the field of labour history who wish to pursue any matters raised here are invited to consult copies of the original thesis in the Borchardt and National libraries.

I have followed another prevailing convention in the matter of spelling. 'Labor' refers to the party and its formal institutions;

'labour' is used to signify the wider movement. Although this has involved some anachronistic usage, I have preferred that convention in the interests of clarity.

Finally, this book is not intended as the last word on Australian labour populism. It will have served its purpose if it finds a place in the continuing debate about the labour movement's ideological heritage.

Peter Love
Yan Yean 1984

Introduction: 'Socialism is Being Mates' – The Populist Vision

The Australian Labor Party developed a theory of capitalist finance called the Money Power. This book traces the changing complexion of that theory from the bank crashes in 1893 through two world wars and the great depression to its culmination in the bank nationalization campaign of 1947–49. In doing that, it offers an explanation of the way that significant sections of the labour movement formed a particular view of capitalism and the means of transforming it into a people's democracy. It shows how existing ideas about nationalism and imperialism, monopoly and democracy, class and race, were woven into an elaborate conspiracy theory, which served to focus and mobilize the discontent of a 'generation that copped the lot' in a succession of major crises. The study concludes with an analysis of how the theory of capitalism that grew out of that process not only reflected the dilemmas confronting a social democratic party, but also contributed directly to Labor's defeat in 1931 and 1949 by reinforcing misleading assumptions about economic and political power in Australia. The main purpose of all this is to develop a model of Australian Labor populism, and so add another dimension to our understanding of the party's ideological heritage.

The most obvious point from which to begin such a study is to explain what the term 'populism' means. That, however, is no simple task. It has been applied to a bewildering array of parties, movements, ideologies and individuals. These have included the American Populist Party, the Russian *narodnichestvo*, Peronism in Argentina, independence movements in Africa and even Maoism in China. It has also been argued that there were strong populist influences in Italian Fascism and German Nazism.

The term 'populism' did not emerge from an attempt to unite these diverse historical phenomena under a generic label. It was first applied, independently, to the movements that arose simultaneously in Russia and the United States towards the end of the nineteenth century. Although profoundly different in many ways, they nevertheless displayed some tantalizing but elusive similarities that have continued to haunt the study of populist movements. To this day there is still debate about what English meaning should be attached to the word *narodnichestvo*.

'Populism' gradually acquired a wider currency in historical analysis, most notably in Latin American studies. This did not simplify the problems of definition: it compounded them. It was apparent that the meaning attached to the term depended upon the movement being examined and the perspective of the person studying it. Richard Hofstadter, for example, wrote about American populism as a troubled liberal in the midst of the Cold War. He detected an ambivalence in his country's populist tradition: 'The impulses behind yesterday's reform may be put in the service of reform today, but they may also be enlisted in the service of reaction'. His account was coloured by the triumph of that reactionary tendency in the early 1950s. Franco Venturi, on the other hand, traced the roots of revolution to the populist and socialist movements in nineteenth-century Russia. Gino Germani's comparative study of authoritarianism, fascism and national populism was also inspired by personal experience. After growing up under Italian Fascism he went as a political refugee to Argentina, where he encountered Peronism.[1] These and many similar studies have enlarged our understanding of the respective traditions. Some, such as Germani, have opened wider theoretical horizons, which can be applied more generally; but most have focused their attention on one particular cultural tradition and have built their model of populism in the terms of that culture. The difficulty with this is that populism can be variously interpreted as a movement leading to capitalist reaction, revolutionary communism or fascist authoritarianism. Thus, any attempt to define populist movements in terms of the results they may produce is likely to fail.

In 1967 a group of scholars met at the London School of Economics to try to distil some essence from the rather muddy waters of populist studies. They began by looking at specific movements in North America, Latin America, Russia, Eastern Europe and Africa. They then tried to extract some common patterns of meaning from those individual cases in an attempt to define the notoriously vague term. Examining populism as an ideology, Donald MacRae suggested that its most typical feature was an implied theory of personality based on a kind of 'romantic primitivism'. The underlying purpose of that theory was 'to console men in their real discontents and act as a charter for undefined but grandiose projects'. Peter Wiles regarded it as a political syndrome, not a doctrine: 'To me, populism is any creed or movement based on the following major premiss: virtue resides in the simple people, who are the overwhelming majority, and in their collective traditions'. Angus Stewart thought that an examination of its social roots would be a more profitable line of enquiry. He claimed that 'Populism emerges as a response to the problems posed by modernization and its consequences. These problems are most importantly those of economic development and of political authority'. Kenneth Minogue considered it, as a political movement, to be a reaction to 'an awareness of being on the periphery' of economic power. In conclusion, Peter Worsley tried to put these different perspectives together as a general concept. He argued that populism was best understood in terms of a 'twofold ideal-type' whose most logical and consistent forms were the 'celebration of the will of the people and experiment with forms of direct contact between people and leadership'.[2] Although this was a very useful exercise in describing some of the more common elements in the political and ideological forms that the various populist movements have taken, it did not finally succeed in uniting those elements into a comprehensive definition. Like many other general concepts employed in social analysis, it remains the subject of debate.

In recent years there have been some interesting developments in that debate. Gino Germani has suggested that populist movements should be seen as part of a wider process of social mobilization. He defines mobilization as a cycle where the pattern of social relations changes rapidly, displacing various sectors from their accustomed position. This tends to change the way they see their role as a group and encourages them to behave differently towards themselves and others. The cycle concludes when some new pattern of social relations emerges and the displaced groups are integrated into the revised structure. Germani sees populist movements as a 'moment' within this process. They represent a transitory stage of social mobilization.[3]

Ernesto Laclau argues that they are best understood in terms of ideological conflict set against the wider background of a struggle between classes for a leading position within society as a whole. Populism begins at the point when popular, democratic ideas present a direct challenge to a dominant ideology that has previously constrained or neutralized their influence. Victory in that struggle depends upon how successfully the contending social forces are able to incorporate 'the people' into their ideology as the basis for a sustained mass mobilization. In this process populist ideology appears not as an independent body of social theory, but as an expression of the contradictions within another ideological discourse. Thus movements of very different social character, such as Fascism, Maoism or Peronism, may experience populist 'moments' in the course of their struggle for supremacy. According to Laclau, however, the highest and most enduring form of populism must be socialism, since that is the only system capable of transforming antagonistic classes into 'the people'.[4]

Despite their very different theoretical perspectives, these analyses suggest a common, more general proposition, which provides a starting point for this study. Populist movements are not independent phenomena. They occur as part of wider social processes from which they derive their meaning. The labour movement's populist inclinations will be defined within a process of mobilization and ideological contradiction, but those terms acquire different shades of meaning when applied in the Australian context. Accordingly, the work of Germani and Laclau has been suggestive rather than prescriptive.

To understand the emergence of populist ideas in the labour movement towards the end of the nineteenth century, it will be helpful to look briefly at some of the more consistent elements in the ideology of the two contemporary movements in Russia and the United States. This will serve two purposes. It will provide us with a rough working model of populist ideology to begin our study, and in the American case, it will describe some of the ideas that were introduced directly into the labour movement during a critical period of class mobilization in Australia.

Richard Hofstadter has identified the origins of the Populist Party as an episode in 'the well-established tradition of American entrepreneurial radicalism, which goes back at least to the Jacksonian era'. The agrarian myth carried by that tradition was revived and embellished in the face of new commercial realities. American populism arose from the discrepancy between an idealized conception of the yeoman farmer and the encroachment of advanced capitalist forms in agricultural production and marketing. These were part of international developments in which huge tracts of land in Argentina, Australia, Canada and the American west were opened up during the latter half of the nineteenth century, and this occurred in conjunction with improvements in transportation and agricultural technology. One effect of this was to integrate agriculture into an international market, thus making farmers increasingly dependent upon exports. The almost uninterrupted decline in world prices for rural commodities between the early 1870s and 1890s provided conditions that were conducive to the mobilization of rural discontent. However, the farmers who formed the basis of the Populist Party did not see it in those terms. They identified their troubles with the immediate effects of what wider process, and drew different conclusions about the causes of those difficulties. Their specific grievances centred around 'the appreciation of debts through deflation, the high cost of credit, inequitable tax burdens, discriminatory railroad rates, unreasonable elevator and storage charges'. Drawing upon their agrarian mythology, the Populists developed an ideology to explain all this in terms of an underlying 'corruption' that threatened the very foundations of American democracy.[5]

Unlike the American Populists, the Russian *narodniki* were not a grass-roots movement. They were a loose coalition of vaguely socialist intellectuals whose ideological tradition was founded in the writings of Saint-Simon and Fourier, Proudhon and Herzen. Their movement was born out of the ferment that followed the death of Tsar Nicholas I and the humiliating defeat of the Crimean War. They expressed an abhorrence of the 'moral and political monstrosity' at the heart of their country's social structure, and dedicated their lives to its destruction. In common with the Americans, they developed an ideology to explain the 'corruption' that oppressed 'the people' and constructed a mythology around the Russian peasantry as its antithesis. Unlike the Americans, they attempted to mobilize 'the people' from above, to help the peasantry understand and shape its destiny on the basis of its own institutions and traditions.[6]

In the most general sense, both movements represent a kind of mobilization in response to a wider social crisis. Their point of closest similarity can be found in the logic they employed to explain the social processes that were the source of their discontent.

Most populist ideology tends to construct a view of the world in which familiar practices and institutions have an intrinsic virtue. It is a world inhabited by common people, who in their everyday lives feel secure in the knowledge of how it works and of their place within it. When that accustomed pattern of relationships is threatened or distrubed by unfamiliar circumstances, the typical populist response is to greet the changes with suspicion or hostility and to identify them with something alien.

This does not necessarily mean 'alien' in the strictly nationalist sense. To the Russian populists, the institutions of the Tsarist régime were just as alien to the spirit of the people as were the horrors of Western capitalism. They understood well the oppressive despotism of the Tsarist régime, with its isolated opulence, decadent cleverness and scheming factions. Although not as explicitly chauvinist as the Slavophiles, they saw the régime as a symptom of an imported malaise that had no place in the Russia they envisaged. Equally horrific to them were the 'dark Satanic

Mills' of the industrial revolution in Western Europe. Taking the peasant *mir* as both a symbol and an organizational starting-point, writers like Chernyshevsky argued that Russia could bypass the capitalist stage of development with all its attendant evils. Their socialist vision was one in which village communes, craft co-operatives and producers' associations would form the nucleus of a new society. To bring this about they had to resist the penetration of Western capitalism as well as throw off the yoke of Tsarist oppression; these evils worked hand in hand, through the centralization of economic and political power in small cliques, to thwart the destiny of the people's will.

The belief that isolated élites within their own country were somehow in league with, or had been duped by, foreign influences was particularly strong among the American populists. For them the villains were the monopolistic trusts, the railway and grain companies, Eastern politicians, New York bankers and, most insidious of all, foreign Jewish financiers. In the folklore of American populism it was this last group who were responsible for the most cunning plots to dispossess the people. 'Coin' Harvey's conspiracy theory, which explained the demonetization of silver as the 'crime of 1873', was an example of this.[7]

The tendency to see their troubles as the result of a conscious conspiracy on the part of wicked men is an issue of the most fundamental importance in the logic of populist ideology. It served both to simplify and obscure the causes of discontent. It was much easier for unsophisticated rural people to understand the actions of men than it was to see how a complex social system operated. If it could be established that the system was manipulated by cunning men, its effects could be understood in terms of deliberate human action. For farmers who knew more about evil than social process this provided an intelligible explanation as well as a focus for their resentment. Conspiracy theories were a logical extension of the basic proposition that there was virtue in the familiar, and peril—if not evil—in the unknown. This tended to produce a hierarchy of moral turpitude in which a villain who was known to his victims was likely to be accused of avarice or duplicity, while the more distant and anonymous conspirators were those who hatched the most audacious plots to enslave the people

There was a corollary to all this in the tendency of populist ideology to develop existing myths about the virtues and strength of traditional culture. These myths were often buttressed by the construction of romantic visions of an innocent and harmonious golden age in the past. This was presented as the direct antithesis of a troubled present and an uncertain future. In that process great emphasis was placed on the surviving remnants of traditional culture. For the Russian populists the peasant commune and the *mir* were powerful symbols of the enduring qualities in their indigenous heritage, while the Americans clung to myths about the sturdy independence and honest simplicity of the yeoman farmer. Those myths equated the collective traditions of the common people with the highest forms of social virtue. The peole were both a democratic majority and a moral force. Their identity, so defined, gave meaning and legitimacy to the concept of 'the nation'. This argument reached its logical conclusion in the proposition that the people were the nation.

Populists often preferred to present such arguments in the form of utopian novels, such as Chernyshevsky's *What is to be done?* and Bellamy's *Looking Backward.* These and many similar works shared a millenarian attitude to social change. They conveyed 'a profound and total rejection of the present, evil world, and a passionate longing for another and better one'. The literary convention most commonly used to express this was the projection of the story into a future utopian civilization. There, by the peaceful triumph of sweet reason or from the ruins of some cataclysmic event, the human condition was transformed. In a secular equivalent to the religious cycle of sin, death and resurrection, social reorganization had been accompanied by moral regeneration. An earthly paradise was established in the populist utopia, where a natural, harmonious and just social order enshrined the perfectibility of human nature. Some writers, however, placed less emphasis on the utopia and more on the apocalypse that might precede it. Ignatius Donnelly's *Ceasar's Column* dwelt upon the tendency to barbarism inherent in the existing social system. His lurid tale describes how a brutalized American populace has been driven to revolt against the dictatorship of a ruthless plutocracy. The story reaches its climax when a huge column of corpses resulting from the carnage is encased in cement as a bizarre monument to the uprising. At the very end of the novel a few gentle, decent souls escape by airship to found a Chrsitian socialist state in Uganda.[8]

Underlying these novels, and most other forms of populist ideology, was the proposition that social conflict could be reduced to a struggle between the people and the predators, the nation and conspiratorial cliques. Again, a number of implications followed from that basic proposition. If the troubles that beset the people were the work of malicious conspirators, it was clear that there was nothing inherently wrong with their community and its collective traditions. Their society, the 'real' nation, would prosper in peace and harmony if it could be freed from the alien corruption. The people were not responsible for their difficulties. They were innocent victims. This not only sharpened their sense of grievance against the predators but also diminished self-recrimination. Accordingly, the divisions between farmers, workers, craftsmen and small businessmen were blurred so that all were part of the people. In their unity as the only real nation they could then combine to build a new social order where humanity might be transformed to a higher level of existence.

The other nation described in populist theories of the state had an elaborate demonology, which comprised oppressors and predators, their dupes and hirelings. The nobility and the officials of the Tsarist régime were living symbols of the decadence and corruption at the heart of that system. The Americans saw their economy dominated by commercial monopolies and industrial trusts. These, in turn, were the mere playthings of the Money Power, which controlled the life-blood of industry through financial institutions. As a class, these capitalists were often ranked in ascending order of wealth, power and moral turpitude. Although they struggled with each other in ruthless competition for increasingly centralized economic power, in one way or another, all robbed the people of their land, their labour and their destiny. Politicians who were not crusaders for the people's cause were part of this. Sent off to distant capitals, they betrayed the people's trust by succumbing to bribery and the seductions of office. Infected by the same alien corruption, hireling professors, clever lawyers and even unsuspecting immigrants all became enemies of the people out of greed, malice or duplicity.

One of the enduring symbols in this populist demonology was the 'Shylock' stereotype of the sinister Jew who would stoop to any means in pursuit of wealth and power. Arising from the suspicion and prejudice built up over many centuries in Christian tradition, it appealed to the deeply racist assumption that commercial acumen and devious ways were inbred throughout successive generations. When the logic of populist analysis traced the ultimate source of the people's distress to a conspiracy of international financiers, the symbol of the Jewish banker was often invoked, not only for its familiarity in the popular imagination but also because it located the cause in deliberate human action rather than a complex social process.[9]

The reductionist logic inherent in populist ideology extended to the analysis of both problem and solution. To many American populists, the direct cause of their difficulties was the demonetization of silver in 1873, which had been achieved by nefarious means by a conspiratorial clique of foreign bankers. The solution was equally simple. Since gold was the basis of currency and its scarcity the root of the problem, it was clear that the free coinage of silver would restore a sufficient quantity of currency and so break the grip over the nation held by those who were able to manipulate gold to their advantage.[10] At a more local level, farmers could free themselves from exploitation by grain-elevator companies by setting up co-operative marketing organizations. Similarly, high interest rates could be avoided by establishing people's banks. Institutions such as these were of both practical and symbolic importance, because they not only prevented exploitation by monopoly interests but also enshrined the people's naturally co-operative instincts.

These, however, were specific solutions to particular problems. In the great issue confronting the people—sweeping aside the whole apparatus of the predatory state—something more than piecemeal solutions was required. Above all else they would need direct, resolute and incorruptible leadership. Many populist movements have found that leadership, in charismatic figures like Perón in Argentina, Vargas in Brazil, and Bryan in the United States. For a discontented populace they embodied all the strength and fighting spirit of the hero to lead them against their enemies. In such figures, the logic of populist ideology reached its penultimate stage. The burning questions were finally reduced to a titanic struggle between the people's saviour and the forces of darkness. It was a kind of class war conducted as a religious crusade, where the struggle was about good and evil, justice and iniquity, order and anarchy. All that remained was the triumph of the people's champion, whose victory would usher in the populist millennium.

The People's Party in the United States was regarded as something of a model for the emerging Labor Party in Australia. Referring to the recent formation of the People's Party, the *Hummer* of 19 October 1891 declared:

> It cannot be brushed aside as unimportant, for it isn't. It cannot be argued down, because it proposed a scheme of legislation that appeals in many of its provisions to the common sense of the most intelligent portions of the community. It cannot be denounced as a class movement for behind it stand a labourer, a farmer, an average merchant and a nationalist.

The paper considered that the Labour Electoral League's constituency in New South Wales was virtually identical. It took a similar view of their respective enemies:

> It is said that a number of New York bankers have raised several million dollars for the purpose of disrupting labour organisations

> and the Farmer's Alliance by sending political confidence men among their ranks . . . The same breed all the world over. How like to the above are the actions of the banks in Australia, and the so-called National Associations Employers' Union, etc.

For some time the paper persisted in describing the Labor parties as the United Australian People's Party. The *Hummer* and its Melbourne counterpart published glowing accounts of the success enjoyed by the People's Party. When the United Labor Party of Victoria was established there was a strong body of opinion in favour of calling it the People's Party.[11] Although this signified both knowledge and approval of the American populists in some sections of Australian labour, it was through the literature that populist ideology made its most enduring mark in this country.

During the late 1880s and the early 1890s when the Labor parties were emerging from a more general working-class mobilization, the literature of American populism was one of the major influences in shaping the way that Labor saw itself and its enemies. As Gollan has shown, Bellamy's utopia and Donnelly's apocalypse were given a wide audience through radical papers like the *Bulletin* and the Brisbane *Worker.* While the first provided a kind of catechism by which the uninitiated could be schooled in the basics of the 'socialist' millennium, the second warned of the brutal anarchy that might result from unrestrained capitalism manipulated by a ruthless plutocracy.[12]

Bellamy's socialism, by which humanity would approach the Christian ideal in social organization, inspired William Lane to editorialize in the first issue of the Brisbane *Worker* that the paper aimed,

> as all thinking workers aim, at the securing of a happier state of society, which, though not, perhaps, on the same lines, is imbued with just the same spirit as that which imbues society in Bellamy's *Looking Backward.*

In the same edition he commenced a serialization of the novel. He also founded a Bellamy Society in Brisbane. Reflecting his earlier attachment to Gronlund's *Co-operative Commonwealth,* Lane saw co-operative unionism as the model for how men of good will might come to understand socialism as he did and embrace it as the only enlightened form of social organization. He distilled this notion to the phrase 'Socialism is being mates'—but it was mateship elevated to a religion, and what is more, a religion with the millenarian quality of total transformation in both social and personal relationships.[13] He wrote in the preface to *The Workingman's Paradise:*

> To understand Socialism is to endeavour to lead a better life, to regret the vileness of our present ways, to seek ill for none, to desire truth and purity and honesty, to despise this selfish civilization and to comprehend what living might be. Understanding Socialism will not make people at once what men and women should be, but it will fill them with hatred for the unfitting surroundings that damn us all and with passionate love for the ideals that are lifting us upwards and with an earnest endeavour to be themselves somewhat as they feel Humanity is struggling to be.[14]

On a somewhat less spiritual plane, the young, radical Henry Lawson pointed his readers to what he regarded as the most appropriate instrument of social regeneration. It was 'The New Religion': 'Trades Unionism really aims at the abolition of all unions and class distinctions and when this is accomplished it will be no longer necessary for men to combine against their fellow-men'.[15]

Looking Backward became the standard reference against which the various ideas for social renewal were measured. It certainly seems to have enjoyed a wide circulation. While the Brisbane *Worker* serialized it, the *Bulletin* and the *Hummer* did a brisk trade in selling mail order copies to their readers. For more than a decade it remained prominent on the list of books sold by the various labour papers. Not only was it widely read but, as Gollan has shown, there were many indications that it met a receptive audience. An important element of its popular appeal was the direct and simple way that Bellamy put his case. As one reviewer observed, 'Not that he had anything new to tell, it was his way of telling it, and his mode of presenting it'. There were many Australians who were so taken with Bellamy's vision of utopia that they followed William Lane to Paraguay in an abortive attempt to establish a New Australia. There were others, however, who thought that Donnelly presented a more likely view of the future.[16]

The arrival of *Caesar's Column* in Australia provided a model of what might arise from the overt class struggle that had erupted during the recent maritime and shearers' strikes. In the highly charged atmosphere of the early 1890s it was not difficult to imagine that a Caesar's column might be built from the bodies of tyrants by 'those that they would throttle'. The *Hummer* of 12 March 1892 suggested that while Bellamy had given cause to dispel the fears of socialism, he had said little on how it would come about. He did not

> provide for the shock which, I think, must come before the stubborn Old Order will give place to the New. Caesar's Column shows the other side of the picture – paints in earnest, glowing language, the conditions of things now existing; the soulless worship of Mammon by the powerful minority, the ever-increasing poverty and despair of the vast majority.

The paper went on to give its own description of world affairs coloured with Donnelly's language:

> Read and reflect upon all the schemes for the regeneration of the world: the great and noble efforts being made for the realization of Bellamy's beautiful dream, and ask yourselves whether they can overtake and subdue the selfishness and greed, the ignorance and apathy which are fast drifting the world towards the horrors and despair of a 'Caesar's Column'.

Between 18 February and 5 May 1888 the Brisbane *Boomerang* had serialized an apocalyptic novel by William Lane entitled 'White or Yellow? A story of the race war of A.D. 1908'. It was clearly modelled on Donnelly's *Caesar's Column.* By 1892 the mood of the labour movement was more attuned to what Donnelly had to say than to Bellamy's utopian dream. There were dire warnings that capitalists would find Caesar a sobering prospect, while Lawson's imagination turned to a 'Leader of the Future' who looked ominously like Caesar Lomellini.[17]

In the context of a deepening depression in which industrial strife continued along with the collapse of the banking system, Donnelly's apocalypse might have seemed imminent. His vision of a small clique of plutocrats supported by a hireling army of Demons, who were locked in mortal combat with a desperate Brotherhood of Destruction that had arisen from the brutalized masses, was powerful stuff. It was replete with desperate men and ruthless conspiracy, corruption and violence, revolution and anarchy. In conditions where unionists had been gaoled, shearing sheds burnt down and troops confronting strikers ordered to 'fire low and lay them out', the prospect of a Caesar's Column did not require a great leap of the imagination. But even if it seemed unlikely then that 'blood should stain the wattle' on quite the same scale, it was not so fanciful to see how capitalists could hire men to break unions, nor that bankers might engage in conspiracies against their depositors. The long-term importance of *Caesar's*

Brisbane *Worker*, 14 July 1894
A POLITICAL CAESAR'S COLUMN.
To be erected by the people of New South Wales on July 17, 1894.

This depicts an episode at the climax of the novel where the Brotherhood of Destruction, an underground revolutionary organization drawn from the brutalized masses, rises up against the wealthy and ruthless ruling class. During the ensuing carnage Caesar Lomellini, a leader of the Brotherhood, orders that the corpses be piled up and covered with cement to form a monument to the revolution. Indulging its accustomed hyperbole in pictorial form, the *Worker* declares that the political corpses of Parkes and many others will serve no other purpose than as a monument to Labor's victory at the polls on 17 July. This allusion to Donnelly's novel reflects the paper's confidence that its readers will recognize Caesar's Column as the symbol of a triumphant mass uprising against corruption and plutocracy.

Column, however, was not so much in the accuracy of its immediate parallels to the Australian situation, but more in the way that it helped shape existing attitudes to social conflict into a particular mould. It provided a model within which the events of the early 1890s could be seen as part of a wider process; and it was significant for the interpretation of later events that the process involved conspiracies by the Money Power as a central theme.

It would be wrong, however, to over-emphasize the importance of American populist ideology, as exemplified in the work of Bellamy and Donnelly, within the broad stream of labour thinking during the 1890s. It was one of many currents, which included Fabianism and Christian socialism, labourism and syndicalism, anarchism and Henry George's single tax. Most, including the anarchists, established their organizations, published their journals and competed for the allegiance of an often overlapping membership. As the president of the Sydney Trades and Labour Council told the Royal Commission on Strikes in 1890, the workers looked to changes in social organization but were not agreed on what they should be. Later in the decade, the Sydney *Worker* of 25 December 1897 reviewed 'the issues we split on' with the wry observation:

> One great difficulty of the social, as of every other reform movement, has always been the enthusiastic conviction of the reformer that the fellow who wants reform in a different way is ever so much worse than the one who wants there to be no reform at all.[18]

These apparent theoretical divisions tended to mask a more general pattern of working-class mobilization that had been under way since the late 1880s.

Connell and Irving have sketched the broad outlines of how it happened. From the experience of earlier campaigns around wages, hours and control of the labour market, many workers developed a sense of class interest and identity beyond the narrow horizons of normal union activity. Although craft unions were still the predominant form of labour organization in cities like Melbourne and Sydney, by the 1880s a wider pattern of mobilization was taking place in working-class suburbs. There co-operative networks sprang up within a specific social geography of residence, work and recreation. A distinct working-class culture emerged from the connections between unions, local business, clubs, churches, sporting organizations, pubs and municipal politics. The ethics of collective action and solidarity that grew out of this were reinforced in the struggles occasioned by the depression and strikes of the early 1890s. This working-class milieu bred its own intellectuals, who rose to positions of leadership in the unions and went on from there to build the Labor parties.

Outside the capital cities the pattern was different. In regional towns where economic activity centred around mining, transport or pastoral work, the 'new' industrial unions provided the focus for working-class mobilization. In towns like Broken Hill, bitterly forged traditions of militancy produced a sense of solidarity that spilled over into the whole fabric of community life, and the union virtually ran the town. But it was the shearers and rural labourers who provided the basis for a wider, more integrated mobilization, which extended beyond regional and colonial boundaries. Gollan has traced the rise of their union and its role in expanding both the size and the vision of a self-consciously Australian working class. He has shown how the growing strength of industrial unionism was accompanied by a rising interest in 'socialist' ideas; how that ideology shaped labour's response to its crushing defeat at the hands of the state and mobilized capital in the great strikes of 1890–91; and how those defeats finally pushed the unions into parliamentary politics, where, in a system loaded against it, the Labor Party set about the task of what Bede Nairn has termed 'civilizing capitalism'. The party that emerged from this was, in the words of Connell and Irving, 'a product of class mobilization under hegemony', an assertion of working-class autonomy constrained within the existing framework of social relations, institutions and ideology.[19]

A radical nationalism, which constructed a distinctive Australian identity in terms of class, race and anti-imperialism, played an important role in that mobilization. The ideas took shape in art, popular music, literature and political platforms. Their influence was seen most clearly in the writings of men like Lawson and Lane, Dyson and Furphy, whose work appeared in new radical papers such as the *Hummer* and the *Worker*, the *Bulletin* and the *Boomerang*. It was a nationalism that invoked images of Australia as a virgin continent unsullied by the corruption, ignorance and persecution of Europe. True Australians had the opportunity to build a new and better society in a land with a dead past that bequeathed 'no register of good or evil endeavour to the ever-living President'. If the free and independent spirit of the common people was built upon, the nation would be populated by self-consciously proud Australians, not 'colonials' who would bend the knee to all things British. Patriotism and democracy were allies in the struggle against colonial wealth with its English connections. In this way an Australian ruling class was identified as much by its attachment to Britain as it was by its actions here.

Henry Lawson, referring to 'A Neglected History', suggested that children should be taught the other side of England's legacy to Australia as an antidote to the orthodox accounts that encouraged them to think of the 'mother land' as 'home'. Australia would be better served if

> children learned how the mother land cradled and nursed the nation they belonged to, and the measure of gratitude and respect they owe her for her tender guardianship: if they knew how the present Australian aristocracy (so loyal and sceptre loving) arose, and whence they came; how the Old New South Wales convict slave-holders and tyrants tried to drag Victoria into the sewer while she made efforts for liberty; how the same worthies tried to divert a convict stream into the northern settlement (now Queensland) that they might reap the benefit of convict labour; if the noble efforts of Lang resulted in the freedom of the mother colony, and lastly how Australian honour and interests were sold right and left for mammon.[20]

The determined efforts of the Pastoralists' Federal Council and the Steamship Owners' Association to crush the unions during the great strikes belonged to that same historical tradition. When those efforts were vigorously supported by the power of colonial governments and their courts, there was good reason for working-class nationalists to take the view that a colonial 'aristocracy' buttressed by the trappings of British 'justice' had little to recommend it.

This emerging radical nationalism was also based on long-held ideas of racial superiority. Although racist assumptions were an integral part of the ideology that sustained the Empire they denounced, nationalist labour nevertheless invoked those ideas as an ostensible defence of their embattled position. The fear and suspicion that greeted Chinese immigrants in the 1850s persisted into the 1890s. There it took on a further dimension — the conviction that Australian employers and their imperial brethren would seize the opportunity for greater profit by importing cheap Asian labour. This would not only lead to racial degeneration but would also betray the birthright of native Australians, meaning Australian-born Anglo-Saxons. By a further application of those same racist assumptions, Aborigines were regarded as a barely noticeable nuisance that would soon be extinct. In the 'New Religion' of Lawson's unionism there would be no place for the Chinese. They would 'have to be either killed or cured — probably the former. They were brutally dismissed by Lawson, Lane and many others as a squalid, disease-ridden race who would imperil

Boomerang, April 1889
THE KERNEL OF THE COLOUR QUESTION.
The Man with the Mortgage, 'You prefer to run with your own colour, Mr. Sugarcane! But where's the white man that'll work for £6 a year? You can't pay whites and pay me too; and unless I'm paid —.' (Sugarcane tumbles.)

In this simple and direct cartoon, the coloured worker waits to cash his annual £6 cheque while the banker instructs the canegrower in economic realities. No matter who the farmer might prefer to employ, the banker presents him with a choice between cheap coloured labour and foreclosure, between economic ruin and racial degeneration. Thus, in the *Boomerang*'s view, banks and mortgage companies value their profit above White Australia. That is the kernel of the colour question: the banks will betray the people's destiny.

the 'new order' being built within the 'great white state'. According to the *Boomerang*, the British Government's rejection of Queensland's Chinese Restriction Bill was a blatant example of imperial hostility to Australian nationalism:

> The vetoing by Downing Street of the Chinese Restriction Bill as determined upon by the representatives of the Queensland people is a move of the gravest moment. It is not only an announcement that Trade is still the sole god of the British Empire . . . It is a declaration thrown into the teeth of the Australian Nationality movement that the mere Trade interests of Manchester warehousemen and Calcutta opium dealers must ever dominate the inherent rights of the self-sustaining Australian communities . . . It is a Power with which we have absolutely nothing in common, whose aspirations are as distinct from our aspirations as day is from night . . . In it are embodied the Shylock lust for gold and the patrician lust for power and pomp and place; these lusts sway with uncontested strength the senile and decrepit body of an expiring oligarchy.[21]

This was further proof of the conspiracy between capitalist greed and imperialist ambition to dispossess the Australian people.

This variety of nationalism, which was such an important part of labour ideology in the 1890s, had a distinctly populist colour. It was moulded, in part, by visions of a new society that might be built in a vast, uncorrupted continent by men whose independent and egalitarian spirit enshrined the rugged virtues of populist mythology. These images were shaped to some degree by the literature of American populism and embellished by local writers like Lane and Lawson who transformed them into recognizably Australian symbols.[22] In the negative sense, it was defined by its rejection of Old World corruption, imperial pomp and class distinction. In this new land the common man might be his own master and make his own future. But the imperialists, in league with local capitalists, pastoralists and bankers, presented an ominous threat to that grand vision. Caring nothing for Australia, since their hearts and minds were in the Old Country, they would betray the worker, the farmer and the 'little man' by flooding the country with cheap Asian labour. This would pollute the 'white race' and break down the conditions of life so hard won by the people from recalcitrant employers and a harsh land. In crushing the unions they were destroying the one great force that stood between them and their determination to sell Australia's destiny for sordid profit. They would offer up to Mammon the birthright of White Autralians so that they and their friends at 'home' might live in decadent idleness and fawning deference to a redundant aristocracy. In this context, it is not surprising that there were many people in the labour movement who listened when they were told that the bank crashes of 1893 were yet another episode in the familiar story of capitalist greed and imperial design, in which the unbridled avarice of predatory monopolies was exemplified by the Money Power.

1

'A Means of Robbery much Simpler than Burglary' — The Bank Crashes

The depression of the 1890s left a profound impression on the minds of a whole generation of Australians and accentuated a number of concerns that helped shape the nation in the twentieth century. The widespread unemployment and social distress occasioned by the slump added an urgency to the existing belief of many liberal and labour reformers that it was the proper role of governments to intervene in the economy to mitigate the worst excesses of late-nineteenth-century Australian and Imperial capitalism. The partiality of governments and the courts in favour of the employers during the maritime and shearers' strikes sharpened the labour movement's sense that Australian society was divided along class lines. Although the notions of class were rough-hewn, the experience was sufficient to accelerate labour's entry into politics in an organized and formal way. The rhetoric that accompanied this often had a radical sting, but the burden of most Labor platforms was essentially reformist. With the culmination of the financial crisis in the bank crashes of 1893, and the means by which several of those institutions subsequently reconstructed, came further confirmation that the rich and powerful were able, in a class-divided society, to protect the interests of themselves and their friends at the expense of 'the little man'. This idea rested easily within labour's general perception of capitalism as a collection of predatory monopolies, which must be constrained by governments embodying the interests of 'the people'. The most appropriate agent for this was the supremacy of labour in politics, either in its own right or in coalition with reforming liberals.[1]

The bank crashes, on which so much of this sort of attention focused, were the result of structural weaknesses in the colonial economies, compounded by drought, encouraged by careless borrowing and precipitated by reckless speculation. During the 1880s the Australian colonies had come to depend increasingly upon external funds, which disguised a large deficit in the balance of payments on current account and helped to sustain domestic liquidity. This dependence was such that during the 1880s capital inflow equalled almost half of Australia's merchandise imports and the massive programme of public and private investment combined, which made the economies particularly vulnerable to external factors. In the latter half of the decade, for example, the level of debt service charges accounted for over one-third of export revenue.

The pastoral industry, which provided a substantial portion of this revenue, encountered severe difficulties during the early 1890s. Between 1889 and 1894, over-production of wool and over-stocking of pastures combined with falling wool prices on overseas markets to reduce rural income. These structural and market problems were compounded by prolonged drought.

From 1891 the decline in export earnings was accompanied by a rapid fall in capital inflow, which removed the main external prop to the colonial economies and set in motion a downward spiral. During the 1880s capital inflow alone was worth more than double the debt service charges, but in the following decade new borrowing only accounted for half of these charges. The main effect of this was that, for the first time since the 1870s, Australia had to service its external debt from its own shrinking financial resources.

The severity of the subsequent crisis was, to a large extent, determined by the way that borrowed money was used in both the public and private sectors. A substantial proportion of public investment was channelled into railway construction, which, while making a contribution to the sum of national capital assets, did not produce the kind of immediate return necessary to avoid a crisis. In the private sector, the boom of the 1880s had developed on the shaky basis of over-investment in the pastoral industry, urban building and land speculation. When the downturn began, pastoralists found that falling income prevented them from meeting their mortgage payments, which in turn created difficulties for their creditors, who in many cases had also extended themselves beyond prudent levels. Land companies, building societies and even banks of issue, encouraged by the blithe assumption that prices for urban land and houses would continue to rise, were drawn into increasingly speculative activity. They not only advanced credit on grossly inflated land values and built more houses than the demand warranted, but also operated on dangerously low liquidity ratios. The resulting crisis did not occur suddenly or uniformly. There were failures of financial houses from 1889 to 1893 and later. Nevertheless, very little was done to halt the gathering momentum.

The first wave of financial collapses occurred between 1889 and

1892. The institutions concerned were mainly building societies and mortgage and land companies, whose precarious liquidity was seriously undermined with the sharp fall in foreign investment. Most were badly run. Some were criminally mismanaged. Almost all had wildly over-extended themselves. As a result, when land prices fell the whole basis of their credit collapsed. This first bout of failures weakened many of the stronger banks that had invested funds in such companies. It also weakened public confidence in the banking system. From 1891 onwards the desire of depositors to withdraw their money snowballed until it assumed the proportions of a run on the banks in the first few months of 1893. The crisis came to a head in May, when thirteen prominent banks closed their doors and suspended payment. During this time most undertook a process of reconstruction with government approval and assistance.[2]

Immediately after the failures there were allegations that several public figures who were connected with the banks had been party to either reckless or dishonest behaviour. Cannon has shown in some detail the involvement of prominent businessmen, bankers and politicians in the affairs of the failed Melbourne banks, and their part in the dubious arrangements that were made to save themselves and their friends at the expense of depositors. Many people whose savings were locked up at a time when they were desperately needed had good reason to question the probity of leading citizens such as James Munro, Sir Matthew Davies and Sir Graham Berry. Munro's reappointment as Agent General in London amid disclosures about the affairs of the Real Estate Bank in June-August 1892 caused a good deal of comment about his and Davies's association with it. The Victorian Government's intervention in the case against Davies for his involvement in the collapse of the Mercantile Bank of Australia gave weight to the popular view that the Government was looking after its friends. Its persistence in this course, despite the resignation of Solicitor General Isaac Isaacs in protest, was a matter of public scandal. In Queensland, some four years later, Sir Thomas McIlwraith was forced to resign from the ministry after an inquiry found that his private dealings with the Queensland National Bank while a Minister of the Crown amounted to something very close to corruption. These scandals followed the conviction of several lesser figures in the banking industry on charges of conspiracy and the issuing of false balance sheets. All this gave substance to the enduring popular suspicion of financial institutions and their powerful friends.[3]

The direct association between some members of parliament and banks that were to be assisted by government legislation drew strong criticism from Labor politicians. Speaking on the Bank Issue Bill in the New South Wales Legislative Assembly, George Black claimed, erroneously, that a provision of the United States Constitution prevented anyone connected with a bank from taking a seat in the legislature. That provision, he argued, had fallen into disuse because of 'the tremendous power of the banking institutions there, which have created a state within the state, and which exercise an amount of influence altogether against the true interests of the country'.

When the Government took further action in November 1893 to stabilize the banking system with the Bank Notes Bill, McKinnon claimed that those members who were shareholders in banking companies should be prevented from voting on the Bill to 'save the country from being plundered behind the back of the people'. Schey went even further in suggesting that, if this was so, then those who had overdrafts from the banks should not be permitted to vote either, because they were 'under the financial thumb of some of these financial institutions'. Besides, the Bill was class legislation:

> The underlying basis of the Bill is not to do good to the whole community of the country, but to do good to a numerically small financial class . . . To my mind it is the most sublime impudence of the banks, or of any persons acting on their behalf, to ask Parliament to give them any further assistance . . . Have they not laid their paralysing hand upon a large portion of the wealth of the colony? Holding, as they do, the greater portion of the land and wealth of the colony, they have the sublime impudence to ask for further legislation in their interests, and to the detriment of the people.[4]

Commenting upon the manner in which the banks were reconstructing, and the government assistance that they were receiving to do so, the Sydney *Worker* of 29 April 1893 observed: 'As a means of robbery it is much simpler than burglary. There is no danger whatever attached to this sort of plundering the mob, especially when the reconstructors run the Government'.

During a debate about the possibility that some members of the Government might be prosecuted for their part in the collapse of the Mercantile Bank, Labor members of the Victorian Legislative Assembly suggested that its closure was the direct cause of starvation, destitution and suicide among many of its unfortunate depositors. Perhaps they were recalling an item in the Sydney *Worker* of 21 January 1893, which reported the suicide of a South Australian farmer by hanging. In a manner that owed its inspiration to Donnelly's *Caesar's Column*, the paper observed:

> Cause—mortgage. By the way, mortgage means 'death pledge', and to the plundered settler of Australia it is in literal fact a graveyard grip. The farmer hangs himself, but the banker laughs and grows fat. The yeoman—'their country's pride'—are systematically ruined so that the city usurers, speculators, and commission sharks may thrive and subscribe to that brotherhood of destruction, the National Assassins.

It was also argued during the Legislative Assembly debate that those accused should stand trial so that either their names could be cleared or they could be fairly convicted by due legal process. This, it was claimed, was the only way that the public could be reassured that there was not one law for the rich and another for the poor.[5]

The Melbourne Trades Hall Council thought that Parliament should do more than declare a holiday to halt the run on the banks and then merely debate the position of Government members who were involved with the banks. The council wanted the Lord Mayor to convene a public meeting to impress upon Parliament the necessity to take some form of action that would release current accounts locked up in the reconstructing banks, and to authorize the establishment of a State Bank of issue.[6] Some nine months later, when the crisis had begun to subside and details of the various schemes of reorganization became widely known, the Melbourne *Worker* of 10 March 1894 was moved to comment:

> 'There is no money in circulation', is the cry in the highways and byways. Then, where is it? It is hidden away under lock and key, for the purpose of saving, if possible, rotten financial institutions from utter collapse. There are certain banks 'reconstructing'—that is, in plain English, keeping the people's money already within their grasp, and dragging in their advances as fast as is possible. One institution of this tribe of capitalist bankrupts is openly stated to have 'sneaked' deposits and extorted repayments of loans and interest to the extent of over three million . . . Meanwhile, the money sharks are raking in the life's blood of the community, and Parliament looks inanely on while others are quietly reaping the profit of our financial tribulations.

The Queensland Government was more decisive than its Victorian counterpart. Under the leadership of Sir Thomas McIlwraith it hastened to assist the banks, particularly the Queensland National Bank. Parliament passed a number of Acts designed to stabilize the monetary system, the most effective of

Brisbane *Worker*, 20 February 1897
THE QUEENSLAND PROMETHEUS.
Bound for 25 years.

In attacking the long-term financial arrangement between the Queensland National Bank and the Government, this cartoon invokes the Greek myth of Prometheus, who offended Zeus by stealing fire and giving it to man. Zeus had his revenge by chaining Prometheus to a rock, where, during the day, an eagle devoured his liver, which regenerated at night so that the torment would continue. The Queensland taxpayer is to suffer the same fate at the hands of Boodlewraith (McIlwraith) and the bank for the 25-year duration of the financial scheme. Presumably, he will remain there until freed by Herakles in the guise of the Labor Party. The struggle between the people and the banks thus assumes the heroic proportions of classical antiquity.

which pressed the banks into using treasury notes, which were designated legal tender, for which they were required to pay 25 per cent of the face value in gold. The pressure to accept these was applied by the imposition of a substantial tax on the banks' own notes. The measure that caused most comment, and that was to become part of the web of circumstances that led to McIlwraith's resignation in December 1897, was the direct assistance given to the Queensland National Bank. Some years before the 1893 crisis, McIlwraith had made it the Government's main banker, thus assuring it a commanding position in the Queensland economy. When it was forced to close its doors, the Government came to its rescue with the Queensland National Bank Agreement Bill, which proposed to lodge £2.5 million of Government money with the bank for a period of not less than six years.

Such was the power of the bank in the colony's affairs, alleged Hoolan, Labor leader in the Assembly, that whenever he fought an election he not only had to defeat his opponents but found that he 'had to go against the Queensland National Bank'. Dawson, the Labor member for Charters Towers, pointed out that several members of the Government were shareholders in the bank, a situation that he termed 'an unholy alliance', which could only damage 'the honour and reputation of our public men'. Making an oblique reference to McIlwraith, Reid, Labor member for Toowong, reminded the House of an old German proverb: 'petty thieves are hung and great robbers are knighted, and its seems to me that applies to Australian bank managers and statesmen at the present time'. Turley, Labor, Brisbane South, took the argument a step further by asserting:

> We have heard it stated that this depression arose from industrial disputes, from droughts, floods, and various other things. I believe that it is largely owing to the clouds which have been cast upon the characters of certain public men in Australia.

The only enduring solution of the problem, according to the Labor members, was 'for the Government to start a State Bank'.[7]

For the rest of McIlwraith's political career the Labor Party and its press mounted a persistent campaign against him and others associated with what they called 'The Boodlewraith Bank':

> The Bank has financed its political friends, and its political friends have financed the Bank, and between the upper and nether mill-stone the Queensland taxpayer has been ground into dividends . . . During the last few years the Q. N. Bank has practically been the Queensland Government.[8]

In presenting his report to the fourth annual session of the Australian Labour Federation, Albert Hinchcliffe, the general secretary, reminded members that it was part of a wider pattern:

> Let us remember that every advantage now possessed by capitalism —the control of Parliament, the administration of the laws (through their costliness), which are iniquitously unjust in their incidence on the wage earners, and the exploitation of the real producers of wealth—has been obtained through the close association of the manipulators of capital, who care not for the welfare of the workers when profit alone is their object.[9]

The depression in general, and the bank failures in particular, produced an impressive array of interpretations about basic causes. The metropolitan daily press pointed to land and building speculation, and regrettable tendency on the part of the public to panic, the failure of the banks to support each other, and unfavourable overseas influences. The United Trades and Labour Council of South Australia expressed a view typical of most peak councils of the labour movement. When asked by the Parliamentary Select Committee on the Unemployment Problem to state what had led 'to the present dearth of employment in the colony', it gave a detailed answer. J. A. McPherson, secretary of the council and Labor MHA for East Adelaide, blamed 'the failure of private enterprise to fulfil the requirements of production and distribution'. In particular, he cited monopoly of land to the detriment of small agricultural farming; the use of capital for land and mining speculation at the expense of 'legitimate production'; falling prices for staple products; high interest rates; and unsound banking methods leading to the collapse. To solve the problem he suggested a number of Government initiatives, including land reform through increased tax on freehold land; protection for local industry; a programme of expanded public works; encouragement of closer land settlement; Government assistance with commodity marketing; and the establishment of 'a State Bank'. Implicit in this, and the many other Labor platforms it reflected, was the view that the unrestrained tendency of capitalism towards monopoly should be tempered by state intervention. They were not concerned to dismantle the instruments of state power—parliaments, police and the courts—that had so recently mobilized against them in the maritime and shearers' strikes. As their formal entry into parliamentary politics testified, they were more interested in winning control of those instruments and turning them into benevolent agencies to advance the people's welfare.

This was demonstrated in many ways, but most particularly in their preference for reforming legislation as a means to social change and the desire to have industrial disputes arbitrated by judicial process. Even those groups that purported to offer a fully developed socialist critique of capitalism, linked to a radical political programme, tended to commit themselves to the existing political machinery as the means to build socialism in Australia.[10]

One of the perennial concerns within the labour movement during this period was the issue of land ownership. In an effort to illustrate the effects of financial institutions speculating in land and thus preventing closer settlement, the Brisbane *Worker* of 1 February 1896 analysed the pattern of land ownership in Queensland. It claimed that 35 per cent of the colony was in the hands of 'banks, syndicates and mortgage companies'; a further 27 per cent was owned by pastoralists, many of whom were heavily indebted to the banks; and only 2.5 per cent was being effectively used by small holders.

Discussion of this issue in Labor circles was dominated by the single-tax theory of Henry George, whose visit to Australia in 1890 gave a considerable boost to the existing popularity of his economic panacea. Among the somewhat eclectic selection of books that the labour press offered its readers, George's works seem to have been consistent sellers. From the late 1880s onwards the demand for a 'tax upon unimproved land values' became a standard plank in Labor platforms. Although such proposals were not always pure George, all drew their inspiration from his work, despite an occasional confusion between it and ideas of land nationalization.[11]

Single-Taxers were quick to point out the significance of the bank crashes in terms of their theory. Von Hagen, in a lecture at Newtown, argued that the banks' manipulation of land values and their lending policies based upon erroneous ideas of land use were the real cause behind the crisis. He suggested a 'land value tax which will prevent the land speculator'. The Single Tax League's journal *Beacon* interpreted events in the same way.[12]

During October–November 1893 the Melbourne *Worker* ran a series of articles on 'The Land Question', which claimed that the single tax represented the solution to the iniquities of land monopolization. 'Bedrock', writing in the Sydney *Worker* of 5 August 1893, asserted that the basis of the existing economic system rested firmly upon the inflated price of land, for which the only real cure was the single tax. When Henry George died in October 1897, *Tocsin* printed a glowing eulogy to him as a champion of labour. On 11 November 1897, confusing George's theory with land nationalization, it reminded readers of the significance of his message:

> Private ownership of land is undoubtedly the greatest curse of our civilization. It is the primary cause of all poverty, cruelty, misery, degredation, and a whole catalogue of injustices. It is blockade to all true progress.

A correspondent of the Sydney *Worker*, 3 June 1893, saw it in conspiratorial terms:

> The days of those gambling monsters who have lived upon the earnings of the industrious people of New South Wales are numbered ... It is a well-known fact that many of the banks have advanced heavily upon leaseholds that are about to revert to the Crown ... Now that the leases are about to run out, the banks are naturally anxious to regain control over the political machine that they may use it to retain possession of the public lands.

This concern with land ownership had been a preoccupation of liberal and radical reformers for half a century. It represented, as Gollan has shown, a long struggle between two opposed concepts of social organization. There was the aristocratic notion that large-scale holdings symbolized the most appropriate form of economic and social relations in a developing rural economy. The radical view saw this as an attempt to transplant the Old World corruption that so many of them had migrated to escape. Their ideal was to establish an independent yeomanry on small holdings as a tangible expression of social democracy in the emerging new nation. It was this ideological heritage that underlay Labor's policy on land ownership and added weight to its populist inclinations.[13]

The radical and Labor press during the 1890s was peppered with accusations that governments, banks and other capitalists were engaged in acts of conspiracy against 'the people'.

Hard Cash, can ephemeral 'magazine of finance and politics' that asserted under its banner 'Money Rules the World', published detailed articles claiming to show how bankers, governments, clergymen and newspapers were not only deeply involved in shady financial deals but were also party to a vast conspiracy directed against the savings of honest, hard-working people. It exposed alleged manipulation of bank funds by directors, denounced governments for their complicity in fraud, and published long lists of clergymen who were bank shareholders. It looked forward to the day when such villainy would be for ever banished from Australia:

> Meantime it is the duty of every honest man to do his level best in order to destroy for ever the great bands of financial and political scoundrels who, in pursuit of personal gain, have ruined the People and bankrupted the State.[14]

The *Australasian Typographical Journal* of September 1893 discussed the means whereby depositor's funds were locked up to help the banks undertake reconstruction while friends of the directors could gain ready access to money. This went on while the banks 'were baiting the traps to ensnare more victims'. It bemoaned the fact that 'up to the present time the [Victorian] Government has not expressed its intention of introducing legislation with a view to preventing a repetition of one of the most disgraceful conspiracies that was ever hatched by any financial "ring" in the world'. In similar style, the *Shearers' and General Labourers' Record* of 15 June 1893 viewed the bank collapses as an example of the people as prey to avaricious bankers:

> At no previous period in the world's history have the English speaking people been so cruelly victimized and robbed by those who profess to exercise inordinate honesty, the bankers . . . Some half dozen were nobbled and put away, while the scores are allowed to still walk our streets, and what was left by these swindlers is being frittered away. Thus, the too-confiding people who deposited their earnings with these wolves in sheep's clothing find themselves ruined . . . The attack made upon the people has been so sudden, and their position so helpless, that passive resitance alone can be shown. Verily, it has been a stand and deliver surprise by the banking vultures . . . The perpetrators of this dire blow are by law free from punishment, but they cannot hide their diminished heads from the execration of their victims.

In New South Wales, the Sydney *Worker* of 4 November 1893 saw the Bank Issue Bill in the same light. It claimed that the real cause of industrial warfare in the early 1890s was the successful attempts made by the Government 'to fleece Labor in the interests of the bankers'. In the same edition of the paper, Ben Prior, president of the Lake Cargellico Branch of the Labor Electoral League, asserted that the very existence of the banks rested on their 'ability to gull the wealth producers of this country'. He went on to discuss the news that the Government might soon pass a revised form of the Bill that would make bank notes legal tender, and concluded:

> Such a course would be most detrimental to the interests of the masses, and is only another conspiracy of the Fat Person and his colleagues to rob the people.

The Bill was later described as the 'Ned Kelly Bank Law'.

In their 1893 annual report to the Creswick Branch of the Shearers' Union, W. G. Spence and D. Temple spoke of 'the depression and hard times' as being 'aggravated and intensified by financial swindles and capitalistic villainy'. The whole matter of bank reconstruction assumed the proportions of 'a deep-laid conspiracy', whereby the assets of banks could only be made valuable 'by grinding down the wages of the workers'.[15] Hardacre, speaking on the Maritime Strike debate in the Queensland Parliament, discussed a process that had precisely these results. He told the House that the workers at the Tramway Company had been forced to accept reduced wages because the company had to find the money necessary to meet its overdraft to the Queensland National Bank. By refusing to accept a lower interest rate the shareholders of the bank were 'sucking the life-blood out of the company'. The maintenance of high dividends was achieved at the direct expense of the workers.[16]

By the mid-1890s the view that capitalism consisted of a group of predatory monopolies whose interests were fundamentally hostile to those of the people had a general currency in the labour movement. This was symbolized in the names applied to various 'interests'. The generic term for capitalists was 'Fat', 'Fatman' or 'The Fat Person'. Mine owners were 'The Coal Vend'; breweries were labelled 'Bung'; and the banks were commonly referred to as either 'Shylock' or 'The Money Power'. This often led to capitalists being ranked within a hierarchy of moral turpitude. The ranking depended upon the particular issue being considered. After the financial crisis, the choice of supreme capitalist was obvious:

> The greatest monopoly on earth is the monopoly of money for it includes all the others. Cash reigns despotic and supreme. They who possess it, possess land and power and slaves in countless millions. It buys all things—it rules all things. Kings are its bejewelled figureheads—presidents its executive officials and parliaments its committees of tax collectors. Literature is its satellite and religious hypocrisy its auxiliary. In olden times kings were marauding chiefs who fought for the possession of the good things of the earth that money now buys. Today, they who possess the cash divide the spoil and use legislatures, sovereigns, armies and police to divide it for them. To all intents and purposes parliaments are impotent to bring about any fundamental social changes, because they do not command the key of the Nation's Treasure House. They do not control its money, its land, and its machinery. Every parliament in the world exists upon 'hand to mouth' finance and the majority of them are overwhelmed with debts that never can be repaid. In Australia, private persons (banks) possess the nation's cash and the nation's

Brisbane *Worker*, 12 January 1901
THE WORKERS' DESIGN FOR A TRIUMPHAL ARCH.

This conveys the paper's attitude to Australian federation. While the ceremonial parade of dignitaries moves along a deserted street, it passes through the twin pillars of poverty and crime. Two workers, struggling to sustain their burden, support the whole superstructure of rent, interest and profit, law and order, imperialist slogans, the fat capitalist and, supreme above all, the three balls of the pawnbroker. Such is the hierarchy of capitalist imperialism.

> property. Consequently, their whispered ukase is more powerful for weal or for woe, than the parchment resolutions of purchased parliaments. In New South Wales proprietory Banks own the people, body and soul. They own our gold, coal and silver mines. They own the lands, the cattle, the sheep and the farms and the vineyards. They control the steam and the sailing fleets. Every Department of Commerce, Trade and Production is systematically exploited by the Joint Stock Shylocks of Banking and Exchange.[17]

From this it followed that not all capitalists were equal. Some were clearly better than others. John Robertson, arguing a case for monetary reform by the extension of credit to 'enlightened capitalists' to stimulate productive works, put the proposition plainly:

> This reform would soundly and effectually relieve our hopelessly congested labour market, and would tend to attract to our country the true capitalist—the intelligent and humane owner of money and plant; while expelling or reforming the spurious capitalist—the hard-grained, ignorant and sordid dealer in gold and in gold contracts (bonds of one kind and another). These *two kinds of capitalist* are not discriminated; the meaner kind make, through monetary ignorance and sophism about contract, mere catspaws of the better kind. It is the better kind that labour strikes against, because it is nearest. The final profit almost always goes to the more callous gold grubbers and bond collectors; the lower worker being beaten first, the higher falling or transforming later, he doesn't exactly know how.[18]

In subsequent developments of Money Power theory, the relative anonymity of the 'gold grubbers' became a deliberate act of mystification designed to cloak nefarious intentions.

If such capitalists were the workers' enemies and the personification of all that was evil, it was logical that virtue must rest with the cause of labour. Under the heading 'Millennium Means Mateship', the Melbourne *Worker* of 9 December 1893 declared:

> Our cause is a holy one and must triumph. We can hasten the time if we like. The masses have started forward. They may blunder and stumble, but they will reach a better civilization. Mutual trust and confidence both in our future and in each other is all that is needed to ensure success.

In another echo of William Lane, Henry Boote told readers of the Melbourne *Worker* on 7 October 1893 about 'the religion of Labor':

> Yes, O Christian—fellow Christian let me say, for I too follow Christ—yes, Socialism is a religion, humanity wide, excluding from its folds no human being, opening its arms like a tender mother, to the whole world, uttering the sweetest words that were ever spoken: 'Come unto me all ye that are weary and heavy laden and I will give you rest'.

Two months later, W. G. Spence confronted readers of the Sydney *Worker* with the essential moral question: 'Choose ye this day your God. It must be either the Mammon of Capitalism or the Brotherhood of Man'.

Bankers were not only the most greedy and cunning of all capitalists, they were also guilty of hypocrisy in the same way that *Hard Cash* alleged clergymen were false to Christ by their association with banking companies. Supposedly Christian bankers, who 'in their business dealings, worshipped at the Temple of Mammon', were regularly lampooned in prose and verse. The last three stanzas from 'Financial Australia', published in the Melbourne *Worker* on 2 December 1893, are typical:

> He scorns the man who steals for starving wife,
> The bigamist and other wicked ones.
> So he's wedded to a very Christian life,
> But not unto the Tottie whom he runs.
>
> He always goes to Church in pious state,
> Of worldliness you never see a trace;
> But he chuckles while he places in the plate,
> The widow's mite which isn't his to place.
>
> Oh! Keep me from the pious black-clad fraud,
> Who seems all virtue, but is never so;
> Who always bids us 'Lend unto the Lord',
> And sticks to all the 'rhino' here below.

Just as the sturdy worker represented all that was just and righteous, the banker was an embodiment of moral bankruptcy.

For W. G. Spence the lesson of all this was beyond doubt: Labor must destroy the Money Power:

> Usury is robbery, and every private bank, or finance agency are but legalized stealers of the people's labour results. The money power is

> the great power of the age and the sooner it is destroyed the better . . . Financial institutions are absolutely unscrupulous, inhuman and careless as to who sinks, so long as their shareholders get their usury. Labour must become aggressive, and never rest day or night until it has crushed every financial institution out of existence and destroyed usury and land monopoly.[19]

It would be wrong, however, to imagine that Spence and others like him were seriously advocating armed insurrection. Behind his bluster there was a strong commitment to constitutional methods of change.

There was, after all, no need for general revolutionary action. The banks were simply a small, predatory clique whose behaviour was entirely alien to the naturally democratic spirit of Australian society. They could be swept aside by the popular will expressed through the political process as soon as their corrupting influence was widely understood. If only the squatter would see this, he and the labourer could be freed of the burden that interest laid upon both of them. In an article for the Melbourne *Worker* of 21 April 1894, entitled 'The Pastoralists' Union: A Strong Indictment. Interest Kills the Squatter—Not Wages', Spence made a suggestion:

> Now, why don't the P. U. strike at the root of the evil that is driving many of them to ruin? Why don't they organize a boycott of the usurers? Strike against the Banking Vampire, and the AWU will help the P. U. with all its powers. Cutting the price of shearing will not save the squatters from the octopus grip of the Banks . . . The Bona Fide squatter is right enough, but he has foolishly allowed the money handling middle-men to rule him and make a catspaw of him.

This vaguely corporate idea, that although each had his separate and just claims upon the national wealth there was no fundamental conflict of interests between the squatter and the rural worker, had some general currency.[20]

Labour writers commonly depicted the squatter as a victim of the banks. When seasons and prices were bad he had to look for ways of cutting costs to meet his loan obligations, and the only means available to him was to reduce the price of labour. To people like Spence there was a community of interest between 'all who work' that cut across existing social and economic barriers. After all, it was not unusual for a squatter to roll up his sleeves and work alongside his employees even though he was still the 'boss'. This tended to encourage a degree of familiarity that could never be felt towards a bank manager, let alone an anonymous city financier. Moreover, the shared experience of rural life strengthened a vague sense of corporate identity. Accordingly, it seemed reasonable to expect that conflict between pastoralists and shearers might be minimized if they were to unite against the urban Money Power.

> It is time the bona fide squatter took a look at things and stopped the little game, by uniting with the Labour Party, who are trying to secure justice not only for themselves, but for all who work, whatever name they call themselves by.[21]

The implied distinction between those who worked and those who preyed upon them was sufficiently broad to encompass farmers and small businessmen within the first category. This idea was a congenial one for the many shearers who were also small farmers trying to supplement a meagre income with seasonal work. It was also the ideological basis of Labor's electoral success in many rural seats until the emergence of the Country Party in the 1920s. The real enemy in all this—the alien corruption—was monopolistic capitalism, which found its highest form in financial institutions:

> It is in the multitude of industries and of small producers that we must look for our future well-being, not in building up a few Jay Goulds at the expense of the great body of the people; and the manipulation of our credit institutions, whether private or State, must be directed accordingly. In fact, the principle of co-operation which will inevitably be a great factor in the near future, must be brought into play, whether the system of banking be as now in private hands, or in a great measure, or wholly controlled by the State.[22]

The idea that there were interests common to most sections of the community, and that Labor was the political expression of them, was a persistent theme in the party's rhetoric during the 1890s.

Although bankers and other predatory monopoly interests occupied a prominent place in Labor's hall of infamy, there was plenty of room for lesser characters to play the fool to the banker's villain. Among such minor parts a special role had always been reserved for academics of conservative persuasion. In 1894 Professor Morris of the University of Melbourne wrote to *The Times* of London, asking the British people to assist in keeping Victorians from starving by sending some form of help. This was offensive to Labor on two grounds. First, it asked for charity but did not address the real problems that had caused the distress. Second, it offended a sense of independence that held that

Australia was a young and vigorous country, which could face up to its own problems. The 'Bleary-eyed Professor' attracted a salvo of abuse from the *New Order* of 26 May 1894:

> Of all people on economic problems blinder than bats, stupider than backdate politicians, and crankier than lunatics, it is professors. They are par excellence the 'gigantic pudding heads of the world'; as boys they go to school and cram and stuff their brain with the dust of centuries; through a faculty for reproducing the jargon and darkening the air with it they become famous in the universities; and for blinding the people with it they are provided with fat billets and given precedence to at most state ceremonies.

While this may have been good knockabout comedy, it was set against a stern backdrop of anti-intellectualism.

It is also significant that financiers were sometimes cast in the role of 'Shylock', for, although it was only occasionally invoked in the 1890s, there was a degree of anti-Semitism in the way that images of the Money Power were constructed. 'Memorabilia' from 'Bananaland' told readers of the Melbourne *Worker* on 11 August 1894 that Jews had originated the 'evil and immoral' practice of usury, even though it was against Hebrew law. His solution was that private property in both land and goods be abolished, thus tearing asunder the foundations on which usury was built. Commenting on the 1894 election in New South Wales, the *New Order* of 28 July reflected:

> The General Elections are over—heads have been counted and we have voted ourselves again back into slavery—slavery worse than death . . . Division after division will be taken amid the hosannah cheers of Press and Church and Populace whilst the glorious result will be that the rent collector will call around every Monday as usual —that Moses, Cohen and Co. will rake in their per shent, and that every man in New South Wales will be robbed and plundered and swindled out of his rights as usual.

On 13 May 1893 the Brisbane *Worker* alleged that before the Railways Construction Act was passed McIlwraith had cast about to see if there were any syndicates ready to take up land under its provisions. Such was his solicitude toward their interests, the paper claimed, the Premier ensured that 'The Bill itself was submitted to the London Jews before it was rushed through the Queensland Parliament'. The Sydney *Worker* of 4 March 1893 depicted Jews, according to a long-estabished stereotype, as crafty, indolent parasites:

Jews . . . are principally bankers, loan managers, pedlars and pawnbrokers . . . They dress in purple and fine linen and they fare sumptuously every day — but who knows one of them that could not be spared? Did anyone ever see a Jew work? At manual labour, no. It doesn't pay to work when others are so anxious to do it.

Such was the 'Brotherhood of Man' in the 'religion of Labor'.

The same populist idealogy that Labor developed to explain the bank crashes was applied to the Boer War. In New South Wales, W. A. Holman opposed Australian involvement on the ground that it was an unjust war upon an oppressed people into which the Empire had been dragged 'at the behest of a little gang of swindling speculators on the Rand'. Part of his argument was that the conflict had shown how militarism was 'always used by its capitalistic controllers to check the rising tide of socialism and democracy'.[23] In Queensland most Labor leaders were pro-Boer, and the Brisbane *Worker* described the situation with characteristic bluntness: 'It is not the British Empire but international Capitalism that is waging war against the farmer people who dare to stand in its way'.[24] In Melbourne *Tocsin* adopted a similar view, with some embellishments. With its accustomed flourish, the paper described those in the Transvaal who were opposed to Kruger as 'the Land Shark, the Mining Grabber, the Company Swindler, the Bank Robbers (both burglars and directors)'. Against such power the Boers appeared as heroic yeomen defending home and family. Replying to the daily press's satisfaction at an engagement in which seven Boers were killed, *Tocsin* observed:

Only seven homes where the father will never return; seven groups of little ones stretching out appealing hands to God for him who will never again see them; seven wives who will wait in vain for seven brave men, butchered to make a few British soldiers Peers and a few Johannesburg Jews millionaires.

It pursued this theme with an increasing emphasis on the role of Jewish capitalists, who were alleged to have engineered the war for personal profit.[25] On 23 November 1905 it heaped abuse on those whom it saw as the real beneficiaries of the slaughter:

Look at South Africa. Who rules the new British colonies bought with British blood, with a large mixture of colonial folly? For whom did our foolish fellows fight? For whom were the resources of the Empire so liberally poured out? For German Jews, who today own the mines, buy the administrators, square the Imperial Government, and work their properties by cheap Asian labour, and slave labour at that.

Brisbane *Worker*, 22 April 1899
THE CLUTCH OF THE MONEY POWER
'He seizes upon the father, drags the mother from the fireside, and even the little children are the victims of his greed.'

The huge hand of the Money Power is an ominous presence lurking unseen above the heads of the sturdy yeoman farmer and his dependent family. Its malicious intent and threatening power are accentuated by its scale and grasping pose. Caring nothing for the simple virtues of common humanity, it will ruthlessly dispossess the most basic of all social institutions.

The place and the circumstances may have been different, but the enemy was the same as that which confronted them after the bank crashes. Financiers were the same the world over.

By the turn of the century the idea that capitalism consisted in a set of predatory monopoly interests who conspired against the great mass of the people commanded a wide audience in the Australian labour movement. The 'terror of 1893' had taught them that those monopolies were ranked in a hierarchy of power and moral turpitude, with the Money Power supreme above all others. It was a view that led the Sydney *Worker* of 23 March 1901 into an ingenious variety of class analysis:

> The Wage-Earning Class is the only Class which is not a Class. Representing the Body as a Whole, while the other Classes only represent Special Organs, it is the Nation. Therefore, in voting for the Labor Men you vote for those who will most fitly represent you and all others.

2

The People's Weapon – The Commonwealth Bank

Although the bank crashes had convinced many Labor people that the Money Power was the most insidious of all capitalist monopolies, the problem of what was to be done remained. As noted in the previous chapter, the most common Labor proposal was to establish a state bank. The idea was not a Labor innovation. In Australia, advocacy of government involvement in the monetary system went back as far as 1810, when Governor Macquarie suggested such a scheme to the Colonial Office. During the 1840s a Select Committee on Monetary Confusion considered the matter. After the collapse of 1893 several committees of inquiry addressed themselves to the problem of the unstable monetary system.[1]

In 1893 a Select Committee of the New South Wales Legislative Assembly reported that the first step toward reforming the serious abuses that were then evident in the banking system 'would be the establishment of a National Bank of Issue'. A Select Committee of the South Australian Legislative Council considered the part that a state bank might play in stabilizing the economy and alleviating the 'unemployed problem'. The Victorian Parliament established a Royal Commission on State Banking, which reported in 1895 that 'it would be desirable in the interests of the country that a State Bank should be established in Victoria'. An earlier South Australian Royal Commission in 1889 was unable to recommend the formation of such a bank because it could find no agreement among the experts who testified before it. George Cotton, a Labor member of the South Australian Legislative Council, did not share the Commission's confusion. He presented it with a view that was to become a persistent theme among Labor's monetary radicals in the twentieth century—that in times of depression an expansionary monetary policy should be applied to counteract the slump:

> If we had a state bank of issue, it is manifest that this hostile policy of contracting the currency when it was most wanted, would not be followed as it has been in the past.

From the considerable quantity of evidence, reports and recommendations that poured into colonial parliaments only a trickle of legislation emerged. In 1893 Queensland established a state note issue, which the private banks had to accept as part of the arrangement whereby the Government came to their assistance. South Australia set up a *crédit foncier* bank in 1895, and a mortgage department was established by the Victorian Government in December 1896 after much debate and parliamentary manoeuvring.[2]

Although the various Labor parties had not yet developed a detailed scheme, these measures fell well short of the role they envisaged for a state bank. By the turn of the century most Labor platforms called for a state bank, a national bank, or some form of government control over the monetary system. The Australian Labour Federation in Queensland listed as the second of its political aims the need for state control of 'all production and all exchange'. In New South Wales, the platform presented to the electors in 1891 by the Labor Electoral League declared that its members were committed to the establishment of a 'National Bank'. That particular plank steadily worked its way up the platform until, in 1896, it appeared as the second item on the Fighting Platform, which meant that it was intended for action during the course of the next parliament. Two years later it was extended to read, 'National Bank with the sole right of note issue'. The United Labor Party of Victoria advocated 'the establishment of a State bank of issue', a view already favoured by the semi-official organ of the Trades Hall Council, *Commonweal*. The South Australian Labor platform of 1892 and the Tasmanian Labor platform of 1896 both included a plank that proposed a state bank. The 1894 Intercolonial Trades Union Congress held in Sydney resolved that 'steps should be taken as soon as possible to establish state banks of issue in the various Australasian colonies', and went on to urge that private banks have their affairs subjected to close government scrutiny.[3]

The arguments advanced by Labor in favour of a state bank relied as much upon the alleged sins of private banks for their force as they did upon the virtues of state-run institutions. As we have seen, Labor spokesmen were quick to point out the weaknesses of the colonial banks during the crisis. One result of that experience was a deeply ingrained suspicion of the probity of bankers, and a conviction that private banking, by its very nature, was not serving the best interests of the community as a whole. A series of articles that began in the Melbourne *Worker* on 16 September 1893 was representative of this view. In them 'a Banker' argued that, in pursuit of private profit, the banks had conducted their business in

Sydney *Worker*, 27 July 1911
'MOSTLY FOOLS'.
'The right of every person to his freehold,' says the Farmers and Settlers' Association.
'Hear, hear,' says the Land Monopolist, as he reaches for more.
'My blanky oath,' says the Director of the Land and Finance Co., as he grabs the lot.

This purports to explain the process of land monopolization, whereby the 'little man' is deprived of his freehold, first by the big pastoralist, who in turn passes it on to the financial institution. By this means the Money Power comes to exercise control over the land that was originally intended to support the small farmer. The relative size, styles of dress and facial expressions of the three men demonstrate how malevolence increases with the concentration of wealth.

a reckless manner, which not only revealed the basic instability of the system but also endangered the savings of innocent depositors. A further effect of their policy had been to build up 'a few Jay Goulds at the expense of the great body of the people', thus encouraging the development of monopoly interests. As a successful banking system was based on public confidence, it would now be necessary to build a new one in which confidence might properly be placed. The only sound financial institutions that could be developed henceforth were those that were state-run along co-operative lines, to serve the interests of the public, not private individuals. In short, a state bank was the only way to guarantee that the people's money would be safe from the perils of dividend-hungry shareholders and speculating, reckless directors.

According to one Queensland pamphleteer, there was a further, more insidious effect of private banking, which the establishment of a state bank would counteract. As the economic opinions of the banks were those that determined the financial policies of the colonies, it followed that these became the leading ideas, which in turn determined the economic fate of the community. A state bank concerned only for the community's welfare, and operating on an interest rate just sufficient to cover running costs, was the only solution to the problem.[4]

W. A. Holman, giving evidence to the New South Wales Select Committee on the Post Office Savings Bank, argued that a state-run credit institution would relieve the burden of interest on industry that private banks imposed and whatever profits might be made would go to the state. A long-term result of this would be that the private banks would be forced out of business, because of their need to make higher profits to satisfy their shareholders. The primary concern of a state bank would be the national interest, not private profit. Therein would be its virtue and its advantage.

There were some in the labour movement who favoured more radical changes. Most wanted to replace the existing form of currency, in the belief that it was the basis on which the discredited banking system had been built. The American idea of labour exchanges enjoyed some popularity. Under this scheme workers would be paid according to the value they added to the commodities they produced. The goods, in turn, would be priced according to the labour involved in making them. Another means of doing away with the existing currency was suggested by the Sydney *Worker* on 18 December 1897. Taking its inspiration from the distribution system described in Bellamy's *Looking Backward*, the paper advocated the establishment of large, government-run warehouses, which would operate on the barter principle. Michael Flürscheim, a New Zealand currency reformer, developed a scheme that was similar to the labour exchange. He advocated a form of paper currency, which would be issued to workers in proportion to the value that their labour added to the goods they produced. These 'barter notes' could be redeemed by the bearer in exchange for goods or services, after which they would be cancelled. This would permit some flexibility in the quantity of currency, which would have the effect of keeping prices constant through times of economic fluctuation.[5]

The gold standard was often the subject of attacks from monetary radicals. Referring to de Bernardi's *Trials and Triumphs of Labour* as the 'text book of the labour exchange', the *Tocsin* of 6 April 1899 reprinted part of his assault upon the gold standard. Speaking of the Bank of England, he said:

> In front of it, you feel an awe and sombreness very accordant with all our notions of the Old Lady of Threadneedle Street, the image of wealth and power . . . This temple of Mammon is based upon gold, and this basis has often been found to be pre-eminently unstable and dangerous. The gold block within oscillates: and each of its great oscillations is felt like the shock of an earthquake . . . Is there something wrong here? Ought the presence or absence of a few cubic inches or feet of gold in a bank make so vast a difference between national prosperity on the one hand, and national disaster and widespread ruin on the other?

Australian bimetallists also took up the cudgels against gold, arguing that currency based on a rare metal was not only unstable but also prey to cynical manipulation 'to tax the Christian for the benefit of the Jew'. Although the bimetallists made little headway in the labour movement, their views were taken sufficiently seriously to warrant a reply from Bruce Wallace in the *Tocsin* of 17 August 1899. He rejected their arguments as utterly fallacious, and proceeded to commend Flürscheim's 'barter notes'.[6]

This preoccupation with banking and currency did not go unchallenged. Among the various socialist sects there were those who argued that the fundamental cause of the unequal distribution of wealth lay at the very heart of the capitalist system, in the ownership of the means of production, distribution and exchange, from which arose two irreconcilably hostile classes. Only through class struggle could capitalism by overthrown to rectify that inequality.[7] Writing in the Victorian Socialist Party's paper the *Socialist* on 7 December 1907, W. H. Emmett argued that the problems associated with banking and currency were merely symptoms of a greater evil, not causes in themselves. The root cause of financial crisis was not the banks or currency arrangements, but the very nature of capitalism. The emphasis of so many in the labour movement on financial issues deflected attention from the fundamentals:

> To my mind, the most misleading and mischievous pile of rubbish which occasionally obscures this clear issue between the workers and their bosses is the stew, the hash, the bad mental meat, known as the currency and money question, or finance . . . It would make no beneficial difference to this wage slavery if you had a national paper currency.

He may have been right, but it proved to be much easier to print notes than to abolish wage slavery.

The Brisbane *Worker* of 5 January 1907 thought differently. In a thundering tirade against 'the Money Power', the paper depicted it as the nefarious, all-powerful influence that controlled the capitalist system.

> The Money Power! It is the greatest power on earth; and it is arrayed against Labour. No other power that is or ever was can be named with it . . . Kings, parliaments, churches, armies, navies?—pooh! Name them not. The Money Power is a giant that rams all these pygmies into his breeches pocket; or says to them, 'Do this', and they do it; or 'Lie down!' and they lie. It is the overwhelming nature of this supremacy of the Money Power that gives its character to the age we live in. It is the Age of Money. Money sets the standard for us in all the things of life. It orders our daily toil. It draws up our codes of honour. It dictates our tables of morality. It interprets our scriptures. It is its own Zion and its own Moses!

The editorial went on to suggest that the Money Power assailed Labor through legions spiritual and temporal:

> It attacks us through the Press—a monster with a thousand lying tongues, a beast surpassing in foulness any conceived by the mythology that invented dragons, wehr wolves, harpies, ghouls and vampires. It thunders against us from innumerable platforms and pulpits. The mystic machinery of the churches it turns into an engine of wrath for our destruction. And in many ways not manifested on the surface its influence works to our ill—by commercial intimidation, the whispered warning of the banker or mortgagee; by industrial terrorism, fear of the sack hanging like a cloud of doom over the heads of voting multitudes; by social panic-making, a host of petty prejudices and sordid ambitions roused to arms against us as the would-be destroyers of things as they are.

It then went on to locate the source of the Money Power that held dominion over the Australian people:

> Yes, so far as we are concerned, the headquarters of the Money Power is Britain. But the Money Power is not a British institution; it is cosmopolitan. It is of no nationality, but of all nationalities. It dominates the world.

It reinforced this domination by penetrating the human mind:

> The Money Power has corrupted the faculties of the human soul, and tampered with the sanity of the human intellect.

The argument continued with the assertion that the only reason why the whole capitalist system, over which the Money Power exercised total dominion, had not been exploded thus far was because the 'seething elements' that might have provoked its destruction in the 'Old World' had migrated to the United States, South Africa and Australia. It even exercised a degree of control over labour in these new lands by branding as 'extremist' those who sought to eliminate the iniquitous system, while it approved of those 'moderates' who proposed reforms that did not attack its fundamental interests:

> And that is why Labour men and women should stand religiously to their principles, and refuse the baits of compromise and expediency. The Labour party represents the one Movement able to cope successfully with the Money Power; the one moral force not vitiated by it; the regenerative agency destined to pull down the crime stained walls of the Old Order and build up an enduring City of Righteousness.

Such was Labor's most dangerous enemy. This not only drew together the elements of populist demonology that had been established in the 1890s, but also introduced a new aspect to the theory —that the Money Power was both the supreme monopoly within capitalism and the ultimate source of its vitality as a social system.

Despite the urgings of socialists that financial questions ought to be examined as part of a broader analysis of capitalist social relations, the political wing of the labour movement inclined more towards the *Worker*'s view that an analysis of capitalism should begin with finance. In short, they began their analyses from different ends of the problem. This had profound implications for the way the Labor Party approached the major crises that confronted it in the first half of the twentieth century.

When the Australian colonies became a federation in 1901, the newly formed Australian Labor Party began the process of developing national policies on a range of issues for which the Commonwealth Constitution gave the Federal Parliament power to act. Section 51 (xiii) specified 'Banking, other than State banking; also State banking extending beyond the limits of the State concerned, the incorporation of banks, and the issue of paper money'.[8] The Labor Party accepted this opportunity with alacrity. It offered a chance to shape the country's monetary system along lines similar to those advocated for State banks. Accordingly, the focus of debate shifted from the State to the Federal arena.

There was certainly no shortage of proposals. T. J. McBride was one of the first off the mark. Writing in the *Tocsin* on 24 January 1901, he suggested a scheme whereby the Commonwealth Government would issue a paper currency, designated legal tender, through a Commonwealth Bank. Many similar ideas, drawing their inspiration from the debates of the 1890s, were advanced within the labour movement. Such was the strength of Labor opinion in favour of government banking that when a proposal to establish a Commonwealth Bank came before the 1902 Federal Labor Conference it was approved with very little discussion. Senator Higgs moved 'That a Commonwealth Bank of deposit and issue be established, the directors of which shall only be appointed and dismissed by Act of Parliament'. The only real debate on the motion centred around a concern by J. C. Watson, Leader of the Federal Parliamentary Labor Party, that it should be free from political control. Conference duly resolved that the eighth plank of the General Platform should read: 'Commonwealth Bank of Deposit and Issue and Life and Fire Insurance Department, the management of each to be free from political influence'.[9]

A year later J. M. Scott took the idea a step further in his pamphlet *The Circulating Sovereign*. He argued that the whole Australian banking system should be nationalized, leaving only the government bank, which would have all the nation's financial resources at its disposal to fund what he called 'reproductive works'. Such a bank would not only be able to direct credit to projects that would be in the nation's best interests, but would also eliminate the need to raise expensive foreign loans. It would also control the currency, which he saw as the linchpin of financial liberation from the 'bridle that controls us'. The pamphlet was widely quoted, and it appears to have been influential among those Laborites who preferred to fell monopolies with one blow rather than strangle them slowly. There is some evidence to suggest that it

THE "NOSE" HAVE IT.

Labor Call, 4 May 1911
THE 'NOSE' HAVE IT.

This refers to the Fisher Government's unsuccessful attempt to gain control over monopolies at a referendum on 16 April 1911. By a vulgar pun on the anti-Semitic stereotype, Brandt depicts a triumphant banker, with the deeds to monopolies in his pocket, towering over the nation. The familiar symbols of the 'Fat' capitalist are included: the top hat, frock coat, cigar, diamond stud and obligatory corpulence. To emphasize the internationalism of financiers, his victory is hailed by his American colleague.

may have influenced the New South Wales Labor Party's decision to include bank nationalization in its platform in 1905.[10]

The Federal Labor Party was not yet ready for such a radical idea. It was not until 1908 that it adopted a comprehensive scheme for a Commonwealth Bank. King O'Malley, one of Labor's most colourful Federal Members, presented his idea for a 'National Postal Bank' to the 1908 Commonwealth Conference of the Labor Party in Brisbane. It was the first really detailed proposal to come before the party that addressed itself to the technicalities of banking practice as well as the intricacies of Commonwealth–State financial relations. Basically, it was a form of central bank, which would act as a stabilizing influence on the Australian economy. It would be a bank of deposit, issue, exchange and reserve, jointly owned by the Commonwealth and State governments, with the Commonwealth controlling at least half the shares. It was to accept ordinary banking business through Post Office agencies across the country. It would also control the issue of currency, act as managing agent for the national debt, hold the gold reserves of the private banks, and maintain the level of credit in the economy during times of crisis such as 1893. The primary purpose was to give the government effective control over the nation's monetary system. The official report records O'Malley as telling the conference:

> The great question was, to his mind, whether the Commonwealth should establish its own National Postal Banking system and manage its own finances through the regulation of its own money scheme, or continue under the benevolent guardianship of capitalists—lambs in the keeping of wolves.

Although the scheme went perilously close to being bogged in the morass of Commonwealth–State financial relations, its 'general outlines' were eventually approved by Conference, thus making it the basis of federal policy.[11]

Labor's first opportunity to do anything with this grand plan came after the 1910 election, when the ALP commanded a majority in both Houses of the Federal Parliament. Andrew Fisher, who had led the party to victory, did not mention the Commonwealth Bank of anything about Australian notes in his campaign opening. But there were some in the party who left no doubt about their views on banking. The election manifesto of the Political Labour Council of Victoria was unequivocal:

> The Labour parties throughout civilization regard land monopoly, manufacturing combines, commercial trusts, and financial

> institutions as their chief enemies, and against these powerful classes every labour attack is directed ... Banking is one of the frauds by which capitalism bleeds the people.

It went on to remind electors about the events of 1893:

> The smash arrested Australian industry and caused widespread suffering and distress among the people for years, but did little or no harm to the perpetrators. Such a catastrophe could not happen under the Commonwealth Bank.[12]

Not only would the bank prevent financial crises such as occurred in 1893, it would also be so efficient as to force the private banks from their commanding position in the Australian economy. As Frank Brennan told an election meeting:

> The position was that if the Commonwealth Bank were established, and worked on socialistic lines, its rate of interest would be so reasonable that it would attract to it the customers of the Commonwealth, and would become the predominant bank, and the other banks would sink into relative inferiority.[13]

It would thus offer the people two weapons in their struggle with the Money Power: a shield against the anarchy of capitalist finance, and a garrotte to throttle the private banks.

Soon after the election the Government proceeded to 'pasteurize' O'Malley's scheme. The first step in this process was to make the issue of Australian notes a separate matter from the establishment of a Commonwealth Bank. On 26 July 1910 Fisher introduced the Australian Notes Bill into the House of Representatives. The main purpose was to give the Government, through the Commonwealth Treasury, the sole right to issue legal tender notes within Australia. Notes issued by the private banks were squeezed out of circulation by a separate Act, which imposed a tax upon them. Both measures were duly passed after only token resistence from the Opposition and the first notes printed by the Treasury came into circulation in 1913.[14]

While the Australian Notes Bill caused barely a ripple in the political waters, the forthcoming Commonwealth Bank Bill in 1911 was the occasion for a rhetorical splash by a number of Labor publicists. The Sydney *Worker* of 28 September 1911 replied to the opponents of state banking with the assertion:

> The deposits with which banks trade are the accumulated savings of labour which are absorbed by these institutions and used by the

> ruling classes who control them for the purpose of private profit, and to oppress their true owners.

It went on to commend the model of the Argentine national bank, which had been established in 1891 to stabilize that country's monetary affairs. *Labor Call* published a concurrent series of articles that reviewed the various types of central bank to be found in England, Scotland, France, Argentina and Switzerland. The paper did not take too much care in discriminating between them, its point being that they were necessary for a nation's financial stability.[15] Henry Boote, who was already pre-eminent among labour journalists, addressed the question with his customary flourish. To him, the Commonwealth Bank would become a mighty weapon in the hands of the people. It would allow them, once and for all, to smite the Money Power. He began with a familiar proposition:

> The big financial institutions governed the world of Capitalism and, that being so, they governed the Governments too.

After a detailed examination of O'Malley's scheme he predicted:

> It would consolidate the public debts, and by the provision of a sinking fund—criminally neglected by the States—would ultimately extinguish them, and relieve the people of the burden of interminable usury.

Following the usual reminder to readers about the 'terror of 93', he drew attention to what he saw as the real significance of the bank:

> But chiefly the National Bank would be of value as a weapon with which the people would destroy the tyranny of the Money Power, and free themselves from the brutal bondage of the gold-bugs. The despotism of the Lords of the Purse is one that penetrates into every home, and extracts its due from the leanest households. There is no escaping from it. The very infant in the cradle is meat for the ravenous maw of the Money Power. Of all monopolies it is the greatest and most oppressive, for it includes that of land. The big financial institutions in Australia are the big landlords also. The tax of usury it levies on the wealth producers amounts to tens of millions a year, every penny of which goes into the pockets of persons who have done nothing to earn it, and most of whom are absentees, squandering in the giddy circles of London and Paris the

wealth created by the sweat and blood of Australian workers. The National Bank will enable the people to fight against this gigantic monopoly. It will make them masters of their own currency. With the capital at its command it will encourage their energy and skill, not for the profit of useless shareholders but for the common good. Whatever gain results from the transactions of the National Bank will be public gain, and private greed will have no share in it.[16]

It was thus more than a weapon. It was a symbol of the people's determination to shape their own financial destiny. As such, it might become an instrument of social transformation from Money Power barbarism to the socialist millennium. The *Sydney Morning Herald* of 17 November 1911 was also excited by this prospect, but from an opposite political stance. It warned readers that the Bill harboured an insidious design to force all other banks out of business, with the ultimate intention of confiscating the country's wealth.

When Fisher introduced the Commonwealth Bank Bill into Parliament it soon became clear that neither paper had good reason to get agitated. The bank described in the bill bore little resemblance to O'Malley's brain-child, much less the mighty weapon with which the people might finally slay the capitalist juggernaut. It had already lost the right to issue paper currency, and it was not given the powers of a true central bank, a crucial element in O'Malley's scheme. In its essentials it was to operate as a normal trading and savings bank, with the additional responsibility of conducting the Commonwealth Government's banking business. Except in the matters of ownership, and management by a single governor, its appearance differed little from that of an ordinary proprietary bank.[17]

Debate on the Bill was lengthy, with nearly thirty members speaking during the second reading stage, but it was not a particularly heated debate. Fisher argued that, in a field occupied entirely by private institutions, there was ample room for a people's bank. In the course of his speech he did offer a more substantial justification by hinting that it might eventually develop the functions of a central bank. Apart from an objection by some Opposition members to the principle of government involvement in the monetary system, most criticism focused on specific provisions in the Bill. Some thought that management by a governor concentrated too much authority in one man, and suggested a board instead. Others argued that the savings bank department would draw funds from State banks. This was seen as a threat to one of the main sources of loan money for State governments, thus diminishing the financial independence of the States.

Sydney *Worker*, 7 December 1911
HAPPY HOMESTEAD.

This is the kind of modest rural utopia that the radical nationalists were talking about. It is not some grand, extravagant folly like Lane's 'New Australia'. The accompanying poem conveys, nevertheless, the same millenarian vision:

For I'm sickened of the shadows, and I'm wearied of the strife,
And the world is void and vapid in the morning of my life.
But beyond the shades of sorrow perfect benediction lies—
It is Happy Happy Homestead—and Eternal Paradise!

It is also significant that, although this dream is located in the temporal world, it is expressed in the familiar language of religious discourse.

There was also the criticism that if the Government did not intend to make it an institution to smash private finance, as Labor policy implied, then why bother with a bank in the form proposed? Hughes, for the Government, replied to this taunt by suggesting that the Opposition was disappointed because they had been presented with a practical measure rather than a revolutionary one. The critics, nevertheless, had a point. The Commonwealth Bank Bill was, as Gollan has argued, a compromise between the demands of Labor's radicals, the objections of conservative bankers and the Government's perception of what the electorate was ready to accept.[18]

The Bill was duly passed and Labor had its people's bank, albeit in a much diminished form. Despite some initial disappointment for those who had hoped that it would be an all-out assault on the Money Power, it remained as a tangible symbol of the people's determination to free themselves from the depredations of private finance. Many Labor radicals were content to abuse the Bank's critics or unearth plots against it by the agents of Mammon.[19] It was not long before their attention was turned to broader issues involving a world-wide Money Power conspiracy.

3

'The Kingdom of Shylock' – War and Finance

When the European war broke out in August 1914 Australia was in the midst of a federal election campaign. The coincidence of these two events provided an occasion for many effusive declarations of imperial loyalty, and some ugly demonstrations of Anglo-Saxon chauvinism. Four days before hostilities commenced the incumbent Liberal Prime Minister, Joseph Cook, told a Horsham audience: 'Whatever happens, Australia is a part of the Empire to the full. Remember that when the Empire is at war, so is Australia at war'. On the same evening Andrew Fisher put the Labor Party's position to the electors of Colac. He invited them to 'Turn your eyes to the European situation . . . and give the kindest feelings towards the mother country at this time'. He went on to express the hope that international arbitration might avert a disastrous war, 'But should the worst happen after everything has been done that honour will permit, Australians will stand beside our own to help and defend her to our last man and our last shilling'.[1] The question of Australian participation was not at issue. The choice was between two versions of Empire patriotism.

Some sections of the labour press followed their parliamentary leader, while others, less mindful of electoral considerations, were equivocal. The Brisbane *Worker* stood squarely behind Fisher. On 6 August it reminded readers that Australia was as much a part of the Empire as England and went on to assert that England would have come to Australia's aid had it been in peril. With the truculent pride of an adolescent springing to the defence of a parent, the paper declared:

> Australian labor has shown the world many object lessons in the way of standing shoulder to shoulder in time of trouble. And now that war has been proclaimed, Australian labor will stand shoulder to shoulder with old England in her hour of storm and stress.

A day earlier, the Hobart *Daily Post* had urged the faithful to 'Remember your Party, and your Country too!'

There were some tortuous attempts to illustrate the necessity of Australia's involvement. The Brisbane *Daily Standard* of 24 August claimed that although Labor hated war and had nothing to gain from it, Britain's cause was just and the defeat of Germany would provide socialists in that country with the opportunity to rid themselves of a long-endured tyranny.

Henry Boote, editor of the *Australian Worker*, did not share the patriotic fervour that Fisher paraded before the electorate. He reacted, on 6 August, with a mixture of sorrow and apprehension:

> We must protect our country. We must keep sacred from the mailed fist this splendid heritage. But we hope no wave of jingo madness will sweep over the land, unbalancing the judgement of its leaders, and inciting its population to wild measures, spurred on by the vile press, to which war is only an increase in circulation, and every corpse a copper. God help Australia! God help England! God help Germany! God help us!

Statements such as these betrayed a profound ambivalence in labour ideology on questions of nationalism, imperialism, race and class. At the outbreak of war they posed a set of dilemmas. In the following three years, as Fisher's last man and last shilling appeared more like grim prophecy than mere rhetoric, they were resolved in radical populist terms.

Even though many labour people were prepared to accept Australia's participation during the early stages of the war, that did not prevent the labour press from commenting on what had caused it. In doing so, they gave signs of what was to come. The Brisbane *Worker* of 17 September reviewed the Rothschild family's long association with financial houses to illustrate a connection between war and finance. The main point of the article was that without the consent of bankers like the Rothschilds there could be no war. Addressing itself to the subject of 'the war and its causes', the *Australian Worker* of 15 October argued that 'Kaiser Bill' was merely a scapegoat to deflect attention from the root cause, which was the institutionalization of greed in the capitalist system. The argument implied a familiar view about the structure of capitalism and the nature of imperialism:

> The criminal machinations of the great War Trust, the traitorous greed of the international Armaments Ring, the unquenchable lust of the manufacturers for foreign markets, the passionate longing of the merchants for new opportunities of trade—all this it was, awakening the heart to unholy cravings for gain, that plunged the world into war.

W. Wallis, writing in *Labor Call* on 29 October, put it more bluntly: 'Wars are made by capitalists for capitalists, and the majority suffer to enrich the few'.

Most Australian socialists took a similar view. They saw the war not as a grand adventure, but an utter horror. It was not only a brutal illustration of capitalism's evils but also a weapon for capitalists to suppress the working class. Accordingly, the Victorian Socialist Party adopted the policy that Keir Hardie had proposed to the Second International's Amsterdam Congress when he called for a general strike against armament manufacture by workers of all nations, as a means to wage 'war against war'.[2] A. W. Foster spoke for many socialists when he told readers of the Melbourne *Socialist* on 23 October that:

> In the first place there can be no doubt as to what the attitude of every Socialist to war generally is. Each and every one abhors it, and opposes it, not only because of its useless sacrifices, its horrors, and its disastrous after-effects, but also because it is the weapon of the capitalist. It is an instrument in the hands of that class for the exploitation and suppression of the working class. The burdens of the fight are borne by workingmen and suffered by their women. The expropriated have nothing to gain, and much to lose. The exploiters, though they may suffer some temporary embarrassment, yet in the end reap every reward. Finally, war stops the world's march towards the Ideal Commonwealth, which is the hope and objective of every Socialist.

The Sydney *International Socialist* of 8 August had already stated virtually the same view with greater force in an article entitled 'The Mad Drama in Europe'. The Industrial Workers of the World (IWW) took a characteristically tough position. On 22 August their paper, *Direct Action*, urged workers to unite in a general strike against the war and to back that up by refusing to join the armed forces.

Although these ideas found a wider audience later in the war, they did not attract a general following in 1914. The great weight of labour opinion rested somewhere between those who saw the war as a sad but inevitable consequence of capitalist development, which must nevertheless be fought and won, and those who inclined to Fisher's position. Many unionists, in fact, voted with their feet. Of the 54 000 men who enlisted in the Australian Imperial Force during the first five months of the war, 45 per cent were members of trade unions. This was much greater than the proportion of unionists in the adult male population.[3] The electors also expressed a preference for Fisher's version of imperial patriotism by returning the Labor Party to government with a majority in both Houses.

Frank Anstey, a radical Labor Member of the House of Representatives, was among the small minority who spoke out against the war from the beginning.[4] In common with many other Labor activists who had served their political apprenticeship during the 1890s, Anstey saw capitalism in terms of monopoly interests. His first book, *Monopoly and Democracy*, published in 1906, examined how the pattern of public and private investment in Victorian land development had concentrated ownership in a few hands at the expense of yeoman farmers. He regarded this as an inefficient and corrupting process, which prevented 'closer settlement' by smallholders. His argument was an extension of the radical tradition that saw the establishment of an independent yeomanry as both a social ideal and a democratic balwark against the ravages of monopoly capitalism.

This concern with monopolies became a major theme in Anstey's subsequent writings. On 9 April 1914 he turned his attention to European steel and armament trusts, which, he warned readers of *Labor Call*, precipitated wars to reap the benefits of slaughter. They had interests that interlocked with, and were buttressed by, large banks, newspapers, military commanders and churchmen, who assisted them in this ambition. On 18 June he gave the same audience a specific example of what he meant. Following the lead of his radical counterparts in Britain, he claimed that through the interests that both Vickers and Krupps held in the Russian firm of Putiloff, each had ready access to the other's technical secrets. This he asserted, showed that while 'the War Gods' paraded themselves about Britain and Germany as patriots, their primary loyalty was to sordid profit from the means of destruction.[5]

Soon after the war began, he reviewed the British Government's special financial arrangements to compensate private banks for losses incurred by the declaration of hostilities. He offered an elaborate explanation of how government-guaranteed notes issued to the banks meant that the British people were twice robbed. In the first instance, the fact that the notes were issued at all meant that the people, through the Government, were giving the banks money that would normally have been accounted as a business loss. In the second, the banks then loaned the notes back to the Government in exchange for war bonds, which returned a high rate of interest. There was, he argued, a cruel paradox in this when the Government's tender regard for the banks was compared with the way it treated a worker who lost his job.[6]

With this 'lesson' in mind, he addressed the problem of how

Australian Worker, 10 February 1916
HATS OFF! THE 5% PATRIOT.
The Tory daily press applauds the patriotism of the wealthy subscribers to the War Loan in not holding back for higher interest.

Australia was to finance its war effort. Harking back to Labor's original conception of what the Commonwealth Bank should have been, he proposed that its functions be expanded to include note issue and reserve banking. With that accomplished, it could then issue non-interest-bearing notes based on the nation's real wealth. This would avoid the need to raise overseas loans with their attendant heavy interest burdens. If it were also given the powers of a central bank, it would be able to control the country's gold reserves and thus prevent speculative operations that would undermine the monetary system.[7]

Early in 1915 he began to draw these threads together. Referring to the outcome of war, he declared:

> This war will put a millstone of debt around the necks of the producing classes of every country. It will grind them to degrading slavery. It will make the monetary power more powerful and oppulent than ever. All who remain alive from the slaughter will toil to pay the parasitical classes annual tribute for the money invested in blood. All wars—all international wars—are the instruments by which iniquities re-establish their crumbling thrones, by dissipating on battlefields the human virility that threatened their existence.[8]

Between 1915 and 1921 he developed these ideas on monopoly, finance and war into a theory of capitalism that provided the labour movement with its most elaborate analysis of the Money Power. He began with articles in *Labor Call.* These were expanded into the pamphlets *War and Finance* and *The Kingdom of Shylock* later in 1915. Two years later they were combined and enlarged under the latter title. The argument was again revised and extended into its final form in 1921 as the book *Money Power.*

The point from which he began his analysis was stated most clearly in the 'Preliminary' to the 1917 edition of *The Kingdom of Shylock.* Referring to the labour movement, he wrote:

> This movement of ours talks of 'The Means of Production,

This comment on the immorality of making profits from war and the hypocrisy of parading them under the banner of patriotism is typical of the biting irony in Marquet's cartoons. Here he invokes all the familiar symbols of the degenerate Shylock stereotype. Significantly, he replaces the southern cross — the one distinctively Australian symbol on the flag — with that of the pawnbroker. The old woman holding the flag is 'Granny', a conventional personification of the *Sydney Morning Herald.*

> Distribution and Exchange'. Of the first two we read much, hear much—upon the last we are silent in speech and policy. Yet in the modern world the last is fundamental in industry, in statecraft, and in war. It is in coping with the problems of Finance that the world has got to find its regeneration.[9]

From the war years onwards this became the central preoccupation of his political career.

In Anstey's conception of capitalism the Money Power occupied a very particular place, which resulted from the way the system had developed in modern times:

> The 'Money Power' is something more than Capitalism. It is its product, and yet its master. 'Capitalism', in its control of the great agencies of production, is observable and understandable. The other lurks in vaults and banking chambers, masquerading its operations in language that mystifies or dazzles. Industrial Capitalism may roll itself up into great monopolies in production and distribution. *It cannot exist for an hour apart from the powers that hold the 'Monopoly of the Instruments of Exchange'. Modern Capitalism throws ever-increasing power into the hands of men who operate the monetary machine.* These men constitute 'The Financial Oligarchy'. The key to their power is combination and concentration. They control banks, trust companies and insurance. They control the savings of the people. They say to whom the savings shall be lent and from whom withheld. They finance industries in which they are interested, and withdraw facilities from would-be rivals. *Such is the Modern Money Power.*[10]

This view had its ancestry in the unlikely marriage between chapter 10 of J. A. Hobson's *Evolution of Modern Capitalism* and the received wisdom from the 1890s bank crashes.

According to Anstey, the essential feature of modern capitalism that had produced this state of affairs was the 'paperisation of industry', the 'cutting up of industry and countries into stocks and bonds'. Once that process began, 'Quick rich comes no more entirely from the profits of industry, but from the market manipulation of shares'. Following this crucial step, the paper symbols of industry became the playthings of speculators and stock-market riggers who could manipulate the 'savings of the trustful'. The process did not end there. The profits from this speculation were invested and re-invested until the fields of industrial activity were exhausted and money became 'cheap'. To prevent profits and interest rates collapsing, 'International hatreds are stimulated', which in turn led to a point where 'armaments are demanded, loans are raised, and the right to levy perpetual tribute on the nation is given in return'. The inevitable outcome was war, in which the toiling masses were slaughtered while the Money Power grew rich upon their misery and death. As a result:

> To the capitalisation or paperisation of industry is added the capitalisation of the living masses. War stimulates the process. The nation sinks further and further into debt. It is mortgaged. It is cut up into stocks, bonds, and debentures at so much per cent. It is sold in pieces upon the market places of the world, and the right to bleed is sold to the highest bidder—Yankee Doodle, Jap, Jew or Gentile. To carry out these vast flotations and speculations in war or in peace, it is necessary to control the banks. Whosoever controls the banks controls industry. This control is exercised in every country by a small group—the inner circle of great Capitalists. This group is designated 'the Money Power'.[11]

Having thus established its supremacy, the 'Black Masonic Order of Plutocracy' was then able to exercise its 'power of plunder'.

Although the process from which it emerged was universal, the Money Power's appearance had distinct national characteristics:

> In the U.S. it is bold, brutal, barefaced. In other countries it is cloaked, polished, hypocritical, but everywhere an oligarchy of financiers working towards the same despotic end.

That end was to make itself 'the dominant behind the curtain power in the government of modern States'.[12] Thus, according to Anstey, capitalism was not simply an economic system that divided people into mutually hostile classes. It had become something more than that. In the hands of the Money Power it had been transformed into a vast conspiracy to enslave the toiling masses.

Such concentrated power harnessed to this ambition gave ample proof of the Money Power's moral turpitude.

> Men may die but Money makes no sacrifice. It looks upon bloody war as a rich gold mine yielding fat dividends for ever and ever without end. Human bloodsuckers, who risk neither life nor limb nor penny, wax fat on Armageddon.[13]

This added another dimension to the political and economic struggle of the labour movement. It was a moral crusade against an enemy who embodied the worst of human motivations. Anstey's account of modern capitalism's transformation into a cabal of financiers shifted its motive force from the logic of economic interests to malicious acts of human will.

The whole pattern of capitalist development thus derived from a darkness in the heart of a few evil men obsessed by greed and ambition. In his personification of Modern Money Power's ancestry, Anstey invoked a familiar stereotype:

> After Medina came the Jew, Manessah Lopez. He amassed a fortune in the panic which followed the false news that Queen Anne was dead. He 'bought on the slump and sold on the rise'. Then came Samson Gideon and the Goldsmids—Abraham and Benjamin. They were succeeded by the Rothschilds.[14]

This was followed by a history of the Rothschild family, which purported to show their skill in financial manipulation and how it had won them a prominent place in both German and British society.

This anti-Semitism in *The Kingdom of Shylock* was no aberration. It arose from the logic of his analysis combined with the cultural tradition of which he was a part. The vulgarities of Christian mythology had built up an accretion of hatred and suspicion towards Jews over many centuries. The resulting stereotype of the greedy and cunning Jewish financier was a commonplace convention in the writings of British radicals and American populists. It was also, as we have seen, a persistent theme among Australian labour radicals. Having defined the essence of power within modern capitalism in terms of an evil conspiracy, it was hardly surprising that a man of Anstey's background should have chosen to invoke such a stereotype. Indeed, the quotations scattered throughout *The Kingdom of Shylock* and *Money Power* demonstrate his heavy reliance on British and American sources.

The ultimate force of this argument depended on the willingness of his audience to accept the racist assumptions on which the stereotype was based. The frequent repetition of it by others in pamphlets, speeches and labour journals suggests that there were many who shared those assumptions.

Once labour's most insidious enemy had been so identified, all that remained was to sweep him aside, thus clearing the road to the millennium:

> It is not a question of class or of class interests. The class struggle will disappear with the exterminated interests of the predatory cliques. It is a question of the capacity of the State to meet the rising

> tide of its responsibilities. It is a question of the economic re-organisation on lines that will furnish its people with an attractive existence and attract others from abroad. It is a question of how and by what means its territory shall be utilised, its resources developed, its wealth multiplied, so that by its wealth and its people—the abundance of the one and widespread ownership by the other, the essentials of a self-sustained community will be secured.[15]

Anstey's analysis had the dual benefit of simplifying both the problem and the solution. If the quintessence of power and evil in modern capitalism was located in a small predatory oligarchy, then the people's social and moral regeneration could begin with the elimination of that oligarchy. This would permit the development of a benevolent State where the latent forces of social harmony embodied in the labour movement could grow and flourish.

There was nothing original in this line of argument. It had appeared in fragmentary form in a number of places many times before. Anstey's role was to arrange those fragments into a conspiratorial design of global proportions. In telling the labour movement about the Money Power, however, all he really offered was an elaborate demonology masquerading as an analysis of capitalism. By doing so, he simply reflected and strengthened labour's populist tradition.

It was not merely the resilience of that tradition, nor the force of rhetoric from publicists like Anstey, that gave these views a wide currency in the labour movement. As hostilities ground on, the full meaning of modern warfare began to impress itself upon the popular imagination. The seemingly relentless casualty lists steadily eroded the almost innocent confidence that many people felt during the early months. The resulting tensions were reflected in the bitterness surrounding the conscription issue, the Easter Rebellion in Ireland and the 1917 general strike. The general war-weariness that developed out of all this helped to create a climate of opinion much more receptive to radical interpretations of the war.

Long before any of this was apparent, many workers were confronted by more familiar difficulties. In the second and third quarters of 1914 reported trade-union unemployment almost doubled, from 5.7 to 10.7 per cent. This was compounded by an effective wage freeze at pre-1914 levels, set against a rise in food prices of almost 40 per cent between the beginning of 1914 and the latter part of 1915. This drastic cut in real income sharpened the resentment that many people felt when the Commonwealth Government abandoned a proposed referendum on price control in October 1915.[16]

Labor Call, 6 April 1916
STILL HUNGRY FOR OUR BEST.

This is Marquet's answer to the famous recruiting poster featuring Lord Kitchener. Instead of a patriotic challenge, a blood-thirsty militarist

There had been a good deal of comment in sections of the labour movement about alleged profiteering, and although a drastic increase in the money supply seems to have been the primary cause of wartime inflation, there were some cases where firms appeared to be taking advantage of the circumstances to boost profits. In 1915 the Ryan Labor Government in Queensland found that the Colonial Sugar Refining Company and some meat processors had exploited the situation to reap excessive profit. In the case of CSR, the Government responded with the Sugar Acquisition Act, by which it acquired the total crop at a set price. W. F. Finlayson took the allegation a step further when he told the House of Representatives that a small coterie of businessmen in Sydney and Melbourne who controlled Australia's major companies were primarily responsible for the level of prices and wages:

> They hold an absolute control over the means of livelihood of the people. They control not only the wages paid, but what those wages can buy, and the quantities which can be purchased by them. They absolutely control the margin between the wages which they pay to the workmen and the amount which they take back from those workmen for the food which the latter eat. They are the speculators in butter, wheat and sugar.

Nor was it just the worker who suffered at the hands of avaricious speculators. J. K. McDougall later claimed that farmers were exploited in a similar way:

> The farmers of Victoria are being guillotined financially for the profit of Shipping Pirates, Bag Buccaneers, Money Mountebanks and Commission Cormorants. These parasites, protected by law, acquire the profits of exploitery by simple commercial processes and hold them . . . In fact, as things are at present, the country might as well sack Hughes and Hagethorn and their incompetent pals, save their salaries, and allow the Associated Banks and the shipping bosses to run Australia. They are the real masters of this country and its politicians.

---

lunges forward, grasping for still more men to devour. In this, the symbols of Prussian militarism, which artists like Norman Lindsay employed to bolster recruiting, are turned against themselves. The point is to identify both British and Prussian militarism as beasts of the same species. The redesigned German helmet shows who profits from the slaughter of war. It is the same hierarchy that Anstey and his colleagues had been talking about.

By the middle of the war years there was a widespread belief in labour circles that inflation was almost entirely due to profiteering. The 1916 Annual Conference of the Victorian Labor Party thought that the situation demanded drastic action and passed a motion from Meehan and Scullin calling for the confiscation of all war profits.[17]

There were many in the labour movement who followed Anstey's lead in suggesting that of all the forms of wartime profiteering the most extensive and insidious was the money lending of 'Shylock'. The *Australian Worker* of 5 August 1915 took a cynical view of 'The Patriotism of Shylock', arguing that an interest rate of 4.5 per cent on a war loan of £20 million was scandalous, because it meant that the 'moneyed interests' would grow fat on war profits while the workers gave their lives at the front. Urging some 'equality of sacrifice', it concluded: 'The poor are giving their lives. The least the rich can do is give their money'. The following week, to reinforce its point, the paper suggested that as there had been a less than overwhelming response to the loan, it was clear that 'Shylock threatens to strike' in the hope that interest rates on future loans would be raised. It concluded with a warning:

> When Shylock isn't satisfied with this guilt-edged arrangement, and darkly hints of going on strike, it is time that Australia began to devise other and more direct means of paying the piper.

Early the following year, when it became clear that the war loan had in fact been oversubscribed, the paper did not withdraw its comments but took the opportunity to draw another lesson for its readers. On 10 February 1916 it argued that the bulk of the money subscribed had come from 'Fat', who had stolen it, through industrial exploitation and price manipulation, from the real producers of wealth—the workers. The victims of such robbery would in future have to pay 'Fat' interest on that money, which was originally of their own making. These sins were compounded later in the year when the Commonwealth Government announced tax exemptions for the interest payments as an added incentive to loan subscribers. On 15 June 1916 the paper saw it as a direct grant to Greed:

> And the trouble is that if the Federal or State taxes have to be increased this gilt-edged aristocracy will be untouched—unless the Government repudiates its original agreement with Shylock and candidly confesses that it was diddled by the grasping and unpatriotic Money Power of Australia—by the schemers and boodlers who have always been Labor's bitterest and most unscrupulous enemies.

The operation of market forces on capitalist finance thus became part of the Money Power conspiracy.

These ideas on industrial exploitation, war profiteering and financial conspiracy were gradually drawn together into a more general argument, which complemented Anstey's exposition of the Money Power. It began with the assumption that labour and raw materials were the source of all real wealth. Whatever profit capitalists were able to make by employing these in the production of commodities was 'surplus value'. This was derived from a kind of double exploitation. The first involved the underpayment of workers relative to the value of the goods they produced. The second was outright profiteering on the prices charged for those goods. Either way, workers and their families were exploited through low wages or high prices, frequently both. The proceeds of this 'surplus value' became capital, which was then invested at the highest possible interest rate. Individual capitalists did not do this on their own behalf, but put their 'ill-gotten gains' into the care of banks and other financial institutions. This aggregation of 'surplus value' not only provided the life-blood of industrial capitalism but also placed a powerful weapon in the hands of those who could manipulate it through their control of the banks. Those individuals and institutions who controlled this accumulated wealth were the Money Power. That wealth, although nominally the property of other capitalists, had in fact been stolen from the workers who produced it in the first place. The Money Power's ability to manipulate that wealth for its own ends was proof that it preyed upon lesser capitalists and workers alike. The logic of this process meant that armed conflict was an inevitable consequence of the Money Power's operations and a means by which it strengthened its position. It not only made huge profits from the slaughter of the foolishly patriotic workers, but also took every opportunity to subjugate the organized labour movement, which presented the only real threat to its continued existence.[18] It was in exactly these terms that labour radicals chose to interpret the 'real' reason behind the proposal from W. M. Hughes, who had succeeded Fisher as Labor Prime Minister, that Australians be conscripted to fight in Europe.

The controversy surrounding the conscription issue in 1916 grew out of the social tensions that had been developing since the early months of 1915. In addition to the war-weariness already mentioned, there was growing disquiet about the direction in which Hughes was leading the Labor Government. The way he applied the draconian provisions of the War Precautions Act against anyone opposed to his recruiting drives—particularly the Industrial Workers of the World—confirmed radical suspicions about his determination to support the Empire to 'the last man and the last shilling'. The belief that he meant to introduce conscription to bolster flagging enlistments prompted the New South Wales Labor Council, as early as September 1915, to pass a resolution that there should be no conscription of men unless wealth was also conscripted. In the first five months of 1916 the Australian Workers' Union Annual Convention, the Queensland and Victorian ALP Conferences and the All-Australian Trade Union Congress endorsed that view. A motion from Frank Hyett, one of Anstey's protégés, was passed unanimously by the Trade Union Congress. It declared:

> That, as the war policy of the capitalist class consists of the conscription of human life, and unlimited robbery of the citizens of the nation that protects them, this Congress affirms that it is the duty of the Labor Party to reverse the capitalist war policy, and prohibit exploitation of the public.

A number of other related motions reflected the hardening attitude of the movement's industrial wing.[19]

When the radicals' fears were realized and Hughes introduced the Military Service Referendum Bill to the House of Representatives in September 1916, Anstey suggested that its real purpose would be more properly expressed in the title 'Coloured Labour Referendum Bill'. He explained sarcastically:

> One of the advantages to be anticipated from the carrying of the proposed referendum is the advance of our industries by the sending out of the country of 200,000 or 300,000 of our men, and replacing them by coloured labourers. It is unnecessary to elaborate the virtues of the proposal. If we can put cheap Asiatics in the place of the men to be sent abroad the advantage to every industry in Australia must be patent.

This played upon the fear, entrenched in labour ideology since the 1890s, that capitalists would exploit every opportunity to import an 'inferior species of creation' as a way to break down the hard-won living standards of Australian workers. It was yet another example of how race and class were linked within the Money Power's great conspiracy against the Australian people.[20]

The referendum was narrowly defeated on 28 October, following a bitterly divisive campaign, which often provoked physical violence. On 14 November, at the first subsequent meeting of Federal Caucus, the split in Labor ranks was formally completed when twenty-four MPs followed Hughes out of the party room. The Hughes faction joined the Liberals in February 1917 to form the Nationalist Party, and they campaigned for the 5 May election under that banner in a two-party contest against the ALP. Hughes's emphasis on winning the war as the most important expression of imperial loyalty contrasted sharply with Labor's tendency to put 'Australia First'. The result was an overwhelming endorsement for Hughes, with the Nationalists winning 53 of the 75 House of Representatives seats and all 18 Senate places.

Such a dramatic reversal of its electoral fortunes had a number of significant effects upon the labour movement. Although the split had purged the party of its more conservative element, those people also comprised most of its leaders. According to conservative opinion, 'the Labor Party had blown its brains out'. The drastic reduction in its numbers left it little more than a parliamentary rump. This not only altered the political complexion of Federal Caucus, but also shifted the balance of power within the labour movement more towards the unions. The first initiative from the industrial wing began in August 1917, when a dispute in the New South Wales railways quickly developed into a general strike. This gave vent to a great deal of pent-up frustration and resentment. But the unions had not anticipated the vigour with which Nationalist State and Federal governments would suppress the strike and then victimize the men involved. Their first major challenge to Hughes's belligerence resulted in a humiliating defeat. Although it served to widen the audience receptive to radical interpretations of the war, that gain was bought at a very high price.[21]

The existing tensions were heightened during September and October, when the Australian forces in France suffered 38 000 casualties at the Third Battle of Ypres. Hughes responded with a second referendum seeking approval to conscript men for military service in Europe. The campaign leading up to the poll on 20 December was just as violent as the first. Scuffles were commonplace. Many meetings ended with an all-in brawl. The War Precautions Act was used ruthlessly to silence the Government's opponents.[22] This time, however, the labour movement was united in its determination to resist what Henry Boote called the 'lottery of death'. In his view, Hughes was simply the 'mouthpiece' of capitalists whose real objective was 'the militarisation of Labor'. They wanted to 'break the independent spirit of the Australian workers, and accustom them to being disciplined like chain-gangs and sweated coolies'.[23] T. J. Ryan, the Labor Premier of Queensland, who had received a good deal of unwelcome attention from Hughes, saw it in purely conspiratorial terms:

> Here is the sinister motive behind the whole conscription plot—

Brisbane *Worker*, 28 September 1916
HISTORY REPEATED – A FAMOUS ANCIENT RUSE.

Anstey's speech on what he called 'the Coloured Labour Referendum Bill' inspired this cartoon. The farewell party comprises the usual collection of jingoist figures: Hughes, the Fat Man and the patriotic cleric. While they wave the 'brave boys' off, the potential war widow and her children weep. In the foreground, another Fat Person tries to tear down the sign proclaiming White Australia, while the Trojan horse disgorges its cargo of cheap Asian labour. In the usual manner, they are presented as figures of fun and derision. Ominously, the 'brave lads' have been betrayed as this 'lesser species of creation' scurries about to occupy the country they may never see again.

> enslavement of the workers, not reinforcements for the soldiers in the trenches; the destruction of labor organisation in Australia, not the destruction of Prussianism in Europe; military control of the workshop, not military supremacy on the battlefield.[24]

Although not all anti-conscriptionists shared Ryan's view, a majority of the electorate, slightly larger than in 1916, was still not convinced that conscription was necessary, and so rejected it a second time.

By the end of the war the mood of the labour movement had been transformed. The ambivalence about nationalism, imperialism and class that was implicit at the beginning had gone. After four years of hostilities both at home and abroad, Henry Boote may well have questioned which 'splendid heritage' should be 'kept sacred' from which 'mailed fist'. It would be a long time before a union paper would again declare, as the Brisbane *Worker* had on 6 August 1914, that 'Australian labor will stand shoulder to shoulder with old England in her hour of storm and stress'. Men like Anstey now commanded the largest audience within the movement.

The strained relations that were evident in Australia at the end of the war were a pale reflection of the massive upheavals that occurred in most other combatant nations. The 1917 October Revolution in Russia had taken the quesion of socialism out of the realm of speculation and provided a model against which radicals felt they must measure themselves. Following the armistice, Germany had become a republic, amid sporadic revolutionary outbursts. There had been incidents of open rebellion in the British forces, and police strikes in England during 1918–19. Despite the intervention of capitalist countries in the civil war, the spectre of Russian Communism persisted, as all over Europe the old order crumbled under the weight of total war and massive popular discontent. As Kendall remarked, 'The struggle began as a war between governments. It ended as a struggle between classes which, for a while, seemed likely to tear the whole fabric of European society asunder'.[25] Explaining the significance of events in Russia, Anstey told his Australian readers in September 1919: 'Capitalism listens with quaking soul to the drum-beats of the Armies of Revolution. Those beats grow louder and louder—they draw nearer and nearer'.[26]

Although the distant drum of revolution may have echoed across this 'red dawn', the net effect within the Australian labour movement was an increase in industrial militancy, a rise in the temperature of radical rhetoric, and an overhaul of the ALP's platform and objective. Nevertheless, the war years had given a wider currency to the view that 'Wars are made by capitalists for capitalists, and the majority suffer to enrich the few'. It followed from that proposition that so long as capitalism survived so would the threat of future war. It would thus be necessary to overthrow it if enduring peace was to be secured.

In the immediate post-war years the labour movement came the closest it has ever been to making a unqualified declaration that it would be better to abolish capitalism outright rather than try to reform it progressively. Within the industrial wing there was much spirited argument about syndicalism and how the One Big Union was the most appropriate weapon to sweep capitalism into the dustbin of history. Various Marxist sects vied for Comintern recognition of their claim to represent what they imagined to be the revolutionary spirit of the Australian working class. Even the Victorian Branch of the Labor Party entertained a motion from Maurice Blackburn that called for the peaceful overthrow of capitalism.[27]

In the arguments about what was to be done there was general agreement that capitalism was both inefficient and evil. Most discussion still implied the established view that capitalism was comprised of an interlocking set of exploitative agencies, despite the insistence of a growing body of opinion that its essential structure was to be found in the relationship of classes to the means of production.

When the ALP Commonwealth Conference of June 1919 came to discuss the question of banking and finance, the interpretation that most delegates preferred was quite clear. With very little debate, Conference accepted the recommendation of its Banking and Insurance Committee that the party adopt a new plank in its Fighting Platform, to read 'Nationalisation of Banking and Insurance'. The official report records no debate other than the speeches made by the mover and seconder of the motion, McNamara and Clementson. The report paraphrases McNamara's speech:

> At the present time banking and insurance was in the hands of private individuals, and they were able to exercise a power almost greater than that possessed by Parliament itself. Banking and insurance should be controlled by Parliament in the interests of the whole of the people. He instanced that although the banks had under £30,000,000 in capital and property, they exercised control of over £250,000,000 of the people's money, often using it against the interests of the people themselves.

He was talking about the Money Power rather than capitalist

Pro Patria and Myself

Labor Call, 19 October 1916
PRO PATRIA AND MYSELF – PATRIOT AND PARASITE

While the distraught war widow supports herself against the last grim reminder of her husband, the bloated profiteer scowls in mocking contempt of her grief. The woman in her mourning clothes symbolizes the innocent victims of the war. The parasite, from his spats to his top hat, is an instantly recognizable composite of stock visual references. This is typical of many cartoons during the war years that sought to explain the bitter harvest awaiting those who succumbed to patriotic enthusiasm. The parasite serves to inflame resentment against those who profit from that tragedy.

finance. Clementson developed the argument further with another enduring proposition:

> Under the present system prices were inflated when it suited the bank magnates to do so. This affected the cost of living. That was an evil they should suppress. All the great exploitation agencies of the country depended upon the private banks to enable them to perpetuate the evil.[28]

Anstey had told them of the Money Power's machinations, and they had learnt his lessons well. Moreover, their experience of the war years had emboldened them to contemplate more direct action to defeat this most insidious of all their enemies.

4

'Money Power Strangles Australia' – The Commonwealth Bank and Foreign Loans

In the early 1920s there were a number of issues that appeared to confirm what men like Anstey had been saying during the war—that the Money Power was an international menace that posed a direct threat to Australian independence.

The first of these was the 1920–21 foreign exchange crisis. During 1920 a fall in export earnings from primary products coincided with a huge increase in imports, which rose from £99 million to £164 million. There were also substantial interest payments to be made on war loans. The combination of these factors resulted in a massive drain on Australia's sterling reserves, which had to be severely rationed. This crisis had a significant bearing on the short, sharp recession that followed in 1921. The veteran labour journalist Frank Cotton detected a hidden hand at work. When the first signs of the crisis began to appear he told readers of the *Australian Worker*, on 12 February 1920, that:

> The maddest anarchist orator who ever mounted a soapbox at a street corner is a very harmless factor as a social disruptionist, compared with a Money King who can bring about World Ruin to suit his own interests by juggling over rates of exchange . . . If this exchange crisis serves to make us all realise that the real rulers of most civilized countries are master criminals, who keep out of public view, and 'produce bankruptcy and anarchy' it will be worthwhile passing through a long period of suffering to learn that lesson once and for all.[1]

If unstable exchange rates were the result of some form of criminal conspiracy, it was plain that foreign loans would also make the nation vulnerable to financial manipulation.

On 3 June 1920 Maurice Blackburn warned *Labor Call* readers 'Against a Borrowing Policy':

> A Borrowing Government pawns Australia to the Moneylender,

> and gives overseas financiers a vote, generally a secret but always influential vote, on Australian policies. Talk as we may of the dangers of Imperial Federation, its dangers are dwarfed by the dangers of Financial Control. At the back of the financier there lies in reserve all the power of Britain—political, judicial, and, at a pinch, military.

To illustrate the point, he referred to the way in which English financiers had tried to force the Queensland Labor Premier, E. G. Theodore, to amend proposed land tenure legislation as a condition of a loan from the London money market. This, Blackburn suggested, showed how the insistence that new dominions should retain imperial links had at its root sordid financial interest backed by political power. From this he concluded:

> No Australian Government should be prepared to abate the self-governing powers of Australia. But all Australian Governments pursue a policy which, in the long run, will make Australian Parliaments, Executives and Courts the instruments of overseas financiers.

Ten years later this did not seem to be such a wild claim.

The problems surrounding the Queensland loans provided an example of how Australian capitalists and English financiers could combine to bring considerable discomfort to a Labor government that threatened their interests. The Queensland Government had a long-standing dispute with pastoral and financial companies over rent on pastoral leases. This flared up shortly after Theodore became Premier and announced that he was going to London to negotiate new government loans. Before leaving he had defeated his opponents in the Legislative Council by swamping it with Labor nominees; they passed the Land Act Amendment Act, which gave the Government, through the Land Court, the ability to revise rent on pastoral leases without restriction. This drew protests from a meeting of Anglo-Australian banks and finance and pastoral companies in London. Shortly after, a delegation of capitalists and conservative politicians sailed for London to lobby against the Government in the City.[2] In an attempt to discredit this 'Stinking Fish' delegation, the Brisbane *Worker* of 22 April 1920 depicted its members as unscrupulous capitalists who had earned their fortunes by exploiting black labour in the north:

> It would have to be realised, first of all, that Capitalism desires black labor in the cane-fields of the North, and associated with that desire

Labor Call, 5 November 1925
ELECTORS! HERE YOU HAVE IT PLAIN.
Charlton for Australia. Bruce for Flinders Lane.

This advertisement for the 14 November Federal election illustrates the tendency of Labor to depict itself as the party that represents the national interest, as opposed to the conservatives, who stand for narrow class interest. The point is emphasized by the way Matt Charlton's benign presence assumes the same scale as the continent itself. Stanley Melbourne Bruce, on the other hand, is wedged between the dingy buildings of the narrow lane that was popularly believed to be the geographical centre of Australian capitalism.

> is the fact that a capitalist delegation of black labor champions is even now trying to persuade the British Government to take away from the people of this State the right to govern themselves.

When it became clear that Theodore was not going to raise the £3 million he sought, the City's refusal was depicted as an arrogant attempt by British Money Power to dictate the internal affairs of the Queensland people. In a cable from London, Theodore specified the terms that he claimed had been presented to him:

> At these conferences I was given to understand that financiers could not assist Queensland loan unless Government would agree to drastically modify its policy generally, and would specifically—
> 1. Withdraw Pastoral Rents Act unconditionally;
> 2. Abandon Unemployed Workers' Bill;
> 3. Modify recent Tramway Act to suit Brisbane Tramway Co.;
> 4. Modify insurance legislation;
> 5. Amend provisions of Succession Duties Act to meet wishes of English companies.[3]

Such demands were, according to the *Australian Worker* of 26 August 1920, an act of blatant imperialism:

> This action against Queensland on the part of the plutocratic pawnbrokers of England is probably part of the game being played off by British Imperialists in order to stifle democratic Legislation on the oversea Dominions.

This revived a persistent theme in labour ideology—the simultaneous equation of nationalism with democracy and capitalism with imperialism.

Theodore emphasized this theme during the 1920 Queensland election campaign:

> The Queensland Labor Government could get millions of money it it would consent to sell itself to the money lords of London. The Labor Party, however, considers that the political liberty of the people is too priceless a possession to be subject to barter, and it would not stain its honour by agreeing to any such proposal. Our opponents would allow the absentee capitalists to dictate the domestic policy of Queensland, but Labor, on the other hand, stands for complete, independent and untrammelled self government.[4]

The electorate took a different view and deprived him of ten seats, leaving his Government with a slim majority of four.

The London financiers remained obstinate and the best Theodore could do was to arrange a temporary loan of £1 million from the Bank of England. But he was not yet beaten. In 1921 he negotiated a loan of £2.4 million on the New York money market, followed by another £2 million early in 1922. At Scullin's behest, the 1921 ALP Commonwealth Conference drew 'patriotic pride and satisfaction' from Theodore's 'courageous statesmanship' in defence of 'Australian democracy', even though the interest rate was higher than that prevailing in London. But despite all the brave words and triumphant declarations, when he approached the London financiers for a conversion loan in 1924 they had the last word. Although he raised the money, it seems that they had to compromise on the pastoral rents issue, and the other matters mentioned in his cable of August 1920 disappeared from public attention.[5]

His apparent surrender to the Money Power was the subject of considerable comment. The Brisbane *Worker* of 22 May 1924 drew the lesson:

> The long wrangle that Premier Theodore had had in London with the money kings of the Empire should bring home to the people the plain, blunt fact that they will never be able fully to control and direct their own affairs until they take complete charge of the question of finance... As matters stand now, we can only pass such Legislation and govern ourselves in such a way as will not raise the ire of our creditors overseas; and if we are ever to hold up our heads as fair-minded, freedom-loving people, we must do something to terminate this humiliating, soul-destroying state of affairs.

But this was merely a preliminary bout to the main event of 1930–31.[6]

At the same time, the Storey Labor Government in New South Wales was having difficulty with legislation to reform land tenure. There were hints in the British press that the Large Holdings Subdivision Bill might prejudice the Government's access to London funds. This was greeted with the usual denunciations of an imperialist threat in which 'Shylock brandishes his knife'. Although direct opposition to the Bill came from the Legislative Council, the *Australian Worker* could detect an unseen hand at work. On 1 September 1921 'R.J.C.' told the paper's readers that the Council, nominated by previous conservative governments, along with the Governor, who represented 'John Bull alias Money Power', was making a mockery of self-government. The reality of it was: 'We have self-government only when, and while, we do

Australian Worker, 2 February 1927
THE BRITISH 'UNCLE'
'Don't go to him, Sonny! He'll rob yer!'

This refers to the tendency of some State governments to look to Wall Street for loan funds rather than the London money market, which had attempted to make them conditional on the introduction of particular domestic policies. Significantly, both versions of the Shylock stereotype conduct their trade from windows in the same building. This serves to accentuate the irony of one accusing the other of robbery. The contented figure representing New South Wales is a reference by Will Donald to the Little Boy from Manly, which Hop had used in the *Bulletin* to symbolize the young Australian nation.

the autocratic Money Power of England likes'. It was the moving force behind the imperialist design to subvert Australian independence.

Issues such as these added fuel to the smouldering embers of post-war radicalism. Against a background of international revolutionary ferment, coupled with the domestic tensions arising from economic recession, industrial militancy and Labor's poor electoral performance, the labour movement began a systematic reassessment of its role in Australian society. Although the impetus for change came from the industrial wing, the ambit of debate was determined by the politicians, who ensured that whatever action was decided upon could be taken within the existing constitutional framework. It was that framework, after all, that sustained and justified the ALP's existence as a parliamentary party.

For some time there had been pressure on the party to adopt a more radical stance in its Objective and Platform. The 1919 Federal Conference produced a reworded Objective, which presaged the debates of 1921. It began with the accustomed association between 'The cultivation of an Australian sentiment, the maintenance of White Australia, and the development in Australia of an enlightened and self-reliant community'. This convergence of nationalism, racism and Australian independence provided the context in which the party would pursue its vaguely collectivist economic objective:

> Emancipation of human labour from all forms of exploitation, and the obtaining for all workers the full reward of their industry by the collective ownership and democratic control of the collectively used agencies of production, distribution and exchange.[7]

Although the 1919 Objective indicated a gradual shift towards a more socialist stance, it still bore the marks of a radical populist heritage.

By 1921 the more cautious members of the party could no longer resist the pressure from a broad coalition of radical opinion for a thorough overhaul of the Platform and Objective. The ALP Federal Executive responded to that pressure with the suggestion that a meeting of unions be convened to propose ways of bringing the political and industrial wings closer together. It was hoped that such a meeting might formulate 'a forward industrial policy with a view to its adoption by the Australian Labor Party'.[8] When the resulting All-Australian Trades Union Conference met in June 1921 it decided, after some debate, that the objective of the labour movement should be the 'Socialisation of Industry, Production,

Distribution and Exchange'. In discussing the means of implementing this, A. C. Willis argued that 'The real credit of the country was produced by Labor, but it could not function without control of the finances of the country'. He went on to warn that 'Labor must devise the means of taking not only control of industry, but also finance and exchange'. J. Kean endorsed this view when he introduced the report of the subcommittee appointed to examine the question of banking:

> Those who had gone into the political economy of things surrounding a Labor Government would have at once discovered that perhaps the most important thing connected with the life of Australia as a nation, and as it affected the interests of the working class, was that thing called credit.

The subcommittee gave banking a pivotal role in the transition from capitalism to socialism:

> That as the control of the financial institutions of Australia by a capitalist oligarchy stifles free development, prevents the development of a free press, by virtue of the control of advertising, and, by and through their pressure upon and dictatorship of Governments, stifles the full and natural growth of Australian States, we affirm that when the powers of Government will have been captured by a working-class majority, the first essential to a reconstructed Australasia will be the rapid expansion of the Commonwealth Bank, to embrace the entire credit system, and the establishment of a similar bank in New Zealand.[9]

Thus, in matters of finance, the new Objective was to be achieved by time-honoured methods.

The trade union proposals were put to the ALP Commonwealth Conference held in Brisbane in October 1921. As expected, there was a spirited debate about the vagueness of the Objective and the effect that its methods of implementation would have on a timorous electorate. The 'Socialisation Objective' was eventually adopted, along with a resolution that the principal means of achieving it would be through 'the constitutional utilization of industrial and Parliamentary machinery'. A specific method was to be the 'nationalisation of Banking and all principal industries'. Representatives of the workers in each industry and of the community would then be appointed to the respective boards of management. The corporate interests of each nationalized industry would, in turn, be represented by delegates elected to a Supreme Economic Council.

Theodore, who led the conservative faction dominated by parliamentarians, found this an alarming prospect and registered his protest against 'Labor being prostituted by Communism'. Scullin's reply was significant:

> The capitalist system is crumbling, and the world's events point to the end being accelerated. It will bring about chaos. If there was any Conference in history trying to prevent a revolution by force, this conference is doing it at present.

This was what the conference was all about. The political and industrial wings of the movement were close to a split. If the ALP could ride the wave of revolutionary enthusiasm by committing itself to the introduction of socialism through parliamentary action, the labour movement might remain intact and continue in its accustomed role as the leading institution of the working class.

In the end, caution prevailed and the political realists won. Theodore, by an adroit manoeuvre in the appointment of a committee, managed to keep the controversial 'Methods' out of the Fighting Platform. This saved the parliamentarians from the embarrassment of having to advocate a revolutionary programme to an unreceptive electorate. Their victory was finally assured when Conference passed the 'Blackburn interpretation' of the Objective. Although there were not enough votes to have it placed in the Platform, it was nevertheless a substantial qualification to Conference's early boldness. The last of its three points was the important one:

> That the Party does not seek to abolish private ownership even of any of the instruments of production where such instrument is utilised by its owner in a socially useful manner and without exploitation.

This effectively removed the teeth from an already lame 'socialisation tiger'.

Although the labour movement emerged intact from these two conferences, it did so at a price. The ALP had to bear the double burden of an electorally unpopular Objective along with the dilemmas arising from a formal commitment to parliamentary socialism.[10]

There was one matter, however, on which all agreed. At both conferences delegates were of the opinion that government control over the financial system was a fundamental prerequisite for a reconstructed social order. Without such control no signficant changes could be made. The 1921 ALP Conference made no alteration to the second plank of the 1919 Fighting Platform, which called for the 'Nationalisation of Banking and Insurance'. Nor was that cherished instrument of the people's will changed. The General Platform still advocated a 'Commonwealth Bank of Issue, Deposit, Exchange, and Reserve, with non-political management'. Through all its ideological struggles over the question of socialism Labor never deviated from the belief that to defeat capitalism it was necessary to take control of 'that thing called credit'. Indeed, as Matthew Charlton's policy speech for the 1922 federal election showed, what passed as socialism in much of Labor's rhetoric was really a radical populist conception of capitalism:

> The principal industries of Australia are controlled by syndicates, trusts and combines. Interwoven with these are the private banks. The directorates are interlocked, and a common policy evolved. Thus at the head of the economic life of this country are a few men who, by their control of banks, of basic industries, of shipping, of the principal channels of supply, dominate the entire system of industry. They can break or make, and no man or industry is free of their influence. These few men constitute the Supreme Economic Council of predatory capitalism.[11]

This echoed the views of his deputy in the House of Representatives, Frank Anstey, whose book *Money Power* had been published a year earlier.

Throughout the 1920s the Labor press was peppered with articles that claimed to show how the Money Power, Shylock, the Unclean Oligarchy or the Secret Money Junta were the powerful hands that moved governments, controlled industry and dispossessed the people.[12] Most of these articles began with a discussion of war loans. The *Australian Worker* of 4 August 1921 drew attention to a proposed loan of £10 million at 6.6 per cent interest for repatriation purposes. It declared, in a manner that was to become common currency in the early 1930s:

> This is what all the cheers, and the flag-flapping, and the rainbowed promises have come to—Shylock standing at his door demanding his pound of flesh from the men who cheerfully risked their lives on his behalf. Verily, it is a sordid end to a sordid business.

Writing in the same paper on 27 June 1923, W. F. Ahern wondered about the conversion of war loans: 'What is the mystic power that compels the Federal Government to consent to the bleeding of the Australian people in this outrageous manner?'

The Australian Money Power, meanwhile, mounted an attack upon the people through their own bank. The weapon used was the Commonwealth Bank Bill, introduced by the newly installed Bruce–Page Government in June 1924. In the Labor press it was greeted with alarm and outrage. It was 'an attack on the people's bank', and 'astounding plot to loot the Commonwealth Bank and Note Issue', and the means by which 'crafty Money Lords seize the people's bank'.

It was really an attempt to rationalize the bank's operations by increasing its central banking functions, giving it control of the note issue, requiring private banks to settle their exchanges through deposits with the bank, and placing its policy under the direction of a board that represented major 'economic interests' in the community. As Giblin has observed, the primary intention was to address the financial troubles of the time by turning it into a central bank.[13]

Ignoring the fact that some of the provisions went very close to party policy, Labor chose to focus most of its attention on the establishment of the board. In his reply to Page's speech, Matthew Charlton moved an amendment that called for the appointment to the board of financial experts, who would be full-time bank employees. This, he argued, would be preferable to 'the proposal of the Government to appoint persons representing squatting and commercial interests who are diametrically opposed to national banking, being designed more in the interests of private financial institutions than of the people's Bank'. He was followed, on the Labor side, by Makin, who regretted that 'the Government has failed to protect the people of Australia against the rapacious demands of the great money changers'. The other Labor members who spoke—Lazzarini, West, Parker Moloney, Dr Moloney, Anstey, Forde, Fenton and Brennan—presented a similar line of argument. It was Anstey's speech that attracted most attention in the Labor press. In it he made ironic reference to Australian financiers who, he alleged, had made huge profits on loans during the war and now wanted the Commonwealth Bank to rescue them from the results of their own recklessness in allowing liquidity ratios to fall to as little as 20 per cent. If the Bill was passed the Commonwealth Bank would be neither a people's bank nor a true central bank. It would become merely a 'banker's bank'.[14]

The Labor press embellished the politicians' arguments in its familiar style. *Labor Call* saw the Bill as a means by which the private banks, through a willing Government, 'intended making a determined assault on the Bank'. The *Westralian Worker* thought that the bank was about to be pillaged because it had acted as a check on the private banks' exercise of monopoly power. Looking

Australian Worker, 8 May 1929
ANOTHER DESIGN FOR THE CANBERRA COAT OF ARMS.
The Money King, supported by Bruce and Page, with Taxpayer rampant.

The coat of arms, a traditional aristocratic artefact, shows how the long-suffering taxpayer is forced to support the Bruce–Page Government. They in turn support the Money Power, who is flanked by his two most cherished policies, longer hours and lower wages. This not only depicts a familiar picture of the structure of capitalism, but also explains where such a large proportion of taxation goes as a result of the Government's borrowing policy.

to the future, the paper boldly declared that 'The Socialist State in the making commences on the day banking is nationalised in Australia, or any other country'. Invoking the usual biological metaphor, the Brisbane *Worker* saw the Commonwealth Bank as the means to control 'the nervous system of the social organism', and depicted the Bill as the Money Power's attempt to capture it. *Labor Daily*, however, was more concerned to expose an alleged fraud in the note issue department, and to discredit James Kell, the acting governor. The object of that campaign was to show what happened to the bank under 'Tory administration'. In the *Australian Worker*, Henry Boote said it was an attempt to nobble the people's bank, and W. F. Ahern made an ominous prediction:

> The working masses in the Commonwealth will be forced to make the bitter sacrifice—in inflated prices, lower wages, longer hours, intense sweating of brain and brawn, while the Lords of Private Finance go on their way rejoicing.

After the Act had been passed and appointments made to the new Commonwealth Bank Board, Ahern found that it was comprised of the 'Money Trust and their fellows'. As proof, he listed the 'connections' of some Board members: J. J. Garvan, insurance; Sir Samuel Hordern and Sir Robert Gibson, commercial and trading profiteers; J. M. Lees, Financial Ring; and R. S. Drummond and R. B. W. McComas, squatters.[15] Similar allegations were made about the Rural Credits Bill in September 1925.[16]

During the 1920s there was a growing interest in the operations of the Money Power in other countries. The expansion of British and French investment in the Middle East was depicted as the advance guard of an imperialist strategy, which had as one of its ultimate objectives the destruction of White Australia through the importation of cheap coloured labour. Claims were made that the 'Lordly Usurer' had tried to dictate to Ramsay MacDonald in Britain, and that the consolidation of banks in Canada was the first move towards 'financial dictatorship'. Similar disquiet was expressed at what was claimed to be a growing trend towards the expansion of the 'British Vampires and Republican Shylocks' into a world power. It was suggested that the 'World Money Trust' was a primary cause of war, and that it possessed more power than the League of Nations. Through manipulation of the gold standard the Money Power would eventually achieve its ambition 'to crucify humanity upon a cross of gold'.[17]

It was not long before this anxiety about the international and domestic machinations of the Money Power found a specific focus. During 1930–31 the labour movement had occasion to reflect ruefully upon Ahern's prediction about the Commonwealth Bank board, and to ponder Blackburn's warning in 1920 that 'A borrowing Government pawns Australia to the Moneylender, and gives overseas financiers a vote, generally a secret but always influential vote, on Australian policies'.

5

'A Lord of Finance' – The Niemeyer Mission

On 25 June 1930 Henry Boote told readers of the *Australian Worker* 'a Lord of Finance is coming', and observed in an ominous tone:

> Sir Otto Niemeyer is a very important person, no doubt. He is coming here direct from the great Temple of Money Power in Threadneedle Street, charged, we are given to understand, with a solemn and sacred mission having something to do with our financial past and more particularly with our financial future.

His apprehension was well founded. Within a year, the circumstances surrounding the Niemeyer mission from the Bank of England led to a political crisis in which Labor governments presided over an economic policy designed to reduce the living standards of their traditional supporters. In the process the mission became the focus of bitter resentment, centred on the familiar theme of a Money Power conspiracy theory that depicted them as 'bailiffs come to repossess Australia as representatives of the British pawnbroker'.[1] The events leading up to their arrival in July 1930, the advice they gave and the convergence of symbols associated with them, provided ample scope for Labor's populist radicals to interpret their visit in a sinister light. By the time they left Australia in November 1930 they had come to represent the embodiment of Money Power demonology in the popular imagination of the labour movement.

Although the Labor Party won the 1929 House of Representatives election with a handsome majority, the Scullin Government took office under the most difficult circumstances. As there had been no election for the Senate, the Nationalist–Country Party coalition retained control of the upper house. In the field of government finance it was also constrained by the Commonwealth Bank board, whose members were largely unsympathetic to Labor policy. While it was obvious that the Government could do nothing about international conditions, it was also clear that its ability to implement domestic policies would require the co-operation of their opponents in both these institutions. It was soon apparent that the Scullin Government was in office but not in power. One of the earliest indications of that fact was the way in which the Niemeyer mission was appointed.

The Australian economy was in a vulnerable position at the onset of the great depression. A high level of debt on the London money market, combined with a heavy reliance on rural commodities for foreign exchange, made it hypersensitive to overseas conditions. When the shock waves from the Wall Street collapse reached Australia via London early in 1930 they brought an abrupt halt to the relatively easy credit that until then had helped service the national debt. In the first quarter of 1930 this was compounded by an alarming reverse in the terms of trade: contrary to the normal seasonal trend, imports greatly exceeded exports. Faced with falling revenue, rapidly diminishing currency reserves, and loan obligations that could no longer be met from new borrowing, the Scullin ministry was confronted by a crisis in government finance.[2]

Fearing imminent default on the London money market, they were persuaded by the Commonwealth Bank to ask the British Government to postpone a war loan repayment of £2.77 million due on 31 March. The Chancellor of the Exchequer passed the request to the Bank of England, which in turn sought more information on Australia's position. If it was satisfied that the Australian authorities were doing everything possible to meet the emergency, the bank promised to recommend the postponement and to find an additional £25 million to honour Australia's London commitments until 31 January 1931. However, it was not convinced by the vague answers it received and deferred judgement on the matter, thus leaving the Commonwealth Bank to cover the £2.77 million at the end of March.

Although this was done and the immediate crisis passed, the Bank of England still required precise information about Australia's difficulties if a long-term solution was to be found. In a cable on 7 April, Sir Ernest Harvey, deputy governor of the Bank, asked Sir Robert Gibson, chairman of the Commonwealth Bank board, to send a 'fully informed' representative to London 'as soon as possible to consider with us [the] best method of dealing with the situation'. But Australia already had such people in London, so Gibson took no action and the matter temporarily lapsed. In the meantime, the Bank of England and the British Treasury kept a close watch on what the Scullin Government was doing. They were increasingly worried by the possible effects of the Government's drastic tariff increases, its slide off the gold standard and the proposed changes to the Commonwealth Bank. All this confirmed a suspicion, long held in British financial circles, that the Australian Government was not addressing the basic problem underlying its balance of payments crisis, namely its domestic 'costs of production'.[3] In a further cable to Gibson on 7 May, Harvey grew more insistent and suggested three options: that they do nothing, that the Government send somebody to London, or 'we could perhaps ourselves send privately an intermediary to Australia if invited to do so and he would be taken into full confidence'.

Gibson, who shared Harvey's alarm at the direction of government policy, preferred the last option. However, he did not want to put it to Scullin and so appear to be dictating economic policy, especially while his reappointment to the board was under consideration.[4] Instead, he suggested that Harvey approach the government through the Australian High Commissioner in London. The Bank of England was equally reluctant to give the impression that it was exerting pressure, but was even more concerned by the possibility that Australia might default. A number of consequences could be foreseen if it was allowed to do so. British bondholders would not only be denied their interest payments but would also feel that the security of their investment was threatened. This erosion of confidence would weaken an already nervous capital market and set a bad example to other debtor nations. From the Australian point of view, as taken by Scullin, it was imperative to retain access to the City if a scheme of reconstruction was to be negotiated. Without that, the imperial relationship on which the Australian economy depended so heavily would be imperilled. According to orthodox opinion there was a mutual, if unequal, interest in maintaining that relationship.

The approach was duly made, and within a week the carefully engineered invitation was received from Scullin. It was then agreed that Sir Otto Niemeyer would lead a mission from the bank to confer with the Commonwealth Government and financial institutions 'with the object of elucidating [a] solution of present and future finance, more especially with regard to its being as between Australia and overseas obligations'.[5] In recognition of the delicate situation it was agreed not to announce Niemeyer's mission until after it had sailed.[6] Accordingly, Scullin informed parliament on 19 June that the mission had been invited and had left England the previous day.[7]

They had good reason to be circumspect. There were influential people in the Labor Party and the wider labour movement who

Australian Worker, 27 August 1930
DEAD MEN PAY NO INTEREST. GIVE ME MY LIVING POUND OF FLESH!

Will Donald invokes two stereotypes to personify the relationship between Australia and its creditors. The British bondholder's top hat, coat and spats identify him as the Fat capitalist, whose determined scowl signifies his intention to claim his 'living pound of flesh' in the familiar manner of Shakespeare's Shylock. Standing upon the grave of 60 000 Australians who died defending the Empire, he demands his bond in contemptuous disregard for their sacrifice. He threatens to cut out the heart of Australia, personified by a woman in classical robes, the traditional symbols of innocence and virtue. His moral bankruptcy is illustrated by the suggestion that her only defence is the gravestone of her dead. Australia is thus at the mercy of rapacious British bondholders.

were becoming restive at the Government's apparent inability to arrest the country's slide into depression. They had seen trade union unemployment rise from an average of 8 per cent during the 1920s to over 10 per cent in 1929 and then soar to 18 per cent by the middle of 1930, with every indication that it would get worse. Nor could the Government do much to help unionists in the disputes on the waterfront, the timber industry and the coalfields of northern New South Wales. Its manifest weakness in these areas was a source of growing frustration, and any hint that it was placing itself in the hands of the Bank of England would have inflamed that mood.

Rank-and-file impatience was evident as early as February 1930 at the All-Australian Trade Union Congress, where delegates declared that unemployment was inherent in the capitalist system and reminded the Government of the Labor Party's 1921 objective to socialize the means of production, distribution and exchange. However, in lieu of revolution, Congress went on to suggest that measures could be taken to prevent widespread unemployment within the existing system. It was argued that people could not consume the goods that flooded world markets because the restriction of credit had eroded their purchasing power and thus aggravated the slump. The Government's responsibility in these circumstances was to provide jobs, or in the last resort, food, clothing and shelter for the distressed. Some delegates thought 'the money-bags in Britain' were behind the crisis and urged the Government to 'use the credit of the Commonwealth' to provide work or sustenance. But they were not clear on exactly what this meant or how it was to be achieved. Nevertheless, they had seized upon a proposition that was to be the central theme in most radical solutions to the crisis. The same idea was raised at the Labor Party's Commonwealth Conference in May, and in Federal Caucus by G. E. Yates, who proposed that £20 million be made available through the Commonwealth Bank for public works.[8]

While this notion of credit expansion was gaining wider acceptance in labour circles, the Government introduced two Bills to change the role of the Commonwealth Bank. The intention was to divide its functions between two separate entities. The Central Reserve Bank Bill would establish an institution with extended central banking powers under a board representing government, employers and labour. The Commonwealth Bank Act Amending Bill provided for the abolition of the existing board, to be replaced by a single Governor in line with the pre-1924 arrangement. The bank would then be free to enter into competition with the private banks according to Labor's original conception.[9] Although they were not initially designed to be the instruments for a 'release of credit', the proposals were soon hailed as such by a number of labour people. A week after the Bills were presented, the veteran labour journalist W. F. Ahern put the view plainly in the *Australian Worker* of 9 April:

> Those at present consituting the Money Power in this country know only too well that a Central Reserve Bank, established in conjunction with the Commonwealth Bank, will take over the mobilisation and control of the financial resources of the Commonwealth and utilise them for the service of the people and the progress of the nation.

He was right. A. C. Davidson, General Manager of the Bank of New South Wales, was worried by the 'large body in the Labor Caucus at Canberra which holds extraordinary theories in regard to money, credit and banking. They wish to make the Reserve Bank a machine for manufacturing notes and credit, regardless of the consequence'. Although he thought an orthodox central bank should be welcomed, he was uneasy about the kind of institution that might emerge under a Labor government. Moreover, it seemed unwise to be making significant changes to the Australian monetary system in the prevailing financial climate. Fearing the consequences that Ahern boldly proclaimed, Davidson joined with other Sydney bankers in arranging for the Opposition majority in the Senate to block the Bills.[10]

While the private banks were quietly organizing resistance to Labor's fiscal heretics, the orthodox solution was being put to the public by conservative politicians, economists and the daily press. In April T. R. Bavin, Nationalist Premier of New South Wales, blunty stated the widely held certitude that as national income had fallen drastically real wages would have to be cut.[11] L. F. Giblin, an academic economist, was more gently persuasive in a series of ten 'Letters to John Smith' published by the Melbourne *Herald* in early July. He argued that wage levels were too high and that, to restore Austalia's competitive trading position and expand employment, it would be necessary for 'John' to accept a reduction in pay. This, he claimed, would place wages on a more sound economic basis from which they could be revived later when conditions improved.

By the time the Niemeyer mission arrived at Fremantle on 14 July 1930, the broad pattern of the ensuing economic debate had already emerged. The conservative view suggested that strict deflation would be necessary if Australia was to compete on world markets and honour its loan obligations. The radical view asserted that living standards and the level of employment were the first priority of governments, and should be protected by some form of inflationary fiscal policy. It was apparent which of these two Niemeyer's party was likely to support, even before it arrived.

The respective backgrounds of Niemeyer, Gregory and Kershaw certainly did nothing to allay the deep suspicion that labour radicals harboured towards anybody associated with the Bank of England. Each in his own way was a pillar of the established orthodoxy.

Otto Ernst Niemeyer was born in London in 1883. He attended St Paul's School, where he won a classical scholarship to Balliol College, Oxford. After taking a first-class honours degree in classics he won first place in the Civil Service examinations of 1906, beating John Maynard Keynes into second place. He was posted to treasury, where his talents were quickly recognized and rewarded. Within sixteen years he rose to the position of Controller of Finance, only one step from the top of the department. In 1922 he became a member of the League of Nations Financial Committee and worked on problems of post-war reconstruction in Europe. Two years later he was knighted. In 1927 he took the unusual step of transferring to the Bank of England, where Montagu Norman was reorganizing the bank's management and control systems. Niemeyer's early work at the bank centred on establishing orderly financial arrangements to assist agriculture, but he retained a strong interest in international financial affairs. He became a director of the Bank for International Settlements, an institution originally set up to handle reparation and debt payments, and to encourage co-operation between central banks. By mid-1930, as a result of this work, he had a reputation in the City that commended him as the most suitable person to instruct the Australian governments in sound financial management. His superiors were apparently well pleased with the way he handled the Australian assignment, because he went on to become their leading international trouble-shooter during the 1930s. After tendering advice to the Australian and New Zealand governments in 1930, he cast a critical eye over the accounts of Brazil in 1931, Greece and Egypt in 1932, Argentina in 1933 and India in 1935. During this period he also served as a member of the Council of Foreign Bondholders, the body responsible for looking after the interests of British loans to overseas countries. In 1941 he led another mission to China, where he advised Chiang Kai-shek's Nationalist régime on its financial difficulties. After the war he assisted in debt negotiations with Germany. He retired from the Bank in 1952, and died in 1971.

Theodore Gregory was born in London in 1890. He was educated at Owen's School and proceeded to further study in

Brisbane *Worker*, 27 August 1930
In the Grip of an Octopus.

This is the *Worker*'s initial response to the publication of Niemeyer's report. It tries to evoke a combination of apprehension and resentment through two devices: the scale of the subject and the association of human types with animal forms. The bald head, fat jowls, thick lips and broad nose of the Niemeyer octopus imply greed and decadence, while the eyes squint with an ominous smugness. The overall effect is vaguely suggestive of anti-Semitic visual conventions, reinforced by the grotesque embrace of the tentacles. This particular conjunction of man and beast is designed to tap deep wells of fear and hatred, and to accentuate that mood with the vast scale of its grasp, which encompasses the whole continent. The abstractions of economic debate are thus transformed into an evil living presence that threatens to strangle the nation.

Stuttgart and at the London School of Economics. At the age of twenty-three he was appointed to the staff of the LSE. As his list of publications on international trade, finance and central banking grew steadily, he was promoted to progressively higher positions until his appointment as Professor and Dean of the Faculty of Economics at the University of London in 1927. Like Niemeyer, he was a member of the Reform Club.

Raymond Newton Kershaw was an Australian, born in Sydney in 1898. Educated at Sydney High School, Sydney University and the Sorbonne, he had served with distinction in the AIF in France during 1917–18. He was the 1918 Rhodes Scholar for New South Wales at New College, Oxford. After five years with the League of Nations Secretariat in Geneva he joined the Bank of England in 1929 as an adviser to the Governors. His special interest in currency problems as well as his nationality commended him to those who chose the members of Niemeyer's mission.[12]

On 20 July, Niemeyer, Gregory, Kershaw and their secretary Miss Wilson arrived in Sydney after a train journey from Perth via Adelaide and Melbourne. Adhering strictly to the terms of his brief, Niemeyer declined to make any comment to the press until he had concluded his enquiries and presented his report to the Commonwealth and State governments. He then settled down to a fortnight's careful study of documents provided by Sir Robert Gibson.

Meanwhile, labour radicals continued to abuse orthodox analysts. On 2 August *Labor Daily*, the organ of Jack Lang's majority faction in the New South Wales Labor Party, poured scorn upon academic economists who advocated deflationary policies:

> The Brigdens, the Giblins, the Coplands are adrift in chaos. These economic doctors, who at less disastrous times prescribe so glibly for the ills of Society, are lost in the tangled jungle of their own economic incoherencies. They are, as it were, the intellectual apostles of Capitalism . . . They have girded themselves in shining armour, and preached hope and salvation to all men, if only they allow Capitalism to work out its benevolent destiny.

But this was merely a taste of things to come. Niemeyer's assessment of Australia's economic destiny was still a matter for speculation.

On 5 August he addressed a meeting of the Loan Council in Canberra, where he offered a preliminary report on the country's gloomy prospects, but the text was not revealed. It was agreed that he would present a full report to a conference of Premiers two weeks later. Immediately after the meeting he returned to Sydney, where he resumed his study. On 18 August the Premiers of all States assembled in Melbourne, but Scullin was too ill to attend, so the Commonwealth was represented by the Deputy Prime Minister, J. E. Fenton, and the Treasurer, J. A. Lyons. Both were from the conservative faction in federal Caucus. In the afternoon Niemeyer delivered his devastating analysis.

He began with a rebuke couched in a thinly veiled Dickensian allusion: 'It is a serious problem, the practical solution of which is not rendered any easier by the natural optimism of the Australian. So long as it is generally believed . . . that something will turn up, it will be difficult to face the realities of the situation'.[13] After cataloguing a history of reckless borrowing by Australian governments he pointed to the dangerous way that they had been financed by overdrafts and short-term Treasury Bills. The decline in domestic savings had merely compounded the problem of external debt. As a result, Australia's credit in London was lower than any other Dominion's 'and even lower than that of some protectorates'. Following a brief discussion of the adverse trade position he moved on to the central point of his report—that Australian costs of production were too high compared to those of its trading partners, particularly England, where costs had fallen much more quickly. This situation was largely due to protectionist policies, which had encouraged low productivity in manufacturing industry. The combination of these domestic and overseas factors meant, in short, that Australia was living beyond its means. If the position was to be improved living standards would have to fall. This would require a reduction in domestic costs, especially wages, increased productivity, and stringent economies in government finance. He reminded them that his very presence indicated a desire in London to assist a Dominion, but 'Australia must reassure the world as to the direction in which she is going, financially and economically, and no one else can do that for her.'

The underlying message in all this was that Australian policies had disturbed the natural pattern in its imperial relationship with the British economy. Its proper role was to supply rural commodities. The desire for economic development based on secondary industry was an 'exploded doctrine' that had led to its present difficulties, as indicated by artificially high wages, excessive protection and massive debt. Australia's only hope of salvation lay in a return to its traditional role within the imperial orbit. To 'reassure the world' it must convince the London money market that it was back on its proper course and thus worthy of further credit.

Although the Premiers accepted the central argument of Niemeyer's uncompromising assessment, they spent the next three days haggling over who was to blame and what was to be done. On 21 August Niemeryer's report was finally released to the press along with the 'Melbourne Agreement', in which the Premiers agreed to his suggestions that they cease borrowing and cut expenditure in an effort to balance their budgets. On the same afternoon, amid criticism that he was deserting a sinking ship, Scullin left for an Imperial Conference in London, where he hoped to bolster Australia's standing in the City.

However, some radical members of the Scullin Government had anticipated the substance of Niemeyer's report. Anstey was widely suspected of having engineered an equally uncompromising resolution passed by a Special Conference of Unions and the ALP in Sydney on 21 August. The motion, moved by the union leader 'Jock' Garden, called for a five-year moratorium on overseas interest payments, repudiation of all war debts and 'the mobilisation of the credit of the community to provide work or sustenance for the unemployed and for the revival of industry'.[14] Thus, on the same day, the two main contending views of how to deal with Australia's predicament stood in stark contrast.

Not surprisingly, it was Niemeyer's that commanded most attention. The daily press welcomed his report as a timely and sobering analysis of a situation that dilatory governments could no longer ignore. Bankers thought it a masterly statement of the position. Businessmen were inclined to agree, although some were uneasy about his views on manufacturing industry. Conservative politicians and academic economists, in public, were pleased that he had given the Bank of England's imprimatur to the broad line of argument they had been advancing for some months. The Premiers blamed each other during their conference, and their predecessors in public. Nevertheless, there was a consensus among all these groups that Niemeyer had done Australia a great service in giving fearless advice in a statesman-like manner. It was also agreed that the resolutions contained in the Melbourne Agreement should be rigorously implemented as a basis for economic reconstruction, as an expression of Australia's determination to re-establish its credit in London and, by association, to maintain its national honour. News of the agreement was received with cautious approval in London, where negotiations to ease Australia's short-term debt were reopened. But these came to nothing as the tide of opinion within federal Caucus moved further towards the radical position.

Labor was divided into two increasingly hostile camps. Those ranging from moderate to conservative views were led by Scullin,

Labor Daily, 13 October 1930
WELL AND TRULY EARNED.

George Finey's grim irony draws out the popular association of war debt with Australia's predicament. The pun on the vernacular term 'mug' is a visual rebuke of the country's gullibility in the form of a medal awarded by the Bank of England's gloating directors. The three bars on the ribbon exploit the popular beliefs: that Australia had paid rent to Britain on

Fenton and Lyons, with support from the Labor Premiers Hogan in Victoria and Hill in South Australia. They accepted Niemeyer's unpalatable prescription for the nation's ills as a regrettable necessity, but they were rapidly losing ground to the fiscal heretics, who were commanding an ever-widening audience within the Labor governments and out in the broader movement.

To this radical faction Niemeyer's policy was not simply different from their own: it was the result of a malicious conspiracy against the Australian people. The *Labor Daily* of 23 August set the tone:

> The sublime impertinence of the lately-arrived emissary of Capitalism abroad—Sir Otto Niemeyer—who comes here to tell us that human misery—life even—is as nothing compared with the necessity of providing the London Jews with their fat rakes-off, passes our understanding.

It went on to blame war debts for Australia's difficulties. Four days later the Queensland *Worker* developed this theme, depicting Niemeyer as the emissary of 'London Jews' who had sent him as a bailiff to collect their 'last shilling' in cruel disregard for the sacrifice of 60 000 Australian soldiers in the Great War.

> Not content with all this, it would appear now that extreme pressure is being exerted in other vital directions to make us reduce our standard of living, and Sir Otto Niemeyer's visit is part and parcel of this conspiracy ... Australia is not living beyond her means, despite what Niemeyer or anyone else says, but she is paying too much extortionate interest to London Jews and other War Profiteers.

It was significant that Australia's prodigal borrowing in the 1920s was not acknowledged as part of the problem. As Anstey's *Kingdom of Shylock* had suggested fifteen years earlier, such conspiracies imply innocence on the part of their victims.

However, that did not preclude the existence of traitors at home. Politicians who had signed the Melbourne Agreement, and some

---

trenches during World War I; that it had exported gold to prop up its credit and received only paper in return; and that Niemeyer's objection to the level of Australian tariffs betrayed a desire to give preference to foreign manufacturers in the domestic market. In this Finey reinforces the rhetoric of the Lang machine, which claimed that Australia had been duped into mortgaging its future by an ungrateful Mother Country that is now utterly indifferent to its welfare.

who had not, were branded as weak or treacherous. In the *Labor Daily* of 26 August, 'Jock' Garden declared that 'The emissary from London is exacting the pound of flesh for his masters, and the Australian politicians in yielding to his demands are betraying their country'. On the day after Niemeyer's report was released, the Hobart *Voice* named Scullin and Theodore as 'catspaws of conspirators' and denounced Theodore, whom it 'neither likes nor trusts', as the one responsible for inviting Niemeyer. Depicting the Melbourne Agreement as a 'scurry of scared politicians' the *Westralian Worker* of 12 September attacked all governments for accepting what Niemeyer had put before them in a state of 'abject submission'.

On 3 September Henry Boote directed readers of the *Australian Worker* to the more general lessons of the situation. 'The money capitalist', he declared, was a 'pernicious parasite' who 'completely dominates our civilisation. He is the embodiment of the Money Power'.

> A dozen financiers in London, New York, Berlin and Paris, acting secretly together, can practically do what they like with the trade and commerce of the world . . . Behold an enemy more dangerous than any we fought in the Great War! An enemy aggressive, unscrupulous, callous, resourceful, insidious, cunning—an enemy moreover, aided and abetted by traitors within our gates. Labour will need all its strength, and its courage, and unbroken solidarity, to thwart the nefarious designs of the Money Power.

This thoroughly familiar interpretation fell upon fertile ground in Labor's traditional constituency, where the visible distress of more than 20 per cent unemployment nourished a mood of anger and resentment.

During the New South Wales election campaign of September–October, Jack Lang sought to mobilize this discontent around the slogan 'Men versus Money'. He committed the Labor Party to the maintenance of living standards and a rejection of the Melbourne Agreement. Bavin, who had signed it on behalf of the State Government, promised that the Nationalist–Country Party coalition would adhere to its provisions and do everything possible to balance the State budget. While Bavin offered nothing but the gloomy prospects inherent in the orthodox solution, Lang promised a return to prosperity through an expansionary program that boldly defied the conspiracy to reduce living standards. Although he was careful to distance himself from the 'repudiation' resolution of 21 August, Lang had no hesitation in denouncing the Niemeyer mission as a Money Power conspiracy. In his opening

PROSPERITY FOLLOWS LABOR SUPREMACY

The "Manufactured" depression that high finance has engineered to serve its own interests has produced

(1) Unprecedented Unemployment in the Cities; (2) Stagnation in the Country

THE
Bavin - Stevens Government HAS:

Reduced Wages!

Increased Hours!

Rationed Work!

Attacked Orphans' allowances!

Reduced Widows' Pensions!

Wrecked Workers' Compensation!

Increased Taxation!

And promises, if returned, to further reduce wages and further increase taxation!

LABOR BRINGS PROSPERITY

LABOR PROMISES IF RETURNED TO

Restore the Arbitration Court.

To give every Worker a Fair Deal.

To assist the Orphans, Widows, Mothers, and Injured Workmen in their necessity.

To Restore Confidence, thereby Increasing Trade Returns.

Thus Prosperity and Happiness will once again be the lot of the people

Labor Will Break the Monopoly that holds up Our Fertile Areas and Compel the Big Financial Houses and Absentee Landlords to give our Young Australians a Chance in their Own Country.

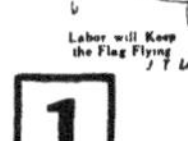

NEXT SATURDAY, 25th OCTOBER

VOTE LABOR No. 1

Labor Daily, 24 October 1930

This is an early example of the Lang machine's tendency to depict its leader as a heroic figure who will lead the people back to prosperity. Significantly, this was before the Lang–Federal Labor split, and that is why he bears the title of the party rather than his own name. After the split it became Lang Labor, and their propaganda began to emphasize him as the charismatic leader who personifies the people's struggle against the Money Power.

speech for the campaign he declared that 'British moneylenders had inspired the move to drag down Australian wage standards . . . and had sent Sir Otto Niemeyer to do it'.

By the time the electors went to the polls on 25 October, Niemeyer had become the central issue in Labor's campaign. Lang and his supporters repeated what the labour press had said about Niemeyer's report. They branded him and Gregory as 'cormorants and vultures of finance' who had 'come to these shores to tell us that we do not know how to govern ourselves . . . that unless we are prepared to enslave ourselves they will cut off our means of existence'.[15] In their rhetoric all the established symbols of Money Power oppression converged around the person of Niemeyer and his mission. The details were specific to the immediate issues, but the essential message was thoroughly familiar. Niemeyer's appointment was the result of a conspiracy between 'London Jews' and 'traitors within our gates', the object being to reduce Australian living standards so that British bondholders might get their full 'pound of flesh' from war loans that were originally raised to defend an Empire that the Money Power owned and controlled. It was an act of moral turpitude to demand that distressed Australians be left to starve while interest payments remained sacrosanct. Moreover, the war loans had already been nourished by the blood of 60 000 Australian soldiers in the Great War. Now, with 'sublime impertinence', an emissary from the Bank of England had come to tell Australians that they were living beyond their means and must henceforth conduct their affairs according to the bank's instructions. Niemeyer was its bailiff sent to repossess Australia. His presence illustrated the Money Power's unrelenting hostility to Australian independence and a callous disregard for the welfare of its people. The only hope of thwarting this conspiracy lay in united resistance behind true Labor men like Lang.

Although this was a perverse analysis of the imperial relationship, it was a very effective way to mobilize discontent in the electorate. The Labor Party led by Lang won a landslide victory, taking more than 60 per cent of seats in the Legislative Assembly.

During this storm of abuse Niemeyer said nothing. He and his party continued to advise governments, bankers, businessmen, economists and some trade unionists on the wisdom of the orthodox solution. After visits to Adelaide, Melbourne, Brisbane and New Zealand, where he cast a critical eye over its financial position, he returned to Sydney near the end of the election campaign. Following Lang's victory, he broke his silence with a brief statement in reply to Labor's allegations. He said that he had been invited to Australia by the Commonwealth Government to advise the Loan Council on its difficulties, and it was up to the Premiers to accept or reject his advice. He was an employee of the Bank of England sent to help Australia out of a financial crisis. Two weeks later he left for England, via Canada and the United States.[16]

Niemeyer's statement could not erase the image created in the popular imagination by labour radicals. The circumstances surrounding his visit matched the entrenched stereotypes of foreign financiers so closely that he became the embodiment of British Money Power in labour's populist demonology. The degree to which these stereotypes were capable of misleading radical opinion was illustrated by an outburst from J. J. Cusack, Labor MHR for Eden-Monaro. Referring to Niemeyer and Gregory after the mission's departure, he told the House of Representatives: 'These lounge lizards—Jew lizards, if you like—seem to have the power to mesmerise our leaders of public thought and make them believe in their financial nostrums'.[17] This was not only racist—it was also wrong. Niemeyer was not a Jew.[18] Nevertheless, it was true that he had given the Bank of England's authority to policies that were explicitly designed to reduce living standards as the price of reviving Australia's credit in London. The resentment that this occasioned coloured the ensuing 'battle of the plans' in a way that reduced popular economic debate to a simple choice between the interests of British bondholders and the welfare of the Australian people.

6

'Finance is Government' — The Scullin Government, the Premiers' Plan and Lang

The tensions that were already apparent in the labour movement during Niemeyer's visit intensified in the following months as political debate hardened around three competing plans for the revival of Australia's economy. The orthodox deflationary policy, supported by the weight of conservative opinion, was eventually formulated as the Premiers' Plan in June 1931. The Theodore Plan, named after Scullin's reinstated Treasurer, proposed controlled inflation to stimulate recovery while ensuring 'equality of sacrifice' for all. The Lang Plan demanded a repudiation of interest payments to British bondholders, a reduction of Australian interest rates and the abandonment of the gold standard. As economic conditions grew worse and political tension heightened, opinion within Labor ranks divided sharply between supporters of the respective plans. Under the pressure of internal divisions and resistance from conservative institutions, the party split into three belligerent factions. Cautious Labor men defended the orthodox solution, a decision that led most of them to join their former political opponents; the majority of moderate Labor members stood by their party's advocacy of the Theodore Plan; Lang's populist revolt attracted a large body of radical opinion. In the ensuing struggle Scullin's administration was defeated and replaced by a United Australia Party Government, which implemented the Premiers' Plan under the leadership of the Labor renegade J. A. Lyons. After five more months of turmoil, during which New South Wales came perilously close to civil war, Lang was dismissed by the Governor, Sir Philip Game. The process that led to these defeats confirmed the view of many radicals that 'finance is government and government is finance'. It also encouraged the belief that Labor's most resolute and insidious enemy was the Money Power, which must be defeated if the Australian people were ever to be truly independent and prosperous.[1]

After August 1930 prosperity seemed a long way off. There was no longer simply a crisis in government finance: there was a depression, which had spread to most sections of the community. All the economic indicators confirmed it. Taxes increased sharply; loan expenditure fell to about a third of its pre-depression rate; wages were cut; rural incomes collapsed and private fixed capital spending all but ceased. In these circumstances working-class people did not need instruction from economists on the meaning of deflation. Their real incomes were declining rapidly. In 1928–29 they fell by 0.9 per cent, in 1929–30 by 1.9 per cent, and in 1930–31 by 5.8 per cent. At the end of 1930 unemployment among trade unionists had risen to nearly 25 per cent, a figure that probably underestimated the situation and certainly took no account of those who had been reduced to part-time work or the apprehension of those who feared that they might be sacked. Moreover, the absence of adequate social security benefits meant that workers who relied entirely on wages to support themselves and their families faced destitution if they lost their jobs. They reacted to this according to temperament and circumstances. Some introspective people blamed themselves for their plight. Others cheerfully 'made do'. Almost all suffered hardship to some degree. There were also many who felt hostility at their condition and sought a focus for their discontent.[2]

In the first few months after the Melbourne Agreement there was a good deal of confusion over what Labor governments could do about this situation. Conservative and moderate Labor members faced a dilemma. They knew that desperately needed relief from the London money market could only come by applying Niemeyer's recommendations, but they also wished to protect their supporters from the effects of that policy. Radicals faced no such difficulty: Labor governments had a primary responsibility for the welfare of the Australian people, and if attending to that involved deferring payment of the nation's debts to rich bondholders, then so be it.

Labor leaders who did not feel themselves irrevocably bound by the Melbourne Agreement responded in two ways: they tried to explain the cause of the crisis, and they cast about for alternatives to deflationary policies. As the initial reaction to Niemeyer's report showed, there was a tendency to blame individuals or institutions—to personify abstract relationships, which could then be explained in terms of malicious intent. Among the more sophisticated members of the labour movement this impulse was often held in tension with a recognition that there was something wrong with the economic system that produced these periodic crises. As the party worked its way towards an inflationary alternative to orthodox policy, this tension was resolved in a synthesis

Labor Daily, 18 November 1930
. . . and so on.

Shoemaker's humorous view of the capitalist trade cycle depicts the world economy as a gluttonous diner, enthusiastically overfed by a waiter keen to sell all he can as quickly as possible. The waiter, however, wants nothing to do with the resulting indigestion and flees the scene in alarm. He only returns when he can again serve an excessive meal. Thus, in keeping with popular wisdom, the irresponsible greed of 'business' is the cause of the periodic violent disorders in the world's digestive system.

of financial conspiracy and underconsumptionist economic theory—but it was not an easy process.

By September–October 1930 the Federal and State Labor governments' acceptance of the Melbourne Agreement was coming under increasing pressure. As shown in the previous chapter, even before the Agreement was announced, the orthodox solution had been rejected by the ACTU in February, by the ALP Federal Conference in May, and by the Labour Council of New South Wales in August. In mid-September, following publication of Niemeyer's report and the Agreement, the ACTU convened a Conference of Key Unions. After lengthy deliberation, they called for 'the freeing of the credit resources of the country' and suggested that the Federal Government find £20 million to be allocated through an Economic Council. This would bypass the Loan Council, which was 'merely an instrument in the hands of the money sharks, loan mongers, and capitalists generally'. The conference also proposed 'a reduction in all interest rates in order to make available to industry cheap money'. A concurrent Special Conference of the Victorian ALP put forward an almost identical programme to combat the 'deliberately created' financial stringency.[3]

One month later the Federal Executive of the ALP, mindful of the frustration and anger that the impotence of the various Labor governments was causing among the rank and file, declared its attitude. The 'derangement of the economic system', the Executive asserted, was being used by 'mercenaries and unscrupulous employers to attack the wage and living standards of the workers'. Addressing itself to the Melbourne Agreement, it warned that 'The action of any Government in lowering the standards of workers cannot be too strongly condemned', and directed attention to the planks of the ALP platform dealing with 'banking, insurance and arbitration'. It argued that the Niemeyer policy was a deliberate attempt to increase the purchasing power of those receiving interest at the expense of the workers. The Executive proposed a five-point plan, which called for a 'back to work campaign' on the basis of an increase of credit to industry on a lower interest rate and the 'utilisation of the nation's credit' to liquidate loan commitments as they fell due, along with an adjustment of Australia's war debt to Britain in line with the conditions applying to other dominions and Britain's debt to other countries.[4]

By the end of October the position of men like Scullin, Fenton, Lyons, Hogan and Hill who had been party to the Melbourne Agreement was becoming more isolated. The Agreement had not only been denounced in the labour press and in a flood of pamphlets, but also by the ACTU, the ALP Federal Executive, the

Victorian ALP Conference, the Labour Council of New South Wales and the Tasmanian and Queensland Parliamentary Labor parties. In addition, Lang had just won the New South Wales election on a platform that explicity rejected the Agreement. With Scullin still in London, and the Federal Government under the less authoritative leadership of Fenton and Lyons, the stage was set for a Caucus revolt.

It began with Theodore, the Government's original Treasurer, who had been replaced by Lyons while allegations of corruption during his period as Premier of Queensland were being investigated. Theodore made his move on 28 October during a Caucus debate on the Government's proposals to implement the Melbourne Agreement. Using George Gibbons as a front, he fired the first shot in what became known as 'the battle of the plans'. He proposed a scheme for mild, controlled inflation in the domestic economy, supported by greater control over Australia's external financial dealings. It was the first instalment of the Theodore Plan, which was developed in successive stages to its mature form in March 1931. It represented a direct challenge to Niemeyer's orthodoxy by offering the promise that gentle inflation might stimulate business activity and revive employment, and at the same time, allow Australia to meet its foreign debt obligations.

The plan owed a great deal to the influence of R. F. Irvine, a former Professor of Economics at Sydney University, who had discussed with Theodore in early September 1930 the need to develop a well-argued alternative to deflationary policy. Before then as McFarlane shows, he had inclined towards the orthodox view. Also, as Cook points out, his conversion to expansionary policy was in happy conjunction with his ambition to regain the Treasury, consolidate his power base in the New South Wales branch of the party at the expense of Lang, and capture leadership of the change in Caucus economic thinking. The change of mood was formalized two days later when Caucus voted 26 to 14 in favour of his proposals. This was a major defeat for Lyons and Fenton, who felt themselves bound by the Melbourne Agreement. It also alarmed Scullin, who sent a cablegram from London opposing the resolution.[5]

The rebellion took a step further on 6 November when a motion from Anstey and Curtin, calling for a £27 million loan repayment to be deferred for twelve months, was carried 22 to 16. This was an even more serious embarrassment to Scullin in London. On 3 December he asked the Bank of England for £5 million to cover maturing Treasury Bills. This was not only to ease the pressure on Australia's balance of payments; he hoped that it would also be interpreted as a sign that the Bank of England supported him in his

Australian Worker, 11 February 1931
'The impression is growing in London that, if Mr. Scullin meets Parliament with a strong policy of economy and retrenchment, a substantial loan will be made available.' — London cable. The Tempter: 'Just do what I wish you to do, Jimmy, and you can have as much money as you want — at the usual price, of course.'

Will Donald's allusion to the Faustian bargain concerns Scullin's trip to London, where he was told by the Deputy Governor of the Bank of England that it would be difficult for Australia to obtain further credit unless the Government adhered to Niemeyer's advice. The implication is that to do so will be to sell the nation's soul into eternal torment.

opposition to the rebellious Caucus majority. Sir Ernest Harvey replied that the Bank could not provide the money, because the Government had departed from Niemeyer's advice. The bank also had 'grave misgivings' about the Government's intentions in the Central Reserve Bank Bill.[6]

Meanwhile, at the Commonwealth Bank, Sir Robert Gibson was equally resolute in the face of Theodore's challenge when Cabinet passed it on to him. On 16 December he told Cabinet that a £20 million expansion of credit would produce inflation that would 'not only fail to improve the situation but will definitely contribute towards plunging the country into more serious difficulties, and, if proceeded with, into final disaster'. The Commonwealth Bank's position was abundantly clear: 'it is not prepared to subscribe to any such policy'. As it appeared that the Melbourne Agreement could not be adhered to, he went on to suggest a further meeting of the Loan Council to formulate a new plan.[7] Both banks were utterly determined that the Government should stick to the dictates of 'sound finance'.

Accordingly, in mid-January 1931 a meeting of the Loan Council, with Gibson present, resolved to convene a Premiers' Conference to lay down a three-year plan for the adjustment of government finances. But while Gibson and a committee of public servants were preparing information for the conference, events took a serious turn for the Federal Government. Following Scullin's return to Australia on 7 January, the Federal and New South Wales Labor parties agreed to contest the Parkes by-election (brought on by the elevation of a Labor MHR, E. A. McTiernan, to the High Court) on the basis of the Theodore Plan. Immediately before the election Scullin announced that Theodore had been reinstated as Treasurer. This provoked the first major split in government ranks, when Fenton and Lyons resigned from the ministry. Subsequently, in mid-March, they joined the Opposition, where they were followed by Guy, Gabb, Price and, later, McGrath. On 7 May, Lyons became leader of the newly formed United Australia Party. These defections of conservative Labor men were repeated in the State parties, particularly in Victoria, Tasmania and South Australia. On 22 January the Arbitration Court added its weight to the tide of orthodox opinion by ordering a 10 per cent reduction in wages. On 31 January the electors of Parkes compounded the Government's troubles by recording a 19 per cent swing to the successful Nationalist candidate.

The Premiers' Conference began on 6 February with no precise plan before it, because, Scullin suggested, they were there to formulate one. Realizing the difficulties confronting him, Theodore cautiously opened his hand on the second day. He put forward his scheme for 'equality of sacrifice' in general terms, hoping that the Premiers would approve it in principle and leave the working out of details until after the Commonwealth Bank's attitude was known. As expected, the bank rejected it on 12 February, and it was duly elaborated to Caucus on 2 March in the light of that knowledge.

The plan comprised a complex set of interrelated measures that aimed at 'the creation of additional bank credit for use in industry and enterprise throughout the country, concurrently with reductions in government expenditure and a reduction of costs in industry'. There would be equality of sacrifice, whereby bondholder's interest would be subject to a special tax, interest rates would be reduced to assist industry, additional credit would be released through normal channels to stimulate business activity, which would increase employment and thus consumption, and the Commonwealth Bank would buy up government securities as a means of reducing the yield on them to 5 per cent. On the overseas account, a drift towards devaluation in the exchange rate was to be permitted, the Exchange Mobilization scheme was to be strengthened to prevent speculation, and attempts were to be made to cover the floating debt in London. The major direct measure, given that the Commonwealth Bank had refused to help with credit expansion, was to be an issue of fiduciary currency—notes without gold backing—up to a limit of £28 million, with £8.5 million to assist wheatgrowers and £1 million per month for unemployment relief work. It was also proposed to press ahead with the Central Reserve Bank Bill, which the Senate had deferred.[8] Irvine and Theodore had produced a sophisticated plan, which recognized the relationship between domestic and external factors, took account of the multiplier effect of credit expansion, and held no fears of deficit budgeting, although it aimed at a balanced budget.

Politically, it offered moderate Labor men an acceptable compromise by which they could be seen to resist deflation yet not actually repudiate Australia's foreign loan obligations. It could thus be sold to the electorate as a plan that ensured 'equality of sacrifice' at home while preserving 'national honour' abroad. As such, it strengthened Theodore's hand in his struggle with Lang for supremacy in the New South Wales branch of the Labor Party.

Lang was well aware of this, and had brought his own plan to the Premiers' Conference. On the Monday following Theodore's careful presentation of his general proposals. Lang put an end to what he called the Conference's 'shilly-shallying' and announced his plan. It would strike at the very heart of the nation's financial troubles—its fixed interest commitments. He proposed:

1. That the Governments of Australia decide to pay no further interest to British bondholders until Britain has dealt with the Australian overseas debt as Britain settled her own foreign debt with America.
2. That, in Australia, interest on all Government borrowing be reduced to three per cent.
3. That immediate steps be taken by the Commonwealth Government to abandon the gold standard of currency, and set up in its place a currency based upon the wealth of Australia, to be termed 'the goods standard'.

Although it lacked the theoretical sophistication of the Theodore Plan, Lang's was nevertheless an astute combination of economic and political objectives.

As Clark has shown, Lang's primary economic concern was to reduce the burden of interest payments on government finances, particularly in his own State. The first two points were explicitly designed to lower the interest payable on foreign and domestic loans. The object of this was to divert a greater proportion of his State's revenue to public works programmes to relieve unemployment, and to meet his existing wages bill without further cuts. The justification was that, as prices and wages were falling while interest rates remained stable, the real value of payments to bondholders was rising. Simple economic justice, supported by nationalist resentment, demanded the redistribution of some of that income from wealthy Britons to poor Australians.

In the week before the Conference, Lang outlined his view on the third point in a series of articles for *Labor Daily* entitled 'Away with the Golden Cross'. Here he was concerned with two basic issues: repudiation and the gold standard. On the former, he revived memories of the 'terror of 1893', when, he alleged, the banks had repudiated their obligations to depositors in the way they 'reconstructed' after the crash. This rhetorical swipe anticipated the response he expected from conservative quarters to the first two points of his plan. On the latter issue, he denounced the gold standard as a tool of international finance:

> It is the power of gold in New York and London that inflates the loan moneys we borrow and deflates the values of our interest payments, so that we are robbed both in borrowing and in paying. When we wipe out the gold standard, when we make our only standard the real wealth of the community, the production of the brains and hands of the people, then, and not till then, we will be a free people—then we will be free of unemployment and usury and distress.

Labor Daily, 4 March 1931
THE ONLY WAY.

In this typical example of the Lang machine's propaganda, Fred Brown reduces the complex problems surrounding economic recovery to a simple and direct issue. Published shortly after the Lang Plan was announced, this cartoon depicts it as the only way that the intolerable burden of debt can be lifted from the nation's shoulders. It issues an implied challenge to the people of New South Wales, whose leader has given them the only means of doing it. Australia's destiny is in their hands.

By issuing currency or credit based on 'the goods standard' governments could free themselves from the grip of the financial institutions, whose control and manipulation of gold was the instrument by which they maintained their domination over governments and people.

The Lang Plan was not simply a financial revolt by a hard-pressed government; it was also a carefully calculated defence of Lang's political base in New South Wales. As Cooksey has indicated, each point was directed at a specific group within this constituency. The first was designed to appeal to those who argued for repudiation, such as the Labour Council of New South Wales, which passed Garden's motion in August 1930. Together, the first two points were intended for those who demanded equality of sacrifice. The third point was directed to the broad sweep of radical opinion that could be expected to respond to the old populist shibboleths about 'The Cross of Gold'. There was a good measure of political cynicism in this last point, for Lang almost certainly knew that Australia has been steadily drifting away from the gold standard since December 1929.[9]

But despite very different emphases and mutually hostile political objectives, the Theodore and Lang plans shared a common heritage in underconsumptionist economics, a theoretical tradition that offered an alternative to the classical school. In Australia the most influential underconsumptionist was the prolific English writer J. A. Hobson. McFarlane has traced the theoretical provenance of the Theodore Plan from Hobson to Irvine to Theodore, and Clark has traced the Lang Plan from Hobson to Douglas to Lang.

According to Adam Smith, the acknowledged founder of classical economics, free competition operating through the 'invisible hand' of market forces would not only reconcile the competing demands of individual self-interests, but would also tend to create the best possible conditions for the most efficient use of resources. It was a school of thought that directed its attention to the act of production, to the supply of goods and services. That preoccupation found its crudest expression in Say's Law which stated that supply created its own demand. But underconsumptionists, having witnessed the development of nineteenth-century industrial capitalism, were not so sanguine about the efficiency or benevolence of the free market. They were more concerned with problems surrounding the question of distribution. Many of them argued that capitalism had an inherent tendency to slump because of its persistent inability to maintain demand for consumption goods. In the absence of offsetting factors such as some form of income redistribution, depression became its normal condition.

Individual writers within the underconsumptionist tradition focused their analysis on different aspects of the problem. Malthus was concerned with the tendency to over-saving, Sismondi with the maldistribution of income, Hobson with the inability to consume and Douglas with distortion of credit. Most, however, were agreed that consumption was both the object and prime determinant of production. How much was produced to meet the demands of consumers determined the level of employment and the amount of income that went to the various factors of production in the form of wages, profit or rent. According to Hobson there was an element of income over and above the price necessary to put whatever was being sold onto the market, be it land, labour or any other commodity. That additional element, which he called 'surplus', was determined by the relative bargaining power of the buyers and sellers. In the sale of labour, he argued that the stronger bargaining position of employers enabled them to secure a disproportionate share of that 'surplus' at the expense of their workers. Since most employers tended to be rich, a substantial part of that extra income was saved. Increasing amounts of income were thus withdrawn from the cycle of consumption and production, going instead into investment. This had two initial effects. The first was a tendency for industrial capital to expand beyond the capacity of its markets to buy the goods it produced. The second was a decline in consumption on the part of the poor, whose share of income would progressively fall. Thus, a downward cycle of falling income and rising unemployment would be set in motion. In the short term, however, this process could be diverted into economic imperialism, whereby excess productive capacity was absorbed in underdeveloped colonial markets. Nevertheless, the time would inevitably come when capital accumulation must halt and the downward spiral of consumption, production, income and employment accelerate into prolonged stagnation.

In the absence of strong trade unions able to force a better share of 'surplus' for workers, Hobson's answer to this process was a periodic redistribution of income to the poor, whose tendency to spend rather than save would restore the balance between production and consumption. It would also prevent additional, unnecessary, capital accumulation. Regular adjustments of this kind would be required to offset the capitalist economy's inherent tendency to slump.[10]

It is significant that underconsumptionist remedies did not require a fundamental reconstruction of capitalist productive relations. They relied, in their essentials, upon a redistribution of income justified on the dual grounds of economic stability and social justice. As such, they held a strong appeal for labour and other vaguely anti-capitalist movements that lacked either the theoretical inclination or the political will to change the whole system.

Prospects for a redistribution of income to the poor in Australia during 1930–31 were bleak. Unemployment continued to rise at an alarming rate. The Arbitration Court gave its formal approval to wage cuts and a weak and demoralized union movement offered only token resistance. In these circumstances it is not surprising that the plans advanced by Labor focused on the only avenue that appeared to be left open—government finance and the 'release of credit'.

Delegates to the Premiers' Conference were prepared to consider any plausible solution that did not involve the stringent measures required by orthodox deflation, but Lang's Plan was too radical and was promptly dismissed. With more hope than confidence, they gave cautious approval to the Theodore Plan and commissioned him to take it to the Commonwealth Bank, but Theodore's proposals meant inflation, which the bank's board regarded as heresy. On 12 February, Gibson bluntly put the bank's position to Theodore:

> Subject to equitable reductions in all wages, salaries and allowances, pensions, social benefits of all kinds, interest and other factors which affect the cost of living, the Commonwealth Bank Board will actively co-operate with the trading banks, and the Government of Australia in sustaining industry and restoring employment.

Stripped of its extraneous verbiage, this was a simple ultimatum: the Government must cut its expenditure before the bank would provide further assistance. Eleven days later a conference of trading banks endorsed Gibson's uncompromising position.

This was seen as the'stick up' that labour radicals had predicted in 1924 when control of the Commonwealth Bank was passed from a single governor to a board representing major economic 'interests'. It was also seen as a compelling reason for the Government to press ahead with the banking legislation it had introduced into the House of Representatives in April 1930.

Having received their answer from the banks, the Premiers reconvened on 25 February. As a reply to Gibson's ultimatum, Theodore asked them to approve an issue of fiduciary currency up to £18 million for rural assistance and job creation. Faced with the banks' threat to refuse any additional finance, they equivocated. After considerable debate the meeting concluded in a deadlock, with Nationalist and Labor Premiers (minus Lang, who had refused to participate) divided along party lines. Even then, two Labor governments gave only conditional approval to Theodore's proposal. The Premiers' Conference had thus, by default, succumbed to the banks' insistence on orthodoxy, leaving Theodore and the Commonwealth Government to try to force their programme through both houses of the Federal Parliament.[11]

Before they had an opportunity to pursue that course, the divisions in the labour movement developed into another bitter split. The tensions were apparent at the Special ACTU Congress of 16–22 February. With more than a quarter of their members unemployed, delegates were becoming impatient at the Federal Government's fruitless attempts to negotiate with the banks. Their general mood was turning more towards direct action. The ACTU Executive urged the Government to declare a state of emergency and use its constitutional powers to deal with unemployment. There were calls for a general strike or overt revolutionary action, because, as one delegate put it, 'The sole power that controlled industry today was money power. Until we captured money power we could not do very much on behalf of the workers'. But the more cautious affiliates, led by the Australian Workers Union, had the numbers. The final resolution was an implied recognition of the ACTU's weakness. It recommended: a reduced working week; union rates for unemployment relief work; adequate sustenance; a rent moratorium; and that child endowment be no bar to the usual relief rates of pay.[12] This left the Lang Plan as the only remaining focus for radical opinion.

The first test of strength between the Lang and Theodore Plans came in the East Sydney by-election. The selected Labor Party candidate, E. J. Ward, supported the Lang Plan, which the New South Wales Labor Party Executive 'wholeheartedly' endorsed. The ALP Federal Executive, on the other hand, declared that the banks had the power to assist the country, and endorsed the Theodore Plan, urging further negotiations with the Commonwealth Bank. It soon became clear that Ward intended to advocate the Lang Plan, so the Federal Executive declared that if he persisted in doing so he was not an approved Federal ALP candidate. The New South Wales Executive replied with a demand that all Federal Members who assisted in the campaign must support the Lang Plan.[13]

In opening Ward's campaign, Lang declared war on three fronts. He began with an attack on 'overseas interests' who had tried to rivet the chains of conscription on Australian manhood in World War I and now wished 'to take the bread from the mouths of your sons and daughters to satisfy the insatiable greed of the financial interests'. He then turned his attention to Gibson and the trading banks, with the assertion that 'There, in that ultimatum, is a declaration of a lock out of the People of Australia by the Australian banking institutions'. After a spirited defence of his plan as 'a sane business proposition', he concluded with a denunciation of the Scullin Government. 'The financial interests have become the law-givers to Federated Australia, and it looks as if many of our Federal legislators are prepared to become the pawns of High Finance.' However, not all were prepared to become 'pawns'. At a rally of 20 000 people in the Sydney Domain on 1 March, Ward and Lang were supported by five 'Federal legislators'—Beasley, Dunn, Eldridge, Lazzarini and Rae.[14]

Federal Caucus took revenge the following day with a 'spill' of all positions, which resulted in the removal of three leading radicals from Cabinet—Anstey, Beasley and Daly. Ten days later Ward won the by-election, but with a majority greatly reduced from that of his predecessor in 1929. When Caucus, in line with the Federal Executive ruling, refused to admit him, the 'Beasley group' walked out. On 15 March the Sydney Metropolitan Labor Conference expelled Theodore and all other Federal Labor MPs under their jurisdiction who had opposed the Lang Plan. A Special Federal Conference of the ALP replied on 27 March by expelling the whole of the New South Wales Executive. The Lang Labor Party emerged from this second major split in the Scullin Government.[15]

While this was in progress it became clear that Lang meant what he said in the first point of his plan. Beginning on 15 March, his government defaulted on interest payments to the Commonwealth and to overseas bondholders at regular intervals until July. By then his State's finances were so depleted that, to pay his wages and salaries bill, he had to seek funds from the Loan Council. This meant rejoining the Council, resuming external interest payments and reducing his expenditure, as laid down in the Premiers' Plan of June 1931.[16]

Despite its difficulties during February and March, the Federal Government persisted with its legislative programme based on the Theodore Plan. On 17 March, Theodore delivered his Second Reading speech on the Fiduciary Notes Bill. A month later the Senate rejected it. In addition, the Government encountered obstruction from Sir Robert Gibson and the Commonwealth Bank board. On 2 April, in reply to a request from Theodore for funds to assist wheatgrowers, Gibson not only refused to help but also warned that 'a point is being reached beyond which it would be impossible for the Bank to provide further financial assistance for the Government in the future'. Theodore replied angrily that this was 'an attempt on the part of the Bank to arrogate to itself a supremacy over the Government in the determination of the financial policy of the Commonwealth'. Early in May, Gibson and the Senate joined forces to defeat the Commonwealth Bank Bill (no. 2), which sought to reduce the gold backing of the currency so that bullion could be exported to London. In an extraordinary move, the Opposition majority in the Senate called Gibson to testify before it on 6 May. His evidence left no doubt that he opposed the measure, and it was duly rejected a week later.[17]

While the Theodore Plan ground to a halt in the face of hostility from the Bank and the Senate, Lang Labor was also in trouble. On 23 April, despite double-page reassurances in *Labor Daily* and soothing words from Lang, the Government Savings Bank of New South Wales collapsed amid a run of panic withdrawals. Since the October 1930 election campaign, confidence in its stability had been steadily undermined by scare tactics from the Nationalist Oppositon, and by press speculation that Lang might use depositors' funds to relieve the pressure on his Government's deficit. It was true that the bank's weakness had been compounded by Lang's failure to repay money owed to it by his Government, and by his subsequent inability to support if from depleted Treasury funds when the run occured. But the Commonwealth Bank's reluctance to come to the aid of its State equivalent also contributed to the collapse. If the Commonwealth Bank or the Federal Treasury had supported the Government Savings Bank, there was the possibility that Lang might have used the funds to supplement his State's finances. This would have enabled him to persist in his default on loan repayments and resist the pressure to rejoin the Loan Council. This gave both Gibson and Theodore a compelling reason to delay any rescue mission. There may have been an element of truth behind R. E. O'Halloran's colourful assertion that 'insidious forces . . . are doing their uttermost to dry up the wellsprings of finance, to make the Government vacate the Treasury benches through want of money'.[18]

By this stage, sectors of conservative opinion were showing signs of alarm at the instability of the Federal Government and the behaviour of Lang Labor in New South Wales. Fearing that the resistance of institutions like the Senate and the Commonwealth Bank might not be sufficient to stem the tide of radical discontent, some prominent citizens formed private armies to secure law and order, defend private property, uphold 'constitutional government' and maintain imperial loyalty. Throughout rural New South Wales the clandestine Old Guard prepared to suppress urban revolution, and the facist-inspired New Guard openly paraded its intentions in suburban Sydney. Some imperial representatives also expressed disquiet at the trend of events. In May, the British

Trade Commissioner suggested to his superiors in London that Australia's financial affairs be put in the hands of 'an expert and impartial Financial Commission from the United Kingdom', which would supervise a process of reconstruction. This was quite unnecessary, because the advocates of 'sane finance' in Australia were beginning to mobilize their forces. The previously divided Opposition in the Federal Parliament had gathered behind Lyons under the banner of the United Australia Party. In South Australia a group of leading conservatives organized a coalition calling itself the Emergency Committee. According to a member of that coalition, they were responsible for engineering the appointment of the Committee of Experts to advise the Loan Council. Their object was to ensure that 'the Communist Langs and Irish Scullins' did not stray from the deflationary policy enshrined in the Melbourne Agreement and thus endanger Australia's 'membership as an honest partner in the British Commonwealth of Nations'.[19]

With the assistance of Lionel Hill, Labor Premier of South Australia, the Committee of Experts was appointed by the Loan Council at the end of April, under the watchful eye of Sir Robert Gibson. It comprised five State under-treasurers, along with the economists Melville, Copland, Giblin and Shann. The Theodore Plan having been effectively defeated, their primary task was to devise a scheme whereby governments might balance their budgets by June 1934. This required finding a way of reducing the burden of interest payments that was acceptable to both banks and governments. While it was accepted that wages and prices should fall according to market forces, interest rates were protected from the chill winds of depression by the 'sanctity of contract'. They could not be reduced without the consent of bondholders. Accordingly, the committee consulted a number of commercial and financial bodies about the possibility of converting existing internal loans at lower interest rates before presenting their report to the Premiers' Conference at the end of May. The report recommended a cut of 20 per cent in all adjustable government expenditure, increased taxation, and a reduction of interest rates, since that was the only major source of income in the economy that had not fallen. Their scheme was, in contrast to the Theodore Plan, a deflationary version of 'equality of sacrifice'.

The whole strategy depended on the co-operation of the financial institutions and all the Premiers. After two and a half weeks of often spirited discussion—during which it was found necessary to admit Lyons and Latham, because the Opposition's approval was required for any scheme to pass the Senate—the Premiers agreed upon an essentially deflationary plan. As expected, there was some difficulty with Lang, who wanted to make the loan conversion compulsory, but a compromise was reached whereby governments would cut expenditure by the required amount in their own way after the voluntary loan conversion was completed. The Conference's final resolution became known as the Premiers' Plan. It involved three main elements: a 20 per cent reduction of adjustable government expenditure, with the exception of old age pensions, which were to be cut by 12½ per cent; increased income and sales tax; and a reduction of public and private interest rates, with the conversion loan's rate being lowered by 22½ per cent.

Although there had been considerable difficulty in convincing the Australian banks to accept the cut in interest rates, because of their suspicion that the New South Wales and Federal Governments might not cut their expenditure as agreed, there was at least one banker who could see an advantage in their 'sacrifice'. A. C. Davidson from the Bank of New South Wales considered that:

> if we force the Scullin . . . and Lang Governments to adopt this plan it means that those factors that might normally be turbulent in the community will lead this movement. They will pass the necessary legislation which will naturally be unsavory to their extreme supporters with the probable result that a Nationalist Government will follow and obtain the credit for 'pulling Australia out of the mud'.[20]

He was right.

Predictably, the Premiers' Plan was unpopular with Labor people, especially the provisions that involved wage and pension cuts. On 6 June most ministers 'regretted the necessity for such economies, especially the necessity to interfere with pensions'. On 12 June, after two days of heated debate, Federal Caucus endorsed it by 26 votes to 13. The following day, *Labor Daily* launched an emotionally charged denunciation of the Federal 'Government of Straw', studiously ignoring the fact that Lang had signed the agreement. In accustomed style, the paper invoked images of starving war widows, of the Premiers 'repudiating' the weak and maimed, and of a plan that would hurry pensioners to their graves —'a most desirable and economic result' for those 'who know only the velvet and silk things of life'. During the course of the Premiers' Conference the Hobart *Voice* of 30 May had detected an international conspiracy at work in the Bank of England's 'Norman Plan' for debtor nations, which it feared would presage the 'Norman Conquest of Australia'. Henry Boote reviewed the Plan in the *Australian Worker* of 10 June and concluded that it would save Australia only at the price of national starvation. Two days later the *Westralian Worker* reflected bitterly on the fact that wage and pension cuts were to be compulsory while interest reduction was to be voluntary. E. J. Holloway thought that Cabinet's acceptance of the Plan was a 'Great Betrayal' of those whom Labor represented. Both he and Culley resigned from the ministry in protest.[21]

The Labor Party machine faced the difficult problem of what to do about Labor governments that had agreed to preside over wage and pension cuts. The various State Executives condemned the Plan in slightly different terms, but most focused on the pensions issue. Some declared that Labor parliamentarians who supported it should be expelled. The Federal Executive also denounced the cuts, but pointed out that they were the result of obstruction by the Senate and the banks. It went on to remind party members that a Labor government was preferable to a Nationalist, thus implying that it did not favour expulsion of the Scullin Ministry. The ALP Special Federal Conference of 27 August took a similar attitude. It deplored the policy agreed on by the Premiers, but was not prepared to risk further splits in the party over an issue that was an accomplished fact. Thus the party machine effectively endorsed the Government's capitulation.[22]

An editorial in *Labor Call* on 30 July captured the resulting mood of frustration when it observed:

> The English financial capitalists or bankers, or those who constitute Money Power, have no interest in Australia and its workers beyond what they can get out of them in the way of profit or surplus products . . . And the only limits that will be observed or respected are those which the workers themselves in Australia are capable of enforcing.

The bitter irony was that neither the workers nor their political or industrial leaders were capable of enforcing any effective limits to the general trend of deflationary policy.

From June to November 1931 the discredited and dispirited Scullin Government pressed ahead with its attempts to implement the Premiers' Plan. It lingered on until 25 November, when Beasley's Lang Labor faction seized upon an allegation of impropriety against Theodore as the pretext to bring it down.[23]

During the ensuing election campaign the respective parties advocated the policies to which they were already committed. Lyons for the UAP, and Page for the Country Party, stood for 'sane finance' in the form of the Premiers' Plan, despite some differences of emphasis on the tariff issue.

Australian Worker, 22 July 1931
The World: 'Why did I ever take to drinking this stuff again? Look at the state it's got me into.'

The depressed world hastens his slide into utter destitution by an addiction to the 'fine old gold standard dope'. The landlord of the Bankers' Inn, meanwhile, displays a cheerful indifference to the world's plight. After all, he prospers from the misery inflicted by his wares. According to this temperance view of economic recovery, the world might be saved if only he would foreswear the demon 'gold standard dope'.

Scullin complained about the obstruction of his Government by the banks and the Senate. He took credit for the way that the Premiers' Plan had addressed the balance of payments crisis and promised to restore the wage and pension cuts as soon as economic conditions allowed. The majority of his campaign centred around tariff policy and the need for reform of the monetary system, with the development of a Central Reserve Bank as the main instrument through which a Federal Labor Government would implement counter-cyclical monetary policy. He also looked forward to the day when international co-operation in monetary management would prevent depressions.[24]

Scullin's restraint was not always emulated by his colleagues. In a radio broadcast on 2UE, Theodore attacked foreign banks and pastoral companies, which had been 'exploiting Australian wealth in the manner of an ancient Empire dragging the wealth out of its enslaved tributary States'. J. L. McKenna, ALP candidate for Fawkner, described the banks as 'a gang of heartless ruffians'. Anstey reminded his constituents of how emergency paper currency had been issued to save the banks in 1893, and observed that it was the banks that were now denying it to the Government. Labor's press and platforms across the country resounded with fulminations against 'the local Banks and the Money Lords overseas'. The fight was 'against the dominance of the Money Power'. 'Saturday's issue is Manhood or Mammon'.[25]

In keeping with tradition, Labor speakers reserved some of their most biting invective for their erstwhile comrades. Lang told an Armidale meeting that the Theodore policy had really been drawn up by Niemeyer. On the same evening Theodore, for the benefit of a Darlinghurst audience, defined Lang Laborities as 'hangers-on, intriguers, ex-IWW men, recent arrivals from Russia, ex-Communists, bulldozers and parasites'. References to Lyons were even more colourful.

The Lang Labor policy, presented by Beasley with vigorous support from Lang, followed the slogan 'Man before Money'. They promised to rebuild the whole credit structure of Australia on the basis of nationalized banking, and rejected Federal Labor's Central Reserve Bank as merely another tool in the hands of overseas financiers. They warned that the 'sinister grip of the banks' must be broken if the insidious designs behind the 'dictation from Semitic Britain' were to be thwarted and so allow money to be a 'servant not a dictator'. The election gave the people a chance 'to strike a blow for economic freedom by releasing Australia from slavery to the financial ring dominated by the Bank of England'.[26]

As expected, the election was a disaster for the Federal Labor

Party. They won only thirteen of the 75 seats in the House of Representatives and eight of the 36 in the Senate. Theodore was one of the casualties, losing his seat to Rosevear, the Lang Labor candidate. While this gave them great satisfaction, it was a pyrrhic victory, since they could only command five seats in the House and two in the Senate. The real victors were the conservatives and the advocates of deflation.

Labor's election post-mortems carried the usual denunciations of the Money Power. There was much spirited abuse of Niemeyer, Gibson, the banks and the Senate, and of the various Labor factions by each other. Motives ranging from grand conspiracy to craven cowardice were imputed to the respective protagonists. The most common allegation was that the Bank of England, the Commonwealth Bank, conservative politicians and economists had conspired to impose deflationary policies upon a Labor government as a means to enrich the Money Power at the expense of the people.

If Lang had been unwilling to co-operate with Scullin, he was even less disposed to adopt a conciliatory attitude towards the incoming Lyons Ministry. At the end of January 1932 he again defaulted on payments to overseas bondholders. The Federal Government exercised its overriding powers by introducing special legislation to force New South Wales to make these payments through the Commonwealth. While that legislation was being challenged in the High Court, Lang directed his public servants to conduct government transactions in cash as a way of keeping State money out of Commonwealth hands. This placed the Governor of New South Wales, Sir Philip Game, in a difficult position. Fearing that Lang was acting illegally, he sought advice from the Chief Justice of New South Wales and the Dominions Office on his constitutional responsibilities. Meanwhile there was mounting evidence of imminent civil disorder. Game came under strong pressure from conservative quarters to dismiss Lang. The Old Guard and the New Guard were being mobilized to seize strategic installations. It seemed likely that the Government might soon be unable to pay its employees. There were even some bizarre attempts to barricade the State Treasury against Federal officials. The matter came to a head when Lang refused Game's request that he withdraw a second circular to public servants directing them to withhold State funds. On 13 May, Game added another symbol to Labor demonology by dismissing Lang's Government.[27]

Land did not defy the Governor's viceregal edict, nor exhort his supporters to insurrection. Instead, he accepted the decision with a calmness that surprised many of his friends and enemies. Although he was always ready to play the role of populist demagogue, he had no pretensions to be a revolutionary leader. His preferred weapon was rhetorical fire. Accordingly, he presented himself during the ensuing election as the charismatic figure who would save the people from the ruthless grip of the banks. The *Labor Daily* of 11 June captured the tone of his campaign:

> Between the bankers and the people they sought to enslave and bend to their will there stood forth a man—the leader of the people—Mr Lang...bearing on his proud battle-flag the slogan MAN BEFORE MONEY. Is it any wonder that the people have rallied to that flag, and with a mighty voice that has struck fear into the hearts of the money-changers, proclaimed LANG IS RIGHT!

Here was Horatious to hold the bridge, a St George to slay the dragon, the defender of the weak against the overweening arrogance and ambition of the Money Power.

The whole direction of this campaign developed the Lang Labor position to its logical conclusion. Everything he had said and done since the Niemeyer visit became part of a heroic struggle in defence of the people. He told 'huge and enthusiastic' crowds of how foreigners had cunningly duped cowardly Federal politicians into administering the conspiracy against them. Was not the Premiers' Plan really the Niemeyer Plan? And what was Niemeyer, after all, but the 'Jewish bailiff from the Bank of England' who had presumed to tell Australians how to run their affairs for the exclusive benefit of the Money Power? Lang was defending the 'generation that copped the lot': Australians who had grown up in the 1890s, had cheerfully defended an ungrateful 'mother country' in the European Armageddon, tried to raise their families in the 'hungry twenties', and were now reduced to 'poverty in the midst of plenty' at the hands of the Money Power and its minions. He was the only politician in Australia prepared to stand up to Niemeyer, Gibson, the 'Feds' and the banks. He was 'the Big Fella', 'Greater than Lenin', the defender of 'the People'. His imposing stature, threatening scowl and declamatory gestures combined with this spirited rhetoric to give the speeches a theatrical character calculated to rouse the passions of those who did not pretend to understand economics but knew that finance, especially international finance, was at the heart of the nation's economic troubles and their own. Their only hope was to rally behind the flag proclaiming 'Lang is Right'.[28]

A majority of the New South Wales electorate took a different view. They installed the UAP–Country Party coalition led by Stevens and Bruxner. They may have turned their backs on their only remaining saviour, but they could hardly be blamed, because, as W. J. Duggan, Secretary of the Melbourne Trades Hall Council, pointed out, their minds were in the grip of the Money Power: 'It acts with a subtle and magic influence upon the inner consciousness of the electors, and, together with the anonymous and pungent criticism of the Press, stampeded them in a direction leading to nowhere'.[29] Ironically, the last phrase might equally have been applied to Lang.

Although the defeats suffered by the Scullin and Lang Governments were accompanied by extravagant denunciations of Money Power conspiracy, the accusations were not entirely wrong. At the onset of the depression Australia was economically dependent on Britain in an imperial relationship. This was made abundantly clear during Sir Otto Niemeyer's visit, when the Bank of England's prestige served to bolster that relationship, both financially and ideologically. The Scullin Government could do little to resist the policies advocated by Niemeyer, since it did not control some of the most strategically placed institutions of economic management. The Commonwealth Bank board, initially unsympathetic to Labor policy, moved quickly to outright hostility as the financial crisis developed. The private trading banks followed suit. The Senate, controlled by the parties of political conservatism, frustrated the Government's initiatives, and the Arbitration Court endorsed economic orthodoxy by authorizing wage cuts.

Labor had long been aware of the dilemmas facing a reformist party committed to working within a set of economic, political and constitutional relationships that were loaded against change. This not only undermined its resolve to pursue its objectives but also severely circumscribed its ability to act when circumstances compelled it to do so. Even the economic theory on which its alternative programmes were based reflected these difficulties. The underconsumptionist Theodore and Lang Plans sought to redistribute rapidly diminishing national income to the poor, but both collapsed in the face of resistance deeply entrenched in that apparatus of social relationships. Squeezed between this and the pressure of rank-and-file discontent, the Labor Party, an uneasy coalition at the best of times, split into three belligerent factions.

The eventual demise of the Labor governments was not due to these factors alone.[30] They also lost an intense ideological struggle for popular acceptance of what was possible and proper for governments to do about the depression. In the end, victory—both inside and outside the party—went to the advocates of 'sane finance' and 'national honour'. Behind this, as Lang discovered, were the reserve powers of an imperial Governor, and the brute force of private armies.

The net result of all this was that the Labor Party, by invoking an elaborate Money Power demonology as a metaphor to explain the mobilization of forces in defence of the existing capitalist state, simply reinforced the popular radical wisdom that 'finance is government and government is finance'.

7

The 'A plus B' of Financial Oppression – Douglas Credit

In the early 1930s Australia showed many signs of a society about to come apart at the seams. By 1932 economic activity had declined alarmingly. Trade union unemployment was approaching 30 per cent. Industrial production had been reduced by 70 per cent between 1928 and 1932. Real national product had fallen by 90 per cent during the period 1927–32. These statistics do not convey the grim reality of dole queues, unemployment marches, sustenance work gangs, evictions and hunger. Many Australians experienced one or more of these. More importantly perhaps, most knew that such things were happening. The anxiety that this occasioned could hardly have been allayed by the political fragmentation described in the previous chapter. The industrial and political labour movement was in tatters. Even the victorious conservative parties had just begun an uneasy process of consolidation. On the fringes of political activity an extraordinary array of organizations emerged. Socialists could choose to involve themselves in the Communist Party, the Socialization Units or the Unemployed Workers' Movement, or volunteer for the proposed Labor Army. Those of conservative persuasion were equally well served. They could cast in their lot with the All For Australia League, join the New Guard or the Old Guard, or support any of the numerous short-lived outfits such as the Sound Finance League. Many people in the Riverina, New England and Western Australia were convinced that the creation of new states, or outright secession, was an appropriate response to their difficulties. More reflective individuals could immerse themselves in a flood of journals, pamphlets and leaflets that peddled quick cures for the nation's ills. To the general observer, Australia in 1932 may well have given the impression of general confusion amid an abundance of certitudes, for despite all its material deprivations during the depression, the country was never short of self-appointed saviours.[1]

One of the most active and prominent of such groups was the

Douglas Social Credit Movement, an organization originally set up in the mid-1920s to propagate the financial nostrums of an English engineer, Major C. H. Douglas. According to Douglas, the vast benefits to be enjoyed by the mass of people as a result of industrial and technological progress had been denied to them by a perversion of capitalist enterprise that gave financiers a commanding position in modern production. Indeed, capitalism had been replaced by 'creditism', an evil enshrined in the financial system and manipulated by oligarchies of power-seekers in every country. In 1922 Douglas had declared that financiers not only precipitated wars and profited from them, but also luxuriated on the Riviera contemplating their power over a world they had enslaved. This enormous power had been accumulated by their ability to divert income from the cycle of production and consumption in such a way as to cause a permanent state of underconsumption for the mass of ordinary people. Douglas sought to demonstrate this proposition with the seductive authority of his 'A-plus-B' theorem, which, despite the flood of literature that exposed its fallacies, purported to explain with mathematical precision the root cause of the paradox of 'poverty in the midst of plenty'.[2]

The basis of its appeal lay in the breadth of its scope and the simplicity of its solutions. Douglas Credit told the discontented how the fundamentally sound machinery of capitalist production had been distorted by the financial system; how their freedom had been eroded by financial oligarchies who cynically manipulated fallacious theories; and how this had produced a centralization of economic power such that the basic purpose of production—consumption—had been obscured by mystification and chicanery in the service of power-hungry financiers. The road to salvation lay in the dethronement of these parasites through the redistribution of credit, which would be managed by such instruments of 'economic sanity' as the National Credit Authority, the Just Price, and the National Dividend. Thus would poverty be eliminated, without disrupting the social formation. To those in the 1930s who witnessed orthodox economists defending a system that had manifestly failed, and listened to socialists preaching an entirely new order that presaged greater centralization of economic power, Douglas Credit held a strong appeal. The whole theory, with the quasi-scientific A-plus-B theorem at its core, had 'an almost hypnotic quality for those who were disposed to believe it and were not accustomed to close abstract reasoning'.[3]

It also had an appeal to many in the labour movement who were accustomed to suspecting banks as the 'great behind the curtain power in modern capitalism'. It offered an apparently scientific proof of how the Money Power expropriated its ill-gotten gains in pursuit of wealth and power. It propounded a seemingly technical explanation in reply to those conservative economists who had blinded them with science for so long, and proposed institutions like the National Credit Authority, which could be easily equated with nationalized banking. To the many Labor people who were inclined towards Money Power theory, Douglas Credit could appear as merely another proof of what they had believed all along. It also mapped out a programme for the redistribution of wealth that rested easily alongside vague notions of social equality and economic justice. It is not surprising, therefore, that of all the political parties it sought to influence, the Social Credit Movement made most headway in the Labor Party.

Much of what Douglas had to say in the 1930s was familiar ground to Laborites. The first sentence of his *Monopoly of Credit* offered a propitious beginning:

> It cannot have escaped the observation of anyone interested in the welfare and orderly progress of society that, more especially in the years which have intervened since the close of the European War and the present time, the centre of gravity of world affairs has shifted from Parliaments and Embassies to Bank Parlours and Board Rooms.

Those who still harboured anger and resentment towards Niemeyer, Gibson and all that they represented, could find ample confirmation in what Douglas had to say. His claim that through the 'ingenious and subtle mechanism of money' financiers vied for control of the 'industrial system and the world population' would have struck a responsive chord. Similarly, his assertion that the world could only find its salvation after it had rid itself of the scourge of bankers had a familiar ring.

> It seems difficult to doubt that the effort of those in control of financial policy are primarily, if not entirely, concerned with making the world safe for bankers, rather than making the world safe. By one of those curious ironies which seem to be present in great crises, it happens . . . that the world cannot be made safe without removing the banker, painlessly or otherwise, from the commanding position which he now occupies. The alternative is in fact clear, and nothing effective can be done to protect civilization from its major risks which is not an attack upon the power of finance.[4]

This might easily have been mistaken for a passage from the 1917 edition of Anstey's *Kingdom of Shylock.*

Although Douglas Credit was a late arrival on the scene, it shared the indigenous tradition's obsession with financial conspiracies. 'The hand of the Bankers' could be detected behind almost any economic decision in Australia, from the Premiers' Plan to taxation and tenancy laws. 'The banks, controlling the volume and flow of money, control the lives and destinies of men; and governments eat out of their hands'. The Money Power was, as Labor publicists had claimed so often before, an international menace:

> By far the strongest force in the world at present is the centralized power of finance. It is all the more powerful because it is not generally recognized. Probably nine out of ten bankers have no other motive than to retain the position of material advantage which their business ensures them, but it seems probable that there exists a small minority of men at the head of the international financial hierarchy to whom profit in the ordinary sense is a secondary consideration, who are actuated chiefly by the will to power. They aim quite definitely at a financial hegemony of the world, and their ideal is the servile state.

Instead of this Douglas Credit promised, in vintage populist style, a new world where the exploiter could not exist; where there would be ample good for all; jobs for the unemployed; crime removed; class enmity abolished; and the conditions created where men might act toward each other as true Christians.[5]

Douglas Credit was first discussed in Australia during the mid-1920s, shortly after initial publication in Britain, but it was not until the onset of the depression that the various Social Credit associations were formed in all States.[6] As Berzins has shown, the Douglas Social Credit Movement began by trying to influence all political parties and a number of other public organizations. It tirelessly propagated what it believed to be the manifest virtues of Douglas's theory. For the reasons discussed above, it attracted most support from members of the Labor Party whose own stream of populist thought was thoroughly entrenched by 1930. Party branches heard talks on Douglas Credit; resolutions appeared on ALP agenda papers; it was given an airing in the Labor press; and many party members were simultaneously active in Douglas Credit organizations. As a result, some State branches enquired into the matter. In Western Australia the ALP issued three separate reports on it. In Tasmania the State Conference gave members approval to advocate it so long as they did so in terms of the party's banking policy. In the latter case, several prominent Labor men held senior positions in Douglas Credit organizations. For many of these people there was no conflict of interest involved in the dual allegiance. Were not both committed to extensive financial reform? They were both fighting the same enemy. Besides, it did not really matter whether you set up a National Credit Authority or nationalized all banks under the umbrella of the Commonwealth Bank—it all amounted to the same thing: control of the nation's credit by the people, for the people. At the superficial level it was easy to confuse Social Credit with Lang Labor's 'Socialization of Credit'. The details of how credit would be managed after they had abolished the Money Power could be worked out later. On these general issues many Laborites and Social Crediters were agreed. They were, after all, quite often the same people. Even after Douglas Credit had become a separate political party in 1934, it preferred that Labor's cherished instrument of financial reform—a reconstituted Commonwealth Bank—should be the institution to perform the functions of a National Credit Authority.[7]

The flirtation was relatively short-lived and far from harmonious. While Douglas Credit was generating interest in Labor circles, it was also attracting growing opposition. Early in 1933 Lang Labor placed a ban on dual membership. When Douglas Crediters formally entered the political arena in mid-1934 with the formation of the Douglas Credit Party of Australia, various ALP executives applied the rule that banned membership of another party. In August 1934 the Western Australian and Queensland executives invoked the rule. In the West there was some concern that ALP candidates for the Federal election who were also prominent Social Crediters might compromise the party's chances by advocating Social Credit rather than ALP policy. The Queensland Central Executive saw the Douglas Credit Party as a threat to its strength in rural areas and forbade simultaneous membership. South Australian Labor, still divided between the Federal and Lang factions, finally pronounced against Douglas Credit at the end of 1935. In Tasmania, where the links between the two had been strongest, a number of ALP candidates were endorsed by both parties. At its 1935 State Conference the Tasmanian ALP fell in line with the other States and imposed the ban. Although formal links were severed, attachment to the theory remained strong. With some support from their New South Wales comrades, Tasmanian delegates to the 1936 Federal Conference attempted to have the bank nationalization plank of the Party Platform replaced by 'national control of credit by the community for the community'. As Berzins has pointed out, five of the six

Australian Worker, 11 April 1934
'We will stand four-square against any interference with the banks.' — Prime Minister Lyons.
A New Constabulary Code.
Constable U.A.P.: 'Stand back! Give him a free hand!'

This reflects moderate Labor's attachment to the pluralist view that government's role is to act as an impartial protector of the national interest. Here, Will Donald accuses the Lyons Government of betraying the people's trust in the same manner as a corrupt policeman shielding a criminal accomplice.

Tasmanian delegates were old Douglas Crediters. The reference to a National Credit Advisory Authority in the 1936 banking policy was probably a compromise gesture to these delegates.[8]

The inroads that Douglas Credit made into the ALP were not merely an Australian aberration. In New Zealand, many leading members of the Labour Party were strong advocates of Douglas Credit. Like so many of their Australian counterparts, most members of the New Zealand Labour Caucus had vigorously attacked 'plutocratic bankers' as the agents behind the restriction of credit. A substantial number of these members were converts to Douglas Credit, but unlike Australia, where the matter was dealt with in the State branches, the New Zealand Labour Party was divided over the issue at the highest levels. Between 1932 and 1936 there was an informal alliance between Labour and the Social Credit Movement, a situation requiring considerable political skill on the part of leaders like Walter Nash to prevent a major split. A good deal of publicity was also given to the success of the Douglas Credit Party in the Canadian province of Alberta in 1935. The United Farmers of Alberta, the party that had ruled the Provincial Government since 1921, were defeated in the 1935 election by the Douglas Crediters. The new Government came to power under the Douglas banner, but during the whole of its extraordinarily long tenure it made no real attempt to usher in the millennium that its official rhetoric promised.[9]

In Australia, Labor's brief flirtation with Douglas Credit was never much more than a convenient association of people who thought that the financial system had been the primary cause of the depression and wanted to do something about it. But for some Labor people Douglas Credit had a more enduring appeal. With its declared intention to leave the basis of capitalism largely untouched, and only to eliminate the predatory Money Power, the theory offered an attractive alternative to the more conservative Laborites who had always been uneasy about the party's 'socialization' pretensions. Like many other populist programmes, it was rhetorically radical but the burden of its social analysis remained essentially conservative. Although Douglas Credit made headway within the rank and file, it was never a serious threat to Labor's centres of power. Besides, its decision to constitute itself as a separate party in 1934 provided the ALP machine with the necessary pretext to stamp it out.

As the Australian economy began to climb out of the trough of the depression in the mid-1930s the conditions that sharpened discontent and gave sustenance to populist monetary theories gradually eased. This coincided with the decline of many leading figures who had publicized the iniquities of the Money Power. Anstey had effectively retired in 1931, although he did not resign his seat until 1934. The Federal ALP lost a number of monetary radicals in the drubbing they received at the 1931 election. In New South Wales the Lang machine had begun a slow decline as moves towards a *rapprochement* with the Federal party gained strength. Even Lang was a spent force, despite a brief appearance in Federal Parliament during the late 1940s, when, as a cold-war warrior, the underlying conservatism of his populist stance was revealed for all to see. Except in Tasmania, where Douglas Crediters in the ALP showed their true colours in the bank nationalization campaign, Social Credit was soon to be a dead letter.

This is not to suggest that the Labor Party had lost interest in monetary reform as a necessary condition for the prevention of another depression. As Scullin told an audience in the Richmond Town Hall during the 1934 Federal election campaign:

> The present monetary system has failed. Another must take its place. Control of monetary machinery for private profits must give way to national control for the benefit of all. Change of control alone, however, will not suffice. There must be a change of policy. Money must be made the servant of industry, not its master . . . The superior pose of bankers speaking with self-assured authority cannot dispose of the tragic facts of private monetary control. Let the money masters be judged, not by their words, but by the fruits of their policy . . . In this enlightened progressive age we remain slaves to an obsolete banking system. The nation's economic energies are bound with financial ligatures stagnating the lifeblood of industry.[10]

In this, populist rhetoric and reformist policies converged within the stream of Labor thinking that underlay the Central Reserve Bank and Fiduciary Notes Bills; that advocated, as Scullin did during the campaign, an inquiry into the monetary system; and that was to embrace the Keynesian 'revolution' within a decade. It is possible that Douglas Credit, with its denunciation of the Money Power and its emphasis on technocratic reform (albeit via erroneous theory), provided a point around which populist radicalism and social democratic reformism could converge. Although it was a blind alley, Douglas Credit did offer the hope that by public control of the institutions of capitalism, the system might be made to work better in the interests of 'the people'. In the context of the post-war boom, Keynesian economics appeared to do just that. Despite considerable differences in theoretical sophistication, there was a broad continuity between Hobson, Douglas and Keynes that Labor found congenial—that it would be better to civilize capitalism than to abolish it.

8

'A New Jerusalem' – Keynes and Post-War Reconstruction

When Labor entered the 1934 Federal election campaign it still bore the scars of 1930–32. Its indifferent performance in the preceding Parliament reflected the demoralizing effect of drastically reduced numbers in both Houses and the continuing division between the Federal and Lang factions. The suspicion that each faction had of the other was only exceeded by their mutual hostility towards the array of forces that they called the Money Power. It was clear that before Labor could return to government it would have to reunite its organization and reassess its policy. It was equally plain that the most sensitive issue in that process would be the question of banking and finance.

Scullin approached the problem with characteristic caution. In March 1933 he was given Caucus approval to press for a Royal Commission into the banking system. He subsequently made it a central issue in the 1934 election campaign. Page also sought an inquiry on behalf of the Country Party's supporters, who had their own reasons for dissatisfaction at existing banking policy. Towards the end of the campaign, Lyons reluctantly promised that the UAP would appoint a Commission, but was very tardy in honouring the promise after his Government was returned to power. The names of the commissioners were not announced until 3 October 1935 and hearings did not commence until January 1936.[1]

There was a good deal of scepticism in Labor circles about a Royal Commission appointed by their political opponents. The *Westralian Worker* of 11 January 1935 thought that such an inquiry would have its terms of reference so narrowly cast as to make it virtually useless. *Labor Call*, on 28 February 1935, told its readers that the promised Commission 'cannot be accepted as meaning anything worth-while to Labor'. The paper went on to argue that, like the MacMillan Commission in England, it would not produce anything to help the workers. It would only tell them what they already knew:

> That banking, finance and credit were controlled and operated as profit-making institutions exclusively in the interests of the capitalists concerned, and that the workers had nothing whatever to hope for from such institutions under existing conditions.

On 11 January 1935 *Labor Daily* said that Lyons had only agreed to the Royal Commission under pressure from the Country Party, and suggested that a Parliamentary Select Committee would be more appropriate, particularly as the Government could be expected to manipulate the Commission in favour of the private banks by selective appointments and carefully circumscribed terms of reference. It went on to assert that if the Commission found truth in even half of what Lang said in his book *Why I Fight*, then the 'banks will be driven out of national life by all decent Australians'. In the House of Representatives, Lang Labor members Beasley, Ward and Lazzarini took the same view, claiming that 'Australia came under the domination of the overseas banking ring' and a Commission appointed by its political friends in Australia could not be expected to report anything detrimental to the banks, domestic or foreign.[2]

It was clear that what many Labor people wanted was a thorough enquiry that would expose the role that the banks had played during the depression and recommend major reforms. If there was to be an official enquiry, its purpose should be to tell the nation what Labor already knew. *Labor Call* put it bluntly on 9 May 1935:

> We want a system of money that will allow a distribution of the Creator's gifts to man, instead of one that prevents it. We have the ability to create that change; and let it be done by Australians! It can be done! The only obstacles in the way are the moneyed interests. The moneyed interests are guilty of wilful murder! Slow but sure murder! . . . Money interests are definitely and undeniably the cause of all depression.

A Commission appointed by the UAP–Country Party Government could hardly be expected to agree with that.

The Commissioners appointed by Lyons, despite the inclusion among them of Ben Chifley, did nothing to allay Labor's suspicion that they would whitewash the banks. They were: Mr Justice Napier of the Supreme Court of South Australia, later Sir John Napier, Chief Justice of South Australia (Chairman); J. P. Abbott, a New South Wales grazier and later Country Party MHR for New England, 1940–49; Ben Chifley; R. C. Mills, Professor of Economics at Sydney University; E. V. Nixon, a prominent

Australian Worker, 8 August 1934
Prime Minister Lyons has started his electioneering tour of Australia.
Here comes the Circus!

As the worst of the depression begins to recede, the tone of the cartoons in the labour press begins to lose its bitter edge and become more jocular. Here, Will Donald makes fun of the UAP circus, with its ensemble of performers. The private banks play the accustomed role of ringmaster, the Tory press is the mischievious monkey, and Lyons is simply the clown who beats the drum on behalf of this strange collection of curiosities. About this time cartoons began to appear less frequently in the labour press as the technology of printing made it easier to reproduce photographs to embellish the text of newspapers.

Melbourne accountant; and H. A. Pitt, Director of Finance, Victorian Treasury. It was alleged that Labor's token representative, Chifley, had only been appointed because he would 'take the most moderate Labor view'. It was entirely unnecessary for Lyons to answer the question from Lang Labor MHR J. H. Gander: 'Will the Prime Minister consider the advisability of putting Mr. Frank Anstey on the Commission?'[3]

The Labor press responded in a predictable way. Most papers declared that there could be no social progress until the ignorance and superstition surrounding finance were exposed and the populace came to accept the need to implement Labor policy. According to the *Westralian Worker* and the Brisbane *Worker*, the recent electoral success of the Social Credit Party in Alberta and the Labour Party in New Zealand showed that people in other parts of the world were beginning to see through the fog of superstition. It was left to the *Australian Worker's* Henry Boote to read the traditional lesson. He reviewed the various 'Powers' in modern capitalism, with particular emphasis on the most secret and formidable of them all, the Money Power, which was 'founded on nothing more solid than the financial ignorance of the multitude'. Only a clear-sighted and resolute labour movement could launch an offensive that would destroy the Money Power.[4]

Soon after the commissioners were named, and long before they began taking evidence, a Select Committee of the Tasmanian House of Assembly presented a report on the monetary system. It found that people had been prevented from receiving the benefits of increased wealth in the last thirty years by a lack of purchasing power. The only effective remedy was 'Restoration to the sovereign community of effective control over money in all its forms, and the establishment by the Commonwealth Parliament of machinery which would secure regular equation between the community's production and the community's purchasing power'. The report offered an essentially underconsumptionist argument, taken directly from Douglas Credit theory.[5]

At a Special Federal Conference in February 1936, Lang Labor was readmitted to the Federal Labor Party. This increased the pressure on the party to review its monetary policy so it could face the electorate in 1937 on an agreed platform. Members were mindful of the lessons of 1930–32. They also remembered how Lyons had 'grossly misrepresented' Labor policy during the 1934 campaign. Accordingly, Caucus agreed to a motion from Ward and Scullin that a committee be formed to survey their monetary policy and prepare a report for the forthcoming Federal Conference.

The committee, comprising Curtin, Forde, Collings, Scullin,

Beasley, Rosevear and Lazzarini, presented its report to Caucus on 24 July 1936, just three days before Federal Conference met. The report was divided into three parts: Objective, Principles, and Plan of Action. The Objective reflected the party's continuing attachment to underconsumptionist economics. The overall purpose of monetary policy was to utilize 'the real wealth of Australia to ensure a maximum standard of living consistent with the productive capacity of the Commonwealth through national control of its credit resources and the establishment of an efficient medium of exchange between production and consumption'. In deference to the radicals, particularly the Langites, the Principles envisaged a nationalized banking system controlled by the Commonwealth Bank, operating under conditions laid down by the Federal Parliament. The essential tasks of the new system would be: to maintain purchasing power by enabling Australian primary and secondary industries to work at their maximum efficiency; to control interest rates to reduce the burden on public and private undertakings; and to finance public works at award rates to aid national development. The Plan of Action proposed that the Commonwealth Bank board be abolished in favour of a single governor; that its trading functions be expanded in vigorous competition with the private banks; and that public bodies be required by law to keep their accounts with the Commonwealth Bank. As a token gesture to the Douglas Crediters, the report also recommended the establishment of a National Credit Advisory Authority. This would collaborate with the bank and the Government to provide assistance for home building, agricultural development, with the object of closer settlement, and development of secondary industry aimed at industrial self-sufficiency.

The Langites in Caucus were not entirely satisfied with the report. When it was presented, Rosevear and Beasley moved an amendment that was tantamount to a call for the immediate nationalization of private banking. After this was defeated, Lazzarini and Ward proposed a further amendment, which sought to give the Treasurer power to establish branches of the Commonwealth Bank wherever necessary, and then prohibit 'credit expansion by cheque system' by any other institution in the areas covered by those branches. In essence, this meant nationalization of banking, branch by branch. That amendment also was defeated. The committee's report, with some minor alterations, was duly passed as suitable for presentation to the Federal Conference.[6]

Although the Caucus recommendations were a hybrid of Labor's contending schools of monetary wisdom, they did offer a more coherent alternative to the thirteen diverse motions that had been proposed by the State Executives. The Party's 'monetary confusion' was such that the committee appointed by Conference to deal with the matter was unable to agree on the various agenda items. Instead, the committee accepted the compromise offered by Caucus, even though there had not been enough time to include it on the formal agenda paper. The overriding necessity was for Conference to decide on an acceptable policy for the next election. Curtin, who had replaced Scullin as Parliamentary Leader in October 1935, made this clear when he spoke on the report. He suggested that the Platform remain unchanged and that the report be taken as the electoral programme for 1937. He argued that after three years of Labor government Conference should review what progress had been made towards nationalization and then determine what should be done thereafter. Immediate nationalization of the private banks, he claimed, would cost £70 million, an amount that could be better spent for the relief of unemployment. Instead, he suggested expansion of the Commonwealth Bank as a practical short-term alternative. After some debate, the slightly amended Caucus programme was accepted as an elaboration of existing policy. The ALP thus had a policy that was binding upon all candidates for the 1937 election, irrespective of their factional allegiance.[7]

Despite this clarification, the party did not offer any evidence to the Banking Royal Commission, even though Scullin had first suggested it. The reasons are not clear, but it seems likely that they did not want to put a policy for bank nationalization before a 'rigged' Commission, which could be expected to reject it out of hand. That would have allowed Lyons to enter the election campaign armed with an 'independent' inquiry's judgement that ALP banking policy was unsound. Moreover, as they had not even begun to revise their policy when hearings commenced, Labor probably settled for Chifley, by default, as their voice on the Commission. Whatever their original expectations, Chifley turned out be a remarkably effective spokesman for his party.[8]

The Royal Commission began taking evidence from some two hundred witnesses in January 1936, and after visiting all States, concluded its hearings in September of that year. The commissioners then began writing their report. They heard evidence from the Commonwealth Bank, the trading banks, representatives of various interested organizations and private individuals. All members of the Commission signed the general report and recommendations, which were presented to Parliament in July 1937. Some submitted minority reports differing from their colleagues on specific issues. The main burden of the general report was that the most appropriate banking system for Australia would be one in which private banks continued to operate, but under the firm control of a central bank. Although there were no specific submissions on bank nationalization, the Commission recommended that:

> The most desirable banking system in the present circumstances of Australia is one which includes privately-owned trading banks. The system contemplated is one in which—
> 1. a strong central bank regulates the volume of credit and pays some attention to its distribution;
> 11. the distribution of credit is left to privately-owned trading banks, working for profit, but regulated in the manner already indicated.

To ensure that this system worked smoothly they recommended an extension of the Commonwealth Bank's operations and an increase in its powers as a central bank, particularly over the activities of the trading banks. They went on to suggest reforms to the bank's organization and management. In addition, they criticized some aspects of the role played by the Commonwealth Bank and the private banks in 1931. They also offered some criticism of the circumstances surrounding the collapse of the Government Savings Bank of New South Wales, particularly those Nationalist politicians who sought to undermine public confidence in it. Labor could also take comfort from paragraph 530, which asserted that ultimate responsibility for monetary policy must be vested in the Federal Government, which would require, after due consultation, that the Commonwealth Bank implement Government policy. This was taken as a belated but welcome rebuke of Sir Robert Gibson's obstruction of the Scullin Government and a vindication of Labor's attitude at the time.[9]

Chifley submitted a minority report, in which he argued a highly cogent case for Labor's policy of bank nationalization. He specifically rejected the proposition in paragraph 669 that the best system for Australia was one where private banks continued to distribute credit under the control of a strong central bank. He regarded it as impossible for 'any well ordered progress being made in the community under a system in which there are privately-owned trading banks which have been established for the purpose of making profit'. In private banking systems there was an irreconcilable conflict between the profit motive and the public interest. It must be expected that banks would ultimately consider profit in preference to public interest. He continued:

> Banking differs from any other form of business, because any action —good or bad—by a banking system affects almost every phase of

> national life. A banking policy should have one aim—service for the general good of the community. The making of profit is not necessary to such a policy. In my opinion the best service to the community can be given only by a banking system from which the profit motive is absent, and thus, in practice, only by a system entirely under national control.

By its very nature, he argued, privately owned banking was incapable of ensuring financial stability because 'private banking systems make the community the victims of every wave of optimism or pessimism that surges through the minds of financial speculators'. He then went on to describe how he believed the Commonwealth Bank should function. It should operate as a central bank controlling the volume of credit and currency, which would be distributed through its trading bank department directly to industry. It would also have savings and mortgage departments, as well as an industrial section to provide capital for developing industry. Chifley's final objective was the same as his party's—eventual nationalization by the gradual extension of the Commonwealth Bank's trading operations:

> Even under the system of a government-owned central bank with private trading banks, which has been adopted by the majority of the Commission, I am of the opinion that the trading section of the Commonwealth Bank should be extended, with the ultimate aim of providing the whole of the service now rendered by private trading banks.[10]

In simple political terms, the ALP had fared better than expected in the Commission's report. Although the majority recommendation opposed it, Chifley had, in the words of one economic commentator, presented 'a better case for nationalization than the Majority did for private ownership'.

The criticism of the way orthodox policy was applied in 1930–32 provided the Labor press with an opportunity to repeat the charges they had made at the time. But now they were able to claim the authority of a Royal Commission, appointed by the political advocates of orthodoxy. They made considerable play upon the 'Banking Commission's glaring exposure of base Nationalist treachery' in the collapse of the New South Wales Government Savings Bank. They also alleged that, in refusing to support it, the Commonwealth Bank board had used the panic to help rid itself of Lang. The recommendation that Government policy should prevail over the opinions of the bank board was also cited as a case where Labor had been justified by history. Nevertheless, the

Commission's general finding in favour of private banking was roundly condemned as giving support to the 'discredited system' of monopoly control of industry. Referring to the forthcoming election, Henry Boote urged the people to take 'the great opportunity of October 23' to rid themselves of Lyons:

> [who] is actually proud of this subservience to the Money Power . . . A Federal Labor Ministry is urgently needed to deal drastically with the Fascists of Finance, and put the democratic principle into operation in the creation and control of national credit.[11]

Despite Curtin's careful exposition of Labor's newly revised monetary policy, the electorate returned the UAP–Country Party coalition to office. The Lyons–Page Government drafted Bills to make some relatively minor amendments to the monetary system, but seemed quite happy to let them lapse in the face of objection from the private banks. They subsequently treated the Commission's report with what they considered to be benign neglect. Labor was not even allowed a full-scale Parliamentary debate on the issue.[12]

Towards the end of the 1930s, Labor's attitude to its monetary policy underwent a shift in emphasis. Many party members still believed that eventual nationalization of the private banks was the only long-term solution to the financial instability of the capitalist system, but under Curtin's leadership that belief was tempered by a cautious pragmatism, which had resumed its accustomed prominence in ALP thinking. According to his strategy, party supporters would have to wait until three years of Labor government had elapsed before the question of nationalization could be reconsidered. Even then it would depend on what progress had been made with the policy as revised in 1936.

Meanwhile there had been a major new development in capitalist economic theory, which, although most Labor people were not yet aware of it, promised to strengthen the hand of the party's social democrats. Early in 1936, John Maynard Keynes published *The General Theory of Employment, Interest and Money*. In it he offered a new way of looking at the factors that determine the general level of activity in capitalist economies. He rejected the classical view that the free operation of market forces naturally tend to produce full employment of available resources. The depression had made it abundantly clear that it did not. Instead, he argued that the economic system could exist in a state of 'equilibrium' without full employment. To explain how this came about, he constructed a set of theoretical connections between the various factors that determine the overall amount of goods and services produced within the economy. In doing this he established a relationship between the size of national income and the level of employment. He also examined the proportions of national income that are spent on either consumption or investment, and how those decisions in turn are determined by other considerations, such as the businessman's expectation of profits, the rate of interest on money, and so on. His general analysis of the way in which all these influences react upon each other suggested that the primary cause of unemployment is a lack of 'aggregate demand' for goods and services. Since free market forces are unable to sustain this at a satisfactory level, positive action must be taken to lift it. Keynes took the view that some form of State intervention is the only alternative, either through the encouragement of private spending or by deficit budgeting on the part of governments.

The General Theory reached Australia about the middle of 1936. Professional economists, to whom it was explicitly addressed, were quick to understand its implications. Athough its influence spread more slowly outside the profession, there were some who heard about Keynes and his remarkable new theory at this early stage. Chifley, for example, had made an initial acquaintance with it during the Royal Commission hearings. Others may have remembered references to Keynes's *Economic Consequences of the Peace* in 1919, or *A Treatise on Money* in 1930, or read and discussed his Melbourne *Herald* article in May 1932. But it is unlikely that many Labor people outside the ranks of professional economists actually read the *General Theory*. As H. C. Coombs has observed, 'It was not an easy book'. It would take some time for the uninitiated to assimilate a new technical language that discussed, for example, the relationship of Kahn's 'multiplier' to 'the marginal propensity to consume' and then expressed it in mathematical formulae. It was a daunting task, even to those long schooled in the pseudo-science of Douglas Credit. Nevertheless, as these esoteric terms were gradually translated into the language of practical politics it became clear that, in Keynesian economics, reformist Labor had at last found a respectable theory. Unlike 1930–31, the 'release of credit' would no longer be dismissed as wanton heresy.

There was a good deal in the less technical passages of *The General Theory* that was entirely consistent with Labor's long-held aspirations. Keynes began his last chapter, for example, on a point of basic agreement with the underconsumptionists when he observed that 'The outstanding faults of the economic society in which we live are its failure to provide for full employment and its arbitary and inequitable distribution of wealth and incomes'. But while Hobson's cure for underconsumption tendencies focused on workers gaining a greater share of national income through the agency of strong trade unions, Keynes shifted his prescription away from direct consumption to the role of investment which, in the final resort, could be bolstered by State intervention to sustain general prosperity. Despite these different emphases, they shared the view that, left to its own devices, capitalism was an unstable and unjust economic system. This was the same belief that had sustained the ALP's attachment to underconsumptionist economics. Indeed, Keynes was careful to distinguish his theoretical differences with Hobson and Mummery from his admiration for their 'significant and well-founded criticisms and intuitions' about capitalism. His distaste for the social consequences of unrestrained capitalism, particularly the human waste occasioned by unemployment, was a moral stance shared by Labor people. He also struck a responsive chord with his emphasis on 'the competitive struggle for markets' as a major cause of war. On monetary policy, his views were close to those of men like Curtin who saw bank nationalization as a distant objective to be approached by gradual and practical measures. Keynes thought that 'a somewhat comprehensive socialisation of investment will prove the only means of securing an approximation to full employment; though this need not exclude all manner of compromises and of devices by which public authority will co-operate with private initiative'. In such circumstances there would be no need to establish a system of State Socialism, with its attendant political and constitutional difficulties for an Australian Labor Government, because 'the necessary measures of socialisation can be introduced gradually and without a break in the general traditions of society'.[13]

The Keynesian model offered the prospect of governments striking a balance between capitalism's productive energies and destructive effects, the very problem that had long exercised the minds of Labor moderates. Above all, Keynes provided a theory whereby counter-cyclical policies administered through greatly strengthened instruments of State intervention might iron out excessive fluctuations in capitalist economies, and so provide the conditions for sustained full employment. With the memories of 1930–32 still vivid, this was precisely what Labor wanted if its next Government was not to be a repeat of the Scullin–Lang débâcle.

Labor was not in a position to apply Keynesian theory until the latter half of World War II. Before then it was preoccupied with defence policy and the political instability that followed the death of Lyons in 1939. Soon after the Curtin Government was commissioned in October 1941, Japan entered the war. This direct threat to Australian security forced domestic issues into the background. Curtin's obsession with military and strategic problems, while it was generally conceded to be the correct priority, caused concern among some Labor people that the party's traditional domestic objectives were being unduly subordinated to the war effort. This sort of apprehension came to a head during debate over Curtin's conscription proposal in 1942–43, but as the Japanese threat receded during 1943 the ALP's attention turned more towards post-war planning.

Shortly after taking office the Curtin Government had introduced in piecemeal fashion a number of controls over industry, production, wages and the banking system, in the interest of a co-ordinated war effort. It was recognized, however, that the special powers available to the Government during war could not be retained during peace-time, and that some sort of systematic plan would have to be developed if Labor was to build a post-war world better than the one they had known in the 1930s. Taking up a suggestion first made at the 1940 Federal Conference, the 1942 Special Federal Conference established a committee to consider post-war reconstruction. The committee's report began with the assertion that planning for peace was equally as important as planning for war. It recommended a two-pronged approach—national and international. On a global scale, it urged Australia to assist the International Labour Organization in its preparations for a world where reconstruction and development would be directed towards maintaining peace and security for workers and their families, with particular emphasis on raising living standards and securing full employment. At the national level, it asked the Federal Government to appoint a minister to co-ordinate the planning with the assistance of an eight-member committee, comprising one from each State branch of the ALP and two from the ACTU. Conference accepted the report unanimously.[14] Shortly after, Curtin added Post-War Reconstruction to Chifley's duties as Treasurer, and appointed H. C. Coombs head of the new department.

There were some early difficulties. The States refused to transfer the necessary constitutional powers to the Federal Government, and a subsequent attempt to secure them from the people was denied at the 1944 Powers Referendum. Despite these setbacks, the Government pressed on with its programme, strengthened by its landslide victory at the 1943 election, which gave it a majority in both Houses.

The experience of World War I had demonstrated the necessity of systematic preparation for the transition from war to peace. The depression and the present war had emphasized the need for greater international economic co-operation. This was widely recognized. As early as 1940 administrative machinery had been set up to consider post-war problems. But the most important stimulus came from overseas. The Anglo-American Mutual Aid Agreement of February 1942, particularly Article VII, which dealt with the post-war objectives of world economic relations, forced Australia to consider its role in any realignment that might emerge. If a new world economy was to be created on the basis of agreed national and international objectives, it was clear that Australia's place in it would depend on the way domestic and foreign policies were integrated. The formulation of the White Paper on Full Employment and the eventual ratification of the Bretton Woods Agreement were conducted within this wider context.

During 1944 Australia took part in negotiations designed to stabilize the international capitalist economy after hostilities had ended. The meeting culminated in a conference at Bretton Woods in the United States, where it was proposed to establish an International Monetary Fund and a World Bank. In the course of these discussions Australian representatives displayed a persistent concern for the issue of full employment. The Australian Government had not yet issued any clear statement of how it proposed to pursue that objective at home. It was not until August 1944, after he had returned from a Commonwealth Prime Ministers' conference in London, that Curtin ordered the preparation of a document similar to the British Government's White Paper on Employment Policy.

The people who eventually produced the Government's blueprint for post-war reconstruction were not members of a party committee, as suggested by the 1942 Federal Conference. The substance of the 1945 White Paper on Full Employment came from a group of young, academically trained public servants, including Coombs, G. G. Firth and J. F. Nimmo, whose intellectual development had coincided with the 'Keynesian revolution'. It was they who provided the necessary theoretical sophistication to turn Labor's grand but vague ambitions into a coherent plan.[15]

It was not an easy job. They had to plan an Australian economic strategy consistent with the wider international objectives being decided at places like Bretton Woods. They also had to work within the domestic constraints imposed by the constitutional, political and institutional framework of Government policy implementation. Many things had to be considered: the changing structure of the economy, the effect of overseas influences, the co-operation of the States, the role of various Federal departments, the attitudes of the major parties and the factions within them. It is not surprising that the paper went through eight drafts before Cabinet decided it was ready for presentation to Parliament. Inevitably, it was a compromise document. Some economists found it too general on a number of points and lacking a proper balance in the way it handled major sectors of the economy. Many senior public servants were apprehensive about its implications for their departments. Although most ministers were content to make minor amendments, some were disappointed that it left capitalism largely unmolested. Lazzarini, for example, criticized it on two grounds:

> I understand that it is to be called a "White Paper". That is all to the good, for it is certainly not a red one, and, so far as I can see, it has no colour at all.

He went on to complain that it reminded him of 'those dry as dust economic works we grappled with so heroically in our youth'. He continued:

> Indeed, I am afraid it will leave the ordinary bloke in much the same state of mind as must have been the case of the down and out who was told by an old professor that it was not the province of political economy to tell him how to get a job, but rather to explain to him why he could not get one.

Perhaps he had in mind Giblin's 'Letters to John Smith' in 1930. As an old Lang Laborite, his suspicion of academic economists was entirely understandable, but his objection that they had failed to provide the man in the street with something to 'get his teeth into' was a little unfair. Coombs and his colleagues had done a remarkably good job of translating Keynesian formulations into non-technical language. Lazzarini's complaint betrayed his populist anti-intellectual heritage, which held that any social theory that could not be reduced to words of one syllable was suspect.[16]

Despite many drafts and compromises, the White Paper offered a clear and logical exposition of the Government's fundamental objective, the theory that informed it, and the programme that would implement it. On each of these matters the paper began with a statement of general principle and introduced the specific complications as the argument developed. This was the same basic structure used by Keynes in *The General Theory*. The White Paper began by declaring the Government's commitment to provide the Australian people with the general framework of a full-employment post-war economy. After stating that primary objective, it proceeded to explain the essentials of a Keynesian approach by establishing the theoretical connections between the level of employment and five main components of total expenditure. The degree to which each of these components varied according to changes in economic conditions was examined, first in general and then in detail. The point of that examination was to show how governments would act to regulate both public and private spending so that economic activity could be held at a level that would maintain full employment. This was followed by a consideration of the problems that might be encountered in administering a full-employment economy, particularly the threat of inflation. The paper also acknowledged that special difficulties would arise during the transition from war to peace, and sketched out a general approach for dealing with them, industry by industry. It concluded with a brief discussion of the administrative machinery that would be necessary to handle the enlarged functions of government in a mixed economy with strong and systematic intervention by the State.

When Dedman, who had taken over Chifley's responsibility for post-war reconstruction, tabled the paper in the House of Representatives, he was careful to emphasize that it offered both a vision and a practical programme. He began by referring to the complementary measures already undertaken by the Government at home and abroad. He cited, in particular, the role to be played by the banking legislation recently introduced by Chifley. Its main purpose was 'to ensure that no out-worn financial prejudices or the resistance of vested interests will ever again be a bar to the achievement of full employment'. But this was simply one of many measures that were all part of a wider vision:

> I believe that this White Paper constitutes a charter for a new social order. The old order of the inter-war years had as its prime objective, rigid adherence to a certain financial policy. If this entailed 30 per cent unemployment and dwindling world trade, then, according to the pundits of that day, these were necessary evils. What a miserable social structure they built on their own false foundation!

He went on to affirm the Government's intention to pursue its full employment objective 'with the utmost energy and determination'. To emphasize his point he concluded by paraphrasing William Blake:

I will not cease from mental fight,
Nor shall my sword sleep in my hand,
Till we have built Jerusalem
In "Australia's" pleasant land.[17]

In reciting this, Dedman was not simply indulging in the hyperbole endemic to his profession. His presentation of the White Paper was an occasion of considerable significance. After two depressions and two world wars, a Labor Government was at last in a position to reshape Australian society. It had the parliamentary numbers and the political determination, backed by a genuine popularity in the electorate. Despite some irritation at particular war-time controls, most people had become accustomed to a more planned economy. Many understood the necessity for a systematic approach to economic management in the future. Some, indeed, demanded it.

The young Keynesians in the public service had shown the Labor Party that its instincts about capitalism during the 1930s had been generally right, even though they may have been specifically wrong on certain points of theory. They had convinced the Government that it was possible to civilize capitalism after all. The Australian people need never again be subjected to the vicious cycle of unemployment and war. There would be no repeat of 'a land fit for heroes' where a third of the workers 'were left in unproductive idleness'. They were entering a new era of economic stability and social security. The 'old order' would be gradually transformed by a set of carefully integrated reforms. This new Jerusalem, however, would not be some bold, extravagant folly. It would be a modest, well-designed structure of solid legislative bricks, a shelter for the common people and a monument to Laborist social democracy.

The whole capitalist world was emerging from a succession of traumas with a renewed commitment to international co-operation. The Government's belief that Australia was playing its part in building this 'new order' invested the occasion with a certain grandeur. In the circumstances, a romantic hymn seemed appropriate to herald its arrival.

The Labor press was inclined to agree, although some papers harboured lingering suspicions. The *Labor Call* of 7 June 1945 expressed a cautious optimism tempered by long experience:

> The proposals of the Government mean that capitalism must be bridled; that there will not exist reservoirs of workless that will enable employers to obtain cheap labor. It will, of course, be an advantage to the primary producer and the small businessman to

> have a well-paid and permanently employed working class, but the powerful financial and commercial interests in Australia do not wish to lose any of their power to determine the economic destiny of this country, and so their political mouthpieces can be relied upon to attempt to frustrate the plans of the Government.

This not only reflected Labor's traditional populist conception of capitalism, it also prophesied the fate of the 1945 banking legislation. On 13 June the *Australian Worker* saw the White Paper against a wider background. It argued that all countries should commit themselves to the full-employment objective in the United Nations Charter, because the interdependence of foreign trade meant that full employment at home was as much a matter for international co-operation as it was for domestic policy. It went on to declare that only 'short-sighted capitalist exploiters and their political friends' would oppose such plans, because ultimately only a fully employed and decently paid working class could ensure prosperity for capitalists. But it was not short-sighted capitalist exploiters, nor their political friends, who opposed the international plans enshrined in the Bretton Woods Agreement. The opposition was led by prominent Labor men of populist persuasion.

9

'A Vassal State' – The Debate over Bretton Woods

When discussion of the need for international agreement on financial transactions began in Australia, the Hobart *Voice* was quick to detect an insidious hand at work. On 12 June 1943 it warned:

> Unless human beings are prepared to become the permanent slaves of the Money Power, every free country must be left absolutely free to make its own arrangements for its own currency and for its own modes of finance after this war ... It would be better to be the helots of Hitler, Mussolini and the Mikado than to be the helots of thieves prepared to crucify mankind on a cross of gold as the sarcastic achievement of triumphant democratic victory.

It was this ingrained suspicion of international finance that set the tone for the subsequent debate over Australia's participation in the Bretton Woods Agreement.

The conference at Bretton Woods was convened by the United States Government in July 1944 'for the purpose of formulating definite proposals for an International Monetary Fund and possibly a Bank for Reconstruction and Development'. It was suggested that the IMF would act as an agency to stabilize world trade and currency transactions. The World Bank, as the Bank for Reconstruction and Development became known, would provide cheap loans to war-torn and developing nations. The IMF's capital was to be contributed by member countries, whose quota would be calculated by a formula based on national income, trading performance and foreign currency reserves. If need be, members could then withdraw a percentage of their quota each year to help adjust their trading position. The object of this was to establish a climate conducive to the orderly expansion of world trade and so avoid a repetition of policies such as competitive devaluations, which had bred the chaos of the 1930s. It was also recognized that the IMF's international objectives would have to be reconciled with the demands of individual domestic economies. The World Bank would be primarily concerned with the rehabilitation of devastated countries. In a spirit of enlightened self-interest, IMF members would contribute to the bank's capital to help distressed nations whose economic recovery would stimulate export markets for the donors. The economic consequences of the peace would be entirely different from those that followed the 1919 Paris Peace Conference.[1]

The Australian Government was suspicious of the IMF, in that its decisions might limit domestic policy options, especially on full employment. There was also some concern that the United States had so much influence on the board that it might try to manipulate the IMF to its own advantage. Much of the criticism from within Labor ranks focused on these specific issues. Although the Bretton Woods Conference was held in mid-1944, there was not very much discussion of its implications for Australia in the labour movement until 1946–47. The issues surrounding Australia's participation were still being negotiated in the United States. The Labor Party, meanwhile, was preoccupied with Curtin's death, the consequent leadership election, the end of the war, and the 1945 banking legislation. The ACTU was busy dealing with industrial issues and the domestic aspects of post-war planning.[2]

By early 1946 it was clear that the Labor Party was seriously divided on the question of Australia's ratification of the Bretton Woods Agreement. On this occasion there were two main factions looking for support from the wavering majority. On the one hand, there were those such as Chifley, Dedman, Scullin, McKenna, Armstrong and Foll who favoured ratification but were prepared to acknowledge some disadvantages. On the other, men like Ward, Cameron, O'Flaherty, Finlay, Amour and Aylett saw the IMF as a tool of international financiers who wanted to dictate the monetary policies of smaller nations to their own ends. The advocates of ratification saw it as an essential component in the whole strategy mapped out in the 1945 White Paper. For them, the IMF would be the one international agency capable of preventing a repetition of the great depression. Like Keynes, who had inspired the agreement, they were 'sure that the power of vested interests was vastly exaggerated compared with the gradual encroachment of ideas'. The enlightened self-interest of member nations would make the IMF an agent of rational co-operation in international transactions and a counter to the chaos of unrestrained competition. The pro-IMF faction was, in effect, the party's Keynesians. Their opponents were less sanguine about the force of ideas in the face of vested interests. They were the faction who, with the weight of the past bearing upon them, remembered the Bank of England and Sir Otto Niemeyer, the dangers of a gold standard, and the Premiers' Plan. Essentially, it was a choice between an act of faith and the burden of history.[3]

The optimists campaigned on two fronts. While Chifley exercised his considerable political skills within the party machine to secure the numbers for ratification, Dedman led the public debate for Australian membership. The case for and against, led by Dedman and Ward respectively, was argued in a series of articles syndicated throughout the Labor press. While Dedman stressed the benefits that IMF membership would have for the Australian economy both domestically and externally, Ward depicted it as fraught with dire peril.[4]

In a broadcast on ABC radio on 27 March 1946, Ward opened his campaign against the Bretton Woods Agreement with the declaration:

> The very sovereignty of this nation is in jeopardy . . . Whilst our men and women were making tremendous sacrifices to prevent the establishment of a world dictatorship, the International Financial Interests were working out the details of a plan—more insidious because they laboured unseen—whereby the whole world would come under their domination.

There were clear echoes of Anstey, Boote and Lang in this assertion. The scheme represented a return of many bitterly remembered evils, not the least of which was the gold standard:

> At the time of assuming membership, the parity of a nation's currency in relation to gold will be declared. It must therefore be evident that the Agreement pegs a nation's paper currency to a certain parity with gold, and thus obviously it is the 'Gold Standard', but in a different form from that in which we knew it.

According to Ward, the problem was not simply that the agreement meant an effective return to the notoriously unstable gold standard; it would also be the instrument with which the United States could manipulate currency rates through its virtual monopoly of the world's gold reserves. By this mechanism the USA would be able to exercise control over the economies of other nations, who would then become markets for its surplus production.

Turning his attention to the provision whereby a member nation could have special drawing rights when it was confronted with a 'fundamental disequilibrium' in its balance of payments, he pointed out that it was the IMF that would decide what constituted such a condition. This, he claimed, meant that the Fund could control national economies by telling them when they were eligible for special assistance. He illustrated this claim with the example of a situation where Australia decided to increase social services and decrease the working week to forty hours. Such action would affect the balance of payments, thus enabling the IMF to intervene. This argument was directed to those who could remember another occasion when the agents of international finance had been directly responsible for a reduction in Australian living standards. In a further example, he appealed directly to another enduring shibboleth. Referring to the protection that had been given to the sugar industry as a means of eliminating cheap coloured labour, he declared:

> The Fund, dominated by financial interests which have never been favourably disposed towards high living standards. and who have for that reason repeatedly criticised our White Australia Policy would seize upon this as an opportunity to apply pressure designed to compel the Commonwealth Government to open its doors to a flood of cheap coloured labour.

Having usurped national sovereignty, reduced living standards and sullied White Australia, this agent of international finance would then be in a position to force economic slavery upon the Australian people. The Money Power's long-held desires would thus be realized.

> I am convinced that the Agreement will enthrone a World Dictatorship of private finance, more complete and terrible than any Hitlerite dream. It offers no solution of World problems, but quite blatantly sets up controls which would reduce the smaller nations to vassal States and make every Government the mouthpiece and tool of International Finance. It will undermine and destroy the democratic institutions of this country—in fact, as effectually as ever the Fascist forces could have done—pervert and paganise our Christian ideals; and will undoubtedly present a new menace, endangering world peace ... World collaboration of private financial interests can only mean mass unemployment, slavery, misery, degradation and final destruction. Therefore, as freedom-loving Australians, we should reject this infamous proposal.[5]

This was not just a reiteration of the Lang Labor rhetoric of 1930–32; it was an elaborate statement of Labor's populist theory of imperialism. It distilled all that had been said about financiers during World War I, about overseas loans in the 1920s and Niemeyer in 1930. It appealed to the same fears, suspicions and hatreds that had been inflamed on those earlier occasions. In 1946 it remained a powerful message. Nor was he entirely wrong, as many Latin American countries were to discover during the 1970s and 1980s.

Most of those who opposed ratification argued substantially the same case as Ward. S. W. O'Flaherty, a South Australian Labor Senator, found it alarming that 'the scheme provides for an administrative body to implement the financial plan which would be controlled by the same old Money Power in a new situation'. W. Hodsdon, a prominent AWU member from Western Australia, asked whether Australia was going to allow other financial interests to administer the same sort of medicine that Niemeyer had prescribed. Senator Don Cameron saw the machinations of financial interests behind a whole range of issues, including the gold standard, a growing public debt and military conscription. Arthur Calwell took a similar position. The Australian Railways Union issued a pamphlet that claimed the IMF would give American financiers effective control over the Australian economy. The Melbourne Trades Hall Council Executive, after listening to an address from Ward, pronounced that ratification of the agreement would mean economic servitude for Australia. In a series of four articles entitled 'The A, B, C of Bretton Woods', Jack Lang depicted it not only as a *de facto* return to the gold standard, but also the 'noose in an elaborate plan to give the United States complete control of world trade'.[6]

Many Labor people were equivocal. Senator Nash, for example, thought that the agreement, as it stood, gave the IMF too much power over Australia's domestic policies. He suggested that the Government should not ratify it until the IMF's policy-making machinery was made more democratic. On the other hand, Frank Crean, a Victorian Labor MLA, found the arguments presented by both Dedman and Ward too emotional. On balance, he opted for ratification.[7]

The arguments were not confined to the public forum. There were clear divisions within the party machine, where the debate lasted for more than eighteen months. Chifley first presented the proposal to Cabinet in September 1945. Caucus finally agreed to ratify the agreement in March 1947. In the meantime there was a good deal of spirited argument and manipulation in Caucus, in Cabinet and on the Federal Executive. It was not an easy victory for Chifley and his supporters. Although he managed to secure the approval of Cabinet and the Federal Executive, by a bare majority, he ran into trouble in Caucus. They thought that the matter should be referred to a Federal Conference. He got round that problem by convincing the State Executives in New South Wales, Western

Australia and Tasmania not to request a Special Federal Conference. He thus deprived his opponents of the two-thirds majority required to convene such a Conference. The issue was then resubmitted to Cabinet in February 1947, when it was approved. It came before Caucus again on 5 March, when despite some attempts to delay a decision, a motion in favour of ratification was passed by 33 votes to 24.[8]

During their campaign Chifley and Dedman argued strongly that membership of the IMF was the best protection that Australia could have should the circumstances of 1929 be repeated. Dedman claimed that Australia would be insulated from future depressions by the IMF's stabilizing influence on world trade and by Australia's right to draw upon its reserves in the Fund. He argued that it was vital to Australia's full-employment objective that it be able to sell goods on the world market. The IMF and the World Bank would greatly assist this, by nurturing full employment in other countries, developing backward nations so they could buy exports, stabilizing international exchange rates to sustain confidence in trade, and encouraging countries with large foreign exchange surpluses to spend them on imports. 'The Second World War', he argued, 'became inevitable through the failure of Governments to agree upon measures of economic and financial co-operation.'[9] It was these arguments, backed by Chifley's skilful manipulation in keeping the party united, that won the day.

Speaking on the International Monetary Agreements Bill in the House of Representatives, Chifley concluded his case for the optimists:

> Perhaps the experiment will fail, but no country which has any regard for the cause of humanity can, for some selfish reason, or because some ghosts of the past happen to walk, or because of fears created by their experiences of a financial and economic depression, refuse to become parties to this agreement. If we have any love for mankind and a desire to free future generations from the terrible happenings of the last thirty years, we must put our faith in these organisations.[10]

Speaking for those who could find no reason for faith in the organizations of international capitalism, Lang told the House:

> If we abondon our financial sovereignty we shall become a vassal state ... The important thing for Australia to consider is, what would be the reaction of a Government to the demands made by the director of the International Monetary Fund when he arrived in Australia on such a mission seventeen years ago ... Once we enter

> this International Monetary Fund this Parliament can no longer decide financial policy; it will be decided for us by the fund ... The fund will also effect a return to the gold standard ... Gold is not the basis of trade. Our goods and services are the only real form of exchange. Why should we sign ourselves into bondage? Let us remain a nation of free man.[11]

By that stage, however, Lang's was a lonely voice from the cross-benches. The battle had already been won inside the Labor Party. When the division was taken, only five members voted against the Bill, although Ward and a few other members were conspicuously absent. It was duly passed by the Senate without a division on 25 March. Australia subsequently ratified the Bretton Woods Agreement and entered the IMF as a full member, with all the rights of an original signatory.[12]

10

'Smiting Mammon' – Bank Nationalization

When Dedman tabled the White Paper on Full Employment he told members that the banking Bills, which Chifley had introduced on 9 March 1945, were 'closely linked with the Government's policy for full employment'. Both Bills—the Commonwealth Bank Bill 1945 and the Banking Bill 1945—shared the same basic objective: to extend Government control over the operations of the Australian banking and monetary system. They were inspired by Labor's entrenched belief that a financial system dominated by private banks was prejudicial to the good order and welfare of the nation's economy. They were informed by the broad Keynesian strategy that the Government had recently embraced, and were publicly justified with reference to the recommendations of the Banking Royal Commission.

The underlying inspiration of the Commonwealth Bank Bill was clear in the four main changes it proposed. First, it provided for the abolition of the board, which since 1924 had been regarded by Labor as a device with which the private banks had exercised a self-interested control over the people's bank. The new management was to consist of a single governor, who would call upon an advisory board for assistance. This was not a Royal Commission recommendation. It derived from the Labor folklore that had grown up about the bank under the governorship of Sir Denison Miller between 1912 and 1923. As Giblin, Butlin and Schedvin have observed, that provision was not really based on consideration of the most appropriate formula for the post-war world. It was a kind of ideological revenge for 1930–31. Drawing upon the Royal Commission for support, Chifley indicated as much when he argued:

> In 1931, in the depths of the depression, the Commonwealth Bank and the private banks refused to assist the rehabilitation plan of the Commonwealth and State Governments designed to relieve acute unemployment and to restore industry. The present Government is

> determined to ensure, so far as lies within its power, that this will not be repeated.[1]

The second change provided that in matters of monetary policy the bank should be ultimately responsible to the Government. Where there was a conflict of opinion the Government should prevail, and accept responsibility for that policy. This was a convenient marriage of Labor policy and the Commission's recommendation. Chifley justified it by referring to paragraph 530 of the report, which advocated just such a relationship.

Third, the Bill provided for an extension of the Commonwealth Bank's trading operations in such fields as industrial finance and *crédit foncier* for house-building. This was an adaptation of the party's 1936 revised policy. It rested on the belief that, because of a gentlemen's agreement, the bank had been prevented from competing actively with the private banks for general business, thus restricting its natural development into the dominant financial institution that Labor had long desired.

The fourth and most significant change in terms of post-war planning was the considerable expansion of its powers as a central bank. It had been exercising these powers for some time under the National Security Regulations, but the Bill was to give them legislative permanence. It was proposed that the bank should have incorporated into its charter duties that defined the objectives of monetary management:

> It shall be the duty of the Commonwealth Bank, within the limits of its powers, to pursue a monetary and banking policy directed to the greatest advantage of the people of Australia, and to exercise its powers under this Act and the Banking Act 1945 in such a manner as will best contribute to:
> (a) the stability of the currency of Australia;
> (b) the maintenance of full employment in Australia, and
> (c) the economic prosperity and welfare of the people of Australia

In general terms, the bank was to have two main functions, as a central bank and as a trading bank. The central banking powers, as outlined in both Bills, reflected the Government's primary objective—to give it, via the bank, effective control over the general direction of monetary policy.

The main purpose of the Banking Bill was to define the role that the private banks would play in the new post-war world, and to establish a number of controls over the policies they might pursue. Henceforth, the private banks would have to be licensed by the

Federal Treasurer. This was backed by the provision that they should lodge minimum deposits with the Commonwealth Bank and be guided by it in their policies on advances and investment. The exchange mobilization agreement would be revised so that the Commonwealth Bank could have full access to the private banks' London funds. The Bill also provided for the Commonwealth Bank to manage the affairs of any other bank that was unable to meet its immediate obligations. These last two provisions probably owed their inspiration to the reluctance of the private banks to give the Government access to their London reserves in 1930–31, and to the Commonwealth Bank's lack of support for the Government Savings Bank of New South Wales in 1931.

Parliamentary debate on the Bills was vigorously political rather than technical. Menzies and Fadden attacked them as a blatant attempt at political control of the banking system, which they claimed had stood the test of time. Taunting the Labor Party with its own platform, they dismissed the Bills as not even 'honest nationalization', but strangulation without compensation. Ward was delighted to reply in kind. He launched an assault on financial interests, declaring that their 'one interest in life is Power—Power to rule the World!' He traversed Australian banking history from 1839 to the present, mocking the Opposition's claims that the private banks had served the nation well. Ward concluded his speech by reading into Hansard a long letter from a former Country Party Member of the New South Wales Parliament, who detailed his story of victimization by private banks.[2] Despite a long and occasionally lively debate, Labor's majority in both Houses ensured that the Bills were passed without significant amendment.

Not surprisingly, the legislation was warmly received throughout the labour movement. Although no formal resolution was passed, the ACTU Congress of June 1945 had several motions on its agenda paper that either congratulated the Government or urged it to press ahead with outright nationalization. At the ALP Federal Conference in November there was no specific reference to the Acts except a Federal Executive recommendation that Labor representatives should have a place on the bank's advisory board, A motion was passed, however, that asked the government to consider the nationalization of basic industries.[3]

The Labor press also welcomed the Acts. Most comment centred around a number of familiar propositions. The original Commonwealth Bank (1912–24) was the most effective. It had been handed over to the Money Power in 1924. The bank board had been instrumental in worsening hardship during the depression. The national interest and banking for profit were irreconcilable. If full employment and prosperity were to be established, the people's Government must control the banking and monetary system. On 17 January and 14 March the *Australian Worker* justified the legislation by arguing that a strong central bank was the only way to protect the people's welfare, because 'Money Power has ruled long enough'. The Hobart *Voice* repeated these sentiments on 15 September 1945. The Brisbane *Worker* reviewed the significance of the Acts on 29 January, 6 March and 16 April 1945. It spent considerable time reminding readers about the crashes of 1893, and even reprinted sections from Anstey's *Money Power* to illustrate how international capitalist finance worked. The *Westralian Worker* captured the general mood on 16 March:

> Labor has long regarded it as a duty to recapture the Commonwealth Bank for the nation, to extend its branches, enlarge its utility, augment its power, and make it the servant of industry and the bulwark of the people against those who have despotically manipulated the credit resources of the Commonwealth.

Many Labor papers crowed triumphantly when the Victorian United Country Party and the Victorian Wheat and Wool Growers' Association supported the Bills.

The banking legislation was exactly the kind of reform envisaged by the White Paper on Full Employment in Australia. It introduced specific measures that were part of a wider strategy designed to mitigate the worst excesses of capitalism without disturbing its fundamental structure. The intention behind these two Acts was to help protect the living standards of ordinary Australians. The legislation would not only justify Labor's claim to be the people's champion in their struggle against vested interests, but would also temporarily satisfy the party's more radical elements who would have it nationalize the banks. With the publication of the White Paper, the passing of these Acts, and several other reforms in the offing, Labor people could contemplate the 'light on the hill' with some satisfaction in 1945, believing that the 'new order' was not so far distant. But a small flaw in the legislation, a hasty decision by Cabinet, and the mobilization of their traditional opponents within a chilling Cold War atmosphere, all combined to undermine the whole structure of Labor's 'new Jerusalem'.

The Acts had no sooner been proclaimed than it became clear that the private banks intended to challenge their constitutional validity.[4] The banks quite rightly saw the special accounts provisions contained in sections 18–22 of the Banking Act as the crux of Government control over their activities. These, however, were not the ones used to spearhead the attack. The Melbourne City Council and the National Bank chose instead section 48, which prevented State Governments, State instrumentalities and local government bodies dealing with private banks. The special accounts provisions were mentioned in the Statement of Claims lodged by the council and the bank, even though the substance of the challenge was based on section 48. On 13 August 1947 the High Court, in a five-to-one majority judgment, found that section to be unconstitutional. The Government was thus forced to consider its position.[5]

When Cabinet met on Saturday 16 August, Evatt explained the High Court decision. Chifley, who seems to have given the matter some prior thought, then canvassed two options. They could wait for the banks to challenge the substantial sections of the legislation, or they could seize the initiative and nationalize the private banks. After some initial hesitation, they did what more than fifty years of bitter experience and ingrained suspicion told them they should do: they voted unanimously for nationalization. Although the decision was taken hastily, it was no sudden aberration. It was an act to which experience inclined them, rhetoric exhorted them, policy committed them and frustration impelled them. The question of nationalization had always been one for the future, but now in a single act—inspired more by bravado than a sober calculation of the political consequences—they had done it. We will probably never know what ran through the minds of ministers as they filed out of the Cabinet room, but it is possible that many felt a mixture of apprehension and elation. Apprehension that all might be lost on one rash decision. Elation that at last they were, like true class-warriors, about to join battle with their most powerful and bitter enemy—the banks, finance, the Money Power.

Chifley's terse, forty-two-word announcement read:

> Cabinet today authorised the Attorney-General (Dr. Evatt) and myself to prepare legislation for submission to the Federal Parliamentary Labor Party for the nationalisation of banking, other than State banks, with proper protection for the shareholders, depositors, borrowers and staffs of private banks.

He offered no further explanation. It came as a great surprise to almost everybody. Unlike the 1945 banking legislation, which had been part of a much-discussed general economic strategy, Chifley had done nothing to prepare either the public or his party for the shock. On 14 August he had given an oblique hint to a group of

Commonwealth Bank and Treasury officials. Only two of his colleagues, Evatt and McKenna, knew his intentions at the beginning of the Saturday morning Cabinet meeting.[6]

The immediate reaction of the various interested parties was entirely predictable. Bankers, businessmen, the daily press and conservative politicians were astounded. The decision was variously described as 'a piece of petty pique', 'one of the hardest blows at liberty struck in our time', 'little less than sheer madness', an act displaying 'contemptuous unconcern' for public opinion, and 'a long stride towards totalitarianism' comparable to Hitler's Germany. R. G. Menzies, Leader of the Opposition, sounded the rallying cry: 'Australians are now called to a great battle to defend their freedoms against dictatorship at home'.[7] This was no rehearsal of the everyday clichés of cut-and-thrust political debate. They meant every word of it. For more than fifty years political conservatives had invoked the spectre of Labor's 'socialist tiger' to alarm the more timorous electors. Now, to their astonishment, it was true. Such a beast did exist, and it was about to be unleashed upon them.

Most people in the labour movement greeted the announcement with surprise and outward delight. It was the long-awaited assault upon the bastions of Australian Money Power. Comment in the Labor press displayed its usual flourish. On 18 August 1947 the Brisbane *Worker* congratulated the Government on its 'momentous move' and recalled the attitude of the banks towards the Scullin Government. A week later it quoted a report that 'Wall Street bankers have promised moral support to Australian trading banks in their avowed fight to a finish against nationalisation'. It followed this, under the headline 'Frank Anstey knew', with a reprint of his chapter on 'American Money Power' from the book *Money Power*. The *Workers' Weekly Herald* of 22 August applauded the decision as a climax to the whole process of reform. J. S. Hanlon, who had followed Henry Boote as editor of the *Australian Worker*, told his readers:

> It is a step that will provide both for Australia and Great Britain greater strength, and even though the representatives of home grown and foreign monopolists scream to high heaven with rage, and their legal luminaries move every available court on earth to upset the Government's decision, the economic security of our country and well-being of our people will be assured by the orderly mobilisation of our economic and financial resources for the good of all.[8]

The Hobart *Voice*, which had by this stage adopted a very

conservative Douglas Credit line, struck the only discordant note. It viewed nationalization as an evil equal to communism and socialism. and hoped that 'none of them will ever get a firm hold in Australia'.[9]

Most of the labour movement's peak councils were quick to pass resolutions in support of the Government. The Executive of the New South Wales State Labor Party resolved:

> In the determination to reap profits, the control of the banking system by private interests fosters exploitation of the people and plunges the world into cycles of trade depressions.

It went on to argue that a banking system controlled by the people's elected representatives was the only lasting protection they could have against the ravages of mass unemployment. The Melbourne Trades Hall Council echoed these views, emphasizing the point that nationalized banking would be 'a safeguard against the dictatorial powers exercised by the private banks linked with vested monopoly interests'. When the ACTU Congress met at the beginning of September it declared that bank nationalization was one of the most progressive steps ever taken in the interests of the Australian people. Congress developed the point made by the Melbourne THC:

> It will give small farmers and business people protection from a small group of financiers who exercise a monopoly control over large sections of the economic life of the community, and will give the Government greatly added power to ameliorate the effect of economic crisis and depression.

This familiar appeal to a constituency beyond the ranks of the labour movement was repeated by Dedman in the *Australian Worker* on 1 October 1947. In November the Federal Executive congratulated the Government, deplored the propaganda of its opponents and declared that bank nationalization would further the people's happiness and well-being. In December the Western Australian ALP Congress passed a congratulatory motion, as did the Victorian ALP Annual conference early the following year.[10]

Many Labor leaders echoed the sentiments of their organizations. Albert Monk, Secretary of the ACTU, McNolty, President of the Melbourne THC, and Austin, President of the New South Walcs Trades and Labor Council, all expressed warm support for the Government's move. Leading party members, past and present, joined the chorus. They included Scullin, King

O'Malley, Tasmanian Premier Cosgrove, Queensland Premier Hanlon, Western Australian Labor leader Wise, and P. J. Clarey, Victorian Minister for Labour. The Labor Premiers of New South Wales and Victoria, McGirr and Cain, were conspicuously slow to endorse nationalization. Even Lang was unable to give his former comrades unreserved support. He welcomed the decision, but wanted to know who would control the Commonwealth Bank.[11]

Of all the bold declarations, the Federal Parliamentary speeches show most clearly how heavily the burden of history weighed on the imagination of Labor members. On 16 September Chifley submitted the Banking Bill 1947 to Caucus, which followed Cabinet's lead and approved it unanimously. Two days later, in reply to a censure motion from Menzies, Chifley remarked:

> There are others of us in this House who can remember the circumstances of 1930, when the Members of this Parliament and of the State parliaments, and the governments which they had set up, were subject to a dictatorship, and the dictators were the private banking institutions.

Like most of his Labor colleagues, he was one of 'the generation that copped the lot'. He could recall the distress occasioned by the 1893 bank crashes. As a young railway worker he had been sacked during the 1917 general strike. His memories as a member of the Scullin Government's bitterly divided Caucus were deeply etched. He had been at the centre of the Curtin Government's post-war planning and shared its determination to build a new world free of depressions and wars. If bank nationalization was necessary to that end, then so be it. Casting back fifty-four years, Roly James recalled:

> I was only a child, the youngest of a family of eleven, when the banks failed in 1893, but I remember that my parents lost £100 when the bank in which they had deposited it 'went bung' and they did not get a 'bean'. I am not surprised that only a few years before that Ned Kelly became a bushranger. He was only doing justice when he robbed the banks, because at that period they were robbing the people.

To Calwell, and many other Labor people, the banks occupied the commanding heights of capitalism:

> The private banking institutions are the very basis of finance capitalism, and the Opposition Members of this Parliament stand for the maintenance of that unjust economic and social system

> known as capitalism. They know that if the private banks are broken the capitalistic system will be weakened. They are fighting tonight for capitalism and not for the wage earner, the small farmer and the little businessman . . . Tyrannies have been practised in the past in this country, but there has been no worse tyranny than that of our banking institutions when Australia was in the throes of a depression.[12]

When the Bill came before the House on 15 October, Chifley led for the Government. He began by examining 'modern banking policy', taking paragraph 516 of the Banking Royal Commission as his text. He then proceeded to an exposition of 'the Labor view', that private banking is essentially a class weapon. By means of amalgamation,

> the great power of private banking in Australia has become concentrated in the hands of boards of directors comprising a relatively few men who are responsible for the exercise of their powers not to the nation but only to a limited number of people, some here and some abroad, who have invested money in bank shares.

This 'Labor view' reflected the familiar populist conception of class as a predatory clique. He then surveyed the Commonwealth Bank's history, with particular emphasis on 1924 and 1930–31. The crimes of private banking in the previous sixty years were then recited by the Labor members who followed him. Ward reminded the House of the conspiracy against the New South Wales Government Savings Bank by 'anti-Labor political parties and wealthy interests'. Williams assessed the attitudes of Sir Alfred Davidson and Sir Robert Gibson in the crisis of 1930–31.

Langtry went back to childhood: 'I was a boy at the time of the bank crash of 1893, but I well remember the bitterness and resentment of the people against the banks'. Calwell saw it as a history of oppression:

> The ghastly failure of the banks in the nineties of the last century and the callous and brutal things that they did to people's lives and fortunes in the depressions of the 1890s and the 1930s are indelibly imprinted on the minds of the Australian people. The banks have blighted more lives than the most disastrous droughts; they have blasted more hopes than the most destructive bushfires; and they have broken more spirits than the most devastating floods.

Their crimes were compounded by the conspiratorial way in

which they advanced their narrow class interest at the expense of the people, as Ward had illustrated in his reference to the New South Wales Government Savings Bank. Dedman found further evidence of conspiracy. He claimed that people who wanted to start an enterprise in opposition to big business would be denied finance for it because of the interlocking directorships between banks and big business. From this, it was plain that the Money Power oppressed the small businessman as well as the worker, albeit in a different way. With more passion than originality, Senator Lamp (Tasmania) drew the lesson from this sorry history: 'The Money Power preys upon the nation in times of peace and conspires against it in its hour of calamity'.[13]

Both in and out of Parliament the pattern of argument was similar. The necessity for government control over the banking and monetary system had been acknowledged throughout the world and specifically recommended by the 1937 Banking Royal Commission. Labor had implemented those recommendations in its 1945 legislation but had been challenged by the implacable hostility of the private banks. Their action had forced the Government to assert its authority in the interests of the people. It was clear from the history of private banking in Australia that the interests of this small capitalist clique were necessarily opposed to the national welfare. As Clyde Cameron told his comrades at the South Australian ALP Conference, their party was all that stood between the people and slavery:

> We know that if it were not for the Australian Labor Party the wage slaves of this country would still be under the heel of squatterdom and foreign-controlled financial institutions.

He referred to the claim that bank shareholders should be compensated for 'good will', and asked why moral turpitude must be rewarded:

> To compensate for the removal of an evil means its continuation in another form. What moral claim have shareholders got to claim compensation? Are not these human vampires chiefly responsible for the wars which have taken such heavy toll of life throughout the whole world?

The banks had to be stopped immediately to prevent them from organizing their next conspiracy:

> Already plans are well in hand for the creation of another economic 'recession', when our economic rulers hope to snatch back from us all the gains we have made during the past few years.[14]

The banks, however, were not engaged in a conspiracy. They made an open declaration of war to defend themselves against 'an extreme socialistic trend in the affairs of the country'.

While the Government might have expected resistance from the banks, they were not prepared for the ferocious campaign mounted against them. The banks were quick to marshal their forces. Within a week of Chifley's announcement they had agreed upon a two-year plan designed to rouse public opinion so that the Government would be forced to abandon the legislation or submit it to a referendum. They also planned to challenge the Act in the courts and campaign for the Government's defeat at the 1949 election. Although they failed in their first objective, they were outstandingly successful with the others. Nor did they have to fight alone. Within a very short time they were joined by an impressive army of allies.

The issue presented the Liberal–Country Party Opposition with a happy convergence of principle and self-interest. They were not only fighting for the treasury benches, but for the very ground on which they stood — 'individual liberty' and 'free enterprise'. Bank nationalization was not just a political issue: it threatened the whole system that sustained them. It was more than a campaign: it was a crusade. When the Bill came before the House in October 1947, Menzies described it as 'the most far-reaching, revolutionary, unwarranted and un-Australian measure introduced in the history of this Parliament'. It represented a 'tremendous step towards the servile state'. Their crusade against the socialist infidels took the Federal President of the Liberal Party to London, where English companies with Australian investments were persuaded to make substantial contributions to a fighting fund.[15]

Bank officers had less abstract fears. They saw a direct threat to their jobs. With the financial encouragement of their employers, they quickly mobilized into a tightly organized political machine, which flooded the country with anti-nationalization propaganda. Masses of letters were written to the press and to Parliamentarians. Pamphlets denouncing the dangers of nationalization, socialism and communism were distributed with missionary zeal. Radio was employed to get the message to the public, as were meetings, lectures and rallies. Petitions were gathered in bank chambers festooned with dire warnings. Their union joined the fray, attacking a Labor Government with all the vigour that other unions usually unleashed on the robber barons of capitalist industry.[16]

Other major sectors of Australian capital soon added their voices to the roar of protest. The Associated Chambers of Commerce of Australia, the Associated Chambers of Manufacturers of Australia, the Graziers Federal Council of Australia and the Australian Primary Producers' Union were among the more prominent organizations to register outright hostility to the Government's move against the banks. Various regional groups of employers, retailers, real estate agents, builders, fruitgrowers and 'taxpayers' did likewise. There were even signs that the private armies of the early 1930s were being revived to defend 'traditional freedoms'.

The spectre of 'socialist regimentation' called forth an extraordinary array of groups determined to resist nationalization. In most cases their names signified their cause. They included Citizens' Rights Associations, People's Anti-Socialization League, Democratic Freedom Union, People's Freedom Movement and the United Women Citizens' Movement Against Socialization. All played their part in sounding the alarm by circulating petitions, writing letters, distributing leaflets, organizing meetings and heckling pro-nationalization speakers.

The reaction against bank nationalization was remarkable not only for its intensity, but also for the degree to which it was co-ordinated at the higher levels. In Queensland, Western Australia and Victoria various combinations of business organizations, bankers and conservative politicians formed councils, which co-ordinated the general strategy to defeat the Government. They were united as never before. In New South Wales the Retail Traders, the Employers' Federation and the Chamber of Commerce co-operated in a campaign to place alarmist leaflets in the pay envelopes of all their workers.

It soon became obvious that Chifley and his colleagues had seriously underestimated the ferocity with which the Money Power would defend itself. Labor's most extreme claims about the insidious machinations of the Money Power were equalled or surpassed by their opponents, who suggested that bank nationalization might be only the beginning of a process leading to the socialization of 'the shops or the newspapers, or even, heaven knows, the Churches'.

For their first move the banks chose two instruments that had served them well in the past—the Constitution and the courts. Immediately after the Government had forced the 1947 Banking Act through both Houses of Parliament, the banks challenged its validity in the High Court. But even before the court hearings began in December 1947, the conservative-dominated Legislative Council in Victoria twice refused supply to the Cain Labor Government, and forced it to an election on the bank nationalization issue. Despite Cain's protestations that banking was a Federal matter, the electorate was in no mood to discriminate. All Labor governments had the taint of socialism upon them. The

ALP was defeated in a landslide that left them with only eighteen of the sixty-five Legislative Assembly seats.

After protracted legal argument, during which Evatt objected to one judge and the wife of another holding bank shares, the High Court delivered its decision on 11 August 1948. It found that the 1947 Banking Act contravened section 92 of the Constitution. The Government then appealed to the Privy Council in London, which took a year to hear the case and announce its verdict.[17]

The Labor campaign, meanwhile, made a faltering start and then stumbled to a virtual halt. On the surface it seems strange that, after taking the momentous decision to attack one of its oldest and most formidable enemies, the Labor Party should put up such a half-hearted fight. Were not the banks, as many bold declarations at the time asserted, pivotal institutions in the whole process of capitalist oppression? Was it not the banks that had worsened the depression in cynical pursuit of their own interests? Had they not resisted the Government's every effort to control their operations in the public interest? Although these arguments were often rehearsed during the campaign, the fact remains that, compared to their adversaries, Labor made a poor showing.

Even before the decision was taken, Labor bore a self-imposed handicap. Chifley may have considered the idea of nationalization for some time before putting it to Cabinet, but there is no evidence that he formulated any plans to justify it to the public, nor did he prepare a strategy for the labour movement to defend it. He had, perhaps, inherited the traditional Labor delusion that control of Parliament gave them the power to change the shape of Australian capitalism. Whatever his reasons, a month elapsed before he elaborated on the initial announcement. By that stage the banks and their allies had already organized the beginnings of a full-scale capitalist mobilization.

In New South Wales the ALP State Executive planned a general campaign. The Victorian Central Executive did the same. Support from the other State Executives, however, was either lukewarm or nonexistent. The ACTU and various regional union councils drew up bold plans and began to collect money. Some pamphlets were issued, debates and meetings were organized, resolutions were passed and a few large rallies were held in Sydney. Despite these efforts it was obvious, even in the first three months, that those in the labour movement who favoured nationalization could muster neither the resources nor the fervour of their opponents.

This rather belated campaign had hardly started when things began to go wrong. Some ministers made distinctly unhelpful comments. On one occasion Dedman suggested that a nationalized banking system would require 5000 fewer bank officers.

Chifley, who had recovered some of his political acumen, quickly disowned the statement, as did Dedman shortly after. It was too late. The damage was done. It simply confirmed the bank officers' worst fears and hardened their resolve to fight beside their employers.

Government members and their unionist supporters soon discovered that it was difficult to get a hearing at largely unsympathetic public meetings, where they were often systematically heckled. The Labor Party was also embarrassed by the alacrity with which a number of prominent Communists championed the move. This allowed their opponents to invoke the familiar device of guilt by association, in a rapidly chilling Cold War atmosphere. It also accentuated divisions within the labour movement, where the ALP's Industrial Groups—which had in turn been infiltrated by Santamaria's 'Movement'—were attempting to wrest control of some larger unions from Communist leadership.

By 1948 events were turning against the Government on a wider front. The electorate was becoming weary of the wartime controls that had been continued in the interests of a stable economic transition to peace. The defeat of the 1948 referendum made that abundantly clear. The drawn-out struggle with the doctors over 'socialized medicine', the 1948 rail strike in Queensland, and the disruption of the 1949 coal strike, all served to weaken the Government's position. These difficulties were compounded by the international background, where the Berlin blockade, the struggles in Indonesia and the lead-up to the Korean War increased existing tensions between capitalist and communist nations. All of this strengthened the growing popular perception of bank nationalization as part of that wider struggle.[18]

As the opinion polls began to appear, it was apparent that the Government was steadily losing ground. In Victoria the party recognized this, and aborted its planned campaign when the Cain Government was forced to a premature election on what was plainly an unpopular Federal issue. The subsequent defeat in that election spurred Chifley on to more decisive action. He persuaded the Federal Executive to call on the party faithful to 'go out and fight'. A national campaign was planned, but this too was stopped when the banks' appeal against the 1947 Banking Act came before the High Court. The Executive decided that while the hearings were under way the issue should be considered *sub judice*. It appears, however, that they were making a legal virtue of political necessity. Realizing that they could not halt the momentum of the campaign against them, ALP strategists hoped that it could be deflected into the legal arena, where much of its energy might be dissipated. They were wrong.

The long legal struggle began in the High Court in February 1948, and ended in the Privy Council in July 1949. During that period the banks and their defenders took a different view of what *sub judice* meant. They merely shifted the emphasis of their campaign. Without mentioning the specific matter of nationalization, their advertising in the press, on radio and in films addressed what they saw as the underlying issue. They extolled the virtues of 'free choice' and the 'Australian Way', celebrated the 'Mantle of Greatness' surrounding the achievements of 'free enterprise', and depicted the daily operations of private banks in the most benign light. All the while they were 'girding the loins' for a final assault during the 1949 election.

The Privy Council decision in favour of the banks was announced on 26 July 1949. Evatt claimed that the decision effectively removed nationalization as an election issue, because it had been shown to be constitutionally impossible. Few, if any, believed him.

The champions of 'free enterprise' made sure it was not a dead issue. As polling day drew nearer, their campaign intensified. A full-time army of over four hundred bank officers, supported by thousands of part-time volunteers, campaigned furiously. Vast quantities of literature were distributed to hundreds of thousands of households. In many cases this was followed up by canvassers. The number of anti-Labor meetings increased, as did the attendance. The campaign over the radio was expanded. Newspaper advertisements were larger and more frequent. How-to-vote cards were sent out and rosters drawn up to drive sympathetic voters to the polling booths.

Menzies and Fadden promised that the Liberal–Country Party coalition would save the electors from the horrors of the 'Socialist State', repeal the 1947 Banking Act, undo sections of the 1945 Banking Acts, ensure 'maximum employment' by bolstering private industry, abolish petrol rationing, outlaw Communism and 'put value back into the pound'. The central issue around which all these specific matters revolved was 'Freedom versus Socialism'.

By comparison the Labor campaign was lethargic. Chifley's opening speech made 'no glittering promises'. He was content to stand on the Labor Party's record in office. He acknowledged that bank nationalization was not possible, and promised that Labor would not exceed its powers under the Constitution. He insisted, however, that the Government should still have control over banking to ensure that money and credit were used to the 'best advantage of the community'. Such powers, he claimed, were available under the provisions of the 1945 Banking Acts.

In characteristic style, Ward met the Opposition head on. He was happy to have nationalization as the main issue. As far as he was concerned, if Labor did not have the power to nationalize the banks then they should set out to get it. Most Labor candidates took a more moderate position. Many made it clear that they had no intention of relaxing the existing controls over the monetary system. Some hinted that the Commonwealth Bank might be encouraged to compete against the private banks with such vigour that they would be forced to co-operate with Government policy. The most common response was the same as Chifley's, a retreat to the 1945 legislation accompanied by a dogged defence of Laborist social democracy. There, at least, they were defending their real home ground.

The initial flurry of enthusiasm that followed their decision to 'take on the Money Power' in August 1947 had long passed. After more than two years of relentless pressure from mobilized capital, Labor could do little more than wait for the electoral landslide to engulf them. On 10 December 1949 they were swept from office and replaced by the Liberal–Country Party coalition.

There were some in the labour movement who were beginning to understand the significance of the High Court's interpretation of section 92, the Privy Council's endorsement of it, the mobilization of businessmen, bank officers and many of their customers, the hostility of the daily press and the appeal of the Opposition's message about 'Freedom versus Socialism'.[19] At the same time, there were many more who persisted in a thoroughly traditional interpretation. As Don Cameron told *Labor Call* readers on 21 December 1949:

> The real interests behind the anti-Labor parties are already showing their hand. The Wall Street Journal—the organ of the big financial interests who endeavour to control not only the United States of America, but also the other countries of the world—is jubilant over the anti-Labor parties' success. The financial interests see an opportunity of taking back control of the people's money.

Labor had indeed been defeated by the Money Power, not only as an economic force but also as an ideology.

Conclusion

The main purpose of this book has been to develop a model of Australian labour populism by examining the changing complexion of the ALP's preoccupation with the Money Power. This has been done by looking at a range of issues over the sixty-year period and drawing out a number of elements that have given a particular shape to Labor's conception of the Money Power as the commanding force in modern capitalism. The object of this has been to locate that populist stream in Labor thinking against a wider background of class mobilization and ideological tension.

The bank crashes of the early 1890s mobilized a number of existing ideas into a pattern that sustained a lingering suspicion of banks and the role that they played in the colonial economies. This was overlaid with imported notions that the behaviour of bankers was to be explained by more than economic crises in a dependent economy. It was just as much a matter of avarice compounded by wanton malice towards 'the people'. In the circumstances of a general depression and bitterly fought strikes, bankers who conspired to defraud the public became symbols of capitalist greed and malicious intent in the popular imagination of the labour movement. Representing all the corruption of the Old World, they offended against a vision of what Australia might become if freed from its colonial shackles. Because of their connections with British finance and their attachment to imperial values they were seen to represent class interests inimical to an independent and distinctively Australian national identity. In this way, bankers became symbols of an imperialism that would plant the noxious weed of European class distinction in Australian soil. The manner in which many of them escaped prosecution through the connivance of powerful friends served to inflame popular suspicion and resentment of 'British justice'. Similarly, their associations with colonial capitalists and British-owned pastoral companies gave substance to claims that their interlocking interests amounted to a conspiracy against the Australian people.

Attitudes of this kind coloured the interpretations that some people in the labour movement put upon the Boer War. To labour's radical nationalists it was a war waged upon a small nation of independent farmers by the vast power of British imperialism. Behind the forces of the Empire were the sordid interests of English capitalists and speculating bankers, most of whom were, according to the popular stereotype, scheming Jews. Australian radicals could easily identify themselves with the Boers, who seemed to be fighting the same forces that had so recently determined to crush the independent spirit of Australian unions.

The banking débâcle of 1893 gave added force to the arguments of those who advocated State banking as a means to stabilize the monetary system and protect the people from the usurious exactions of private banks. According to labour ideology the burden of interest was not only an unearned profit to bankers, but also an additional, unjustifiable cost in the productive process. This meant that even honest employers could not afford to pay both interest and high wages. Thus it was not the manufacturer or the pastoralist who forced wages down, but the banker who demanded that he be paid first. It was therefore possible to argue that the boss and the worker were both prey to the greed of the banker, and that they might happily co-exist if they could only recognize and defeat the common enemy. The same argument was often taken a step further with the suggestion that, because employers could not afford to pay their mortgage commitments and union wage rates, they were forced to look to 'scab' labour or, worse still, import cheap coloured labour. Thus, lurking behind the pressure to reduce wages was the banker, whose lust for profit would imperil the sanctity of White Australia. At its furthest extreme, this was depicted as a deliberate policy rather than something that resulted from the logic of capitalist enterprise. Bankers were at the centre of a conspiracy to import Asian labour, so that they might reap greater profits, and at the same time provide their imperial associates in England with cheap raw materials. At this point in the argument they became more than bankers. They were the Money Power.

State banking was regarded by its advocates as the most appropriate instrument for the people to thwart the Money Power's ambition. State banks would operate under conditions set down by Parliament speaking as the embodiment of the people's will. They would be banks that served the common weal, not narrow private groups, and as they were non-profit institutions they would be able to provide cheap credit to individuals and industries that operated in the public interest. Because of their competitive advantage, State banks would eventually force the private banks, and all the evils that followed in their train, out of national life until all that remained was the one national bank owned by the people and operated on their behalf. This was the basic argument behind Labor's original plan for the Commonwealth Bank.

However, as events during World War I showed, it would require more than government banks to defeat the Money Power. Following a well-established body of opinion in Britain, Europe and America, men like Frank Anstey told the labour movement how the forces of international capitalism, manipulated by the Money Power, were both the cause and the beneficiaries of war. He claimed that the 'Kingdom of Shylock', built upon centuries of brutal oppression and cunning speculation, had grown to such proportions that it stood above capitalism, kings and parliaments as a colossus, manipulating all in pursuit of vast wealth and unchallenged power. Its dominion over all was even more insidious because it worked unseen to prey 'upon the nation in times of peace' and conspire 'against it in the hour of its calamity'. Through its control over gold and other means of exchange, along with its ability to grant loans, the Money Power was able to determine the fate of nations, foster international hatreds and provoke wars, where it would 'wax fat upon the blood of the toiling masses'.

As Theodore and others pointed out in the early 1920s, the Money Power would take every opportunity to dictate to governments through its power of the purse. In the Queensland loans issue there was clear proof, for those disposed to see it that way, of how British Money Power in collaboration with Australian capitalists could veto legislation passed by a supposedly independent government. It showed that the people's elected representatives could only do as they liked so long as their actions were approved by the Money Power.

Many people in the labour movement drew the same lesson from the fate of the Scullin Government. According to popular wisdom, it had no sooner been elected than the British Money Power refused supply. When it looked as though the Government might deny Shylock his pound of flesh in favour of the unemployed, the Bank of England sent in the bailiff, in the person of Sir Otto Niemeyer. The arrival of his mission in Australia was seen by many as further proof of the Money Power's contemptuous disregard for the independence of a sovereign nation. He was depicted as the Jewish emissary from the Old Lady of Threadneedle Street, come to tell Australians that they must tighten their belts to pay British bondholders, while thousands of Australians lived in poverty and hunger. The sheer injustice of it all, that 60 000 Australian men were offered up for slaughter in the Great

War to defend the country that now would starve their widows and children so that British bondholders might continue to live in accustomed luxury! Besides, Britain, it was alleged, had settled its war debt with other nations on much more favourable terms than those which it was now enforcing on Australia.

All this was compounded by the obstruction of the Scullin Government by the agents of the Australian Money Power who had seized control of the Commonwealth Bank in 1924. Sir Robert Gibson's flat refusal to supply money for unemployment relief was taken as another sign of the Money Power's utter indifference to the people's welfare and its determination to frustrate a Labor Government. In due course, the Government capitulated and accepted 'the starvation scheme' in the form of the Premiers' Plan, thus signifying its total surrender to the forces of Mammon. Even the Theodore Plan, which proposed to share the burden more equally without undue prejudice to the interests of bondholders, was rejected out of hand as dangerous and inflationary.

Despite this betrayal by their weak and divided Federal Government, the workers had a leader, the saviour of the people, Jack Lang. At least the people of New South Wales might be saved from the grasp of the Money Power by 'the Big Fella'. While the banks conspired against the people and the 'Fascists of Finance' organized private armies to overthrow him, Lang would stand up for them. He would not pay a penny to bondholders while the people lacked work or pensions, while widows and children were forced into starvation and misery. He would cast away the cross of gold that bore down upon the shoulders of the toiling masses. He might have been 'Greater than Lenin', but he too was eventually prey to the Money Power. The traitors in the Federal Labor Party, Theodore in particular, had conspired with Sir Robert Gibson at the Commonwealth Bank to strangle the New South Wales Government Savings Bank and confiscate the people's savings. In this they were merely concluding the 'base Nationalist plot' that had begun with the Opposition's campaign to undermine confidence in the bank. Lang took his revenge upon the Scullin Government by bringing it down, but in the process acquired a more hostile enemy in the Lyons Government, which set in train a series of events leading to his dismissal by the State Governor, who in turn acted on behalf of the Money Power.

While Lang held centre stage in New South Wales, another version of Money Power conspiracy theory was making headway in the labour movement. The followers of Douglas Credit believed that finance played a central role in the productive process. Fnanciers, they argued, syphoned off significant proportions of purchasing power from the cycle of production and consumption, which distorted the otherwise efficient machinery of capitalism. For them, the world would only find its regeneration if the Money Power was abolished in favour of the National Credit Authority, the Just Price and the National Dividend. To the more conservative members of the labour movement who were uneasy about their party's 'socialization' pretensions, this offered the kind of solution to the question of finance that they were looking for. It would remove the baleful influence of predatory finance, yet leave the basic pattern of capitalism untouched. For this reason Douglas Credit appealed to an audience of the discontented, which spread beyond the labour movement to encompass farmers and small businessmen.

During the mid-1940s, however, Labor embraced a much more promising theory of how to stabilize and civilize capitalism. The policy implications of Keynesian economics were in happy conjunction with Labor's long-held desire to do just that. The 1945 White Paper on Full Employment in Australia, and the Bretton Woods Agreement, provided the blueprint for a post-war world free from the threat of depression and war. The 1945 Banking Acts were part of the systematic program mapped out in the White Paper. They strengthened the Commonwealth Bank's central banking functions, expanded its trading operations and abolished its board, which had appeared to act as an agent of the Money Power since 1924.

The international component in post-war planning centred around ratification of the Bretton Woods Agreement. To the inheritors of Labor's populist tradition, the IMF and the World Bank represented the formal institutionalization of international Money Power. In such hands it would be able to dictate economic policy to Australia, force restraint on government spending, press for wage reduction much as Niemeyer had done in 1930, and even throw open the floodgates to cheap Asian labour. Despite these objections, the party's pragmatic reformists won the day and the agreement was eventually signed.

After the private banks successfully challenged the 1945 Banking Act, the Chifley Government responded to its populist heritage by attempting to nationalize Australian Money Power. But despite some fiery rhetoric about the role of private banks in the last two depressions, Labor's campaign was half-hearted, poorly organized and largely ineffective. Lively denunciations of the Money Power, a few meetings of the party faithful, and a trickle of pamphlets, were no match for the forces arrayed against them. The alliance of forces that they had traditionally called the Money Power used all the weapons at its disposal to defeat the move. They found, to their increasing dismay, that they had taken on more than just a few hard-bitten bankers. They faced an inspired Opposition, a dedicated army of bank officers, a bewildering array of guerrilla organizations that conducted ideological skirmishes against them in every town and suburb, almost unlimited funds, a hostile press, a conservative Constitution, and an electorate made suspicious of 'socialism' by a Cold War atmosphere. In the face of such an onslaught, Labor's disadvantages were compounded by their internal divisions. They lacked decisive leadership, there were tactical errors, and all the while their resolve to fight was sapped by the bitter ideological struggle that was to culminate in the great split of 1954–55. Beyond these specific factors lay a more enduring problem, which added a grim irony to their defeat. Although their preoccupation with ideas about the Money Power had pointed to the importance of finance in a capitalist system, the ultimate sterility of that analysis contributed to their failure either to predict or combat a capitalist mobilization when it confronted them.

The main difficulty was that the logic of the analysis led them to a monocausal explanation of complex social processes. They had convinced themselves that the ultimate source of all the crises that beset Australia and its labour movement was a darkness in the hearts of a few powerful men whose supreme ambition was to rivet the chains of economic servitude upon the toiling masses. Their explanations of how this occurred and what was to be done about it revealed the two sides of populist ideology; a tendency to ascribe the blame to some alien corruption, and at the same time to develop and embellish myths about the virtues of their collective traditions. This process generated an abundant store of symbols, which provided a clear focus for the mobilization of discontent.

During the class mobilization that culminated in the crisis of the early 1890s, a number of existing attitudes were marshalled into a pattern in which class, race, nationalism and anti-imperialism assumed a populist configuration. In the labour movement, myths about the honesty, simplicity and egalitarian independence of the Australian worker were elevated by some publicists to a 'religion' of unionism, which was projected as both a symbol of these virtues and an instrument of social transformation. According to that view, the workers, inspired and sustained by this 'religion', could build a new nation free of the Old World corruption and decadence that had brutalized the populace of Europe. In such circumstances it would be possible to build a new race of people—more vigorous, virtuous and free—in a new land.

Many of the myths that permeated nationalist literature of the 1890s flowed over into labour ideology. The celebration of the 'battler' or the 'little man', struggling with stoic heroism against insurmountable odds in a forbidding land, played an important part in that myth-making process. So too did the notion of a sturdy independence supported by the knowledge that in a real crisis 'mates' could be relied on to give support. Allied to this was a fierce egalitarianism, which insisted on judging a man by what he could do, rather than accepting claims to status based on birth, wealth or inheritance. In the emerging labour movement these ideas were overlaid with the notion that all decent men and women were co-operative by nature, and that the most tangible expression of this was the 'religion' of unionism. According to that doctrine the greatest sin a man could commit was to 'scab' on his mates. These values, expressed through the instruments of unions and the Labor Party, became central elements in a sense of class identity.

This convergence of class and national identity relied just as much upon the way it defined the common enemy. The classes opposed to labour were capitalists and imperialists who did not share the values of true native Australians. They were identified as symbols of oppression, treachery and decadence, who would not hesitate to reduce wages, crush the unions or dispossess farmers in ruthless pursuit of wealth and power. They were dangerous men, whose influence extended into almost all the institutions of national life: the parliaments and the courts, banks and business. All of these, in one way or another, were based upon imperial connections. This was compounded by the fact that many had accepted knighthoods, which merely provided a mantle of respectability behind which they continued their illicit activity. It also signified their attachment to Britain as 'home'. In the popular imagination of working-class nationalists they represented decadent trappings of Old World aristocracy, with its noxious pretensions of superiority. These popular suspicions were confirmed when men such as Matthew Davies, James Munro and Thomas McIlwraith were implicated in bank frauds during the mid-1890s. They came to symbolize the imperial corruption that had infected this virgin continent.

This early tendency was significant for later developments in Labor populism, since it inclined the analysis of class more towards individuals and institutions than social structure and process. It was an ideology that spoke of capitalists rather than capitalism—imperialists, not imperialism. As a result, the actions of individuals were seen not so much as a consequence of the social context in which they operated, but more in terms of greed and malice. If malicious intent was the underlying motive in capitalist behaviour, it was not surprising that populist ideology explained its inner logic in terms of conspiracy theories. The analysis became a relatively simple matter of explaining how the conspiracy was perpetrated.

This led to elaborate explanations of plots to deceive governments, mystification of language to befuddle the people and audacious schemes to plunder the toiling masses. It thus became more a catalogue of crimes than a social analysis, an indictment rather than a theory. There were ample demonstrations of this in the way that Labor's populist radicals explained the causes of war. They began with the proposition that international capitalism was comprised of a set of predatory monopolies who had no national allegiance but were concerned only with the concentration of wealth and power in their own hands. These monopolies were interlocked through overlapping directorships occupied by a coterie of evil men who controlled the press, the armamemt industry and the banks. Their tentacles of influence extended to governments, churches, courts and educational institutions, so that they seldom had to resort to brute force to advance their schemes, because they could stampede a gullible populace to international hatreds and wars through their control over the instruments of public persuasion. Perched at the top of this grand conspiratorial design were a handful of men who operated large international financial institutions. It was they, the Money Power, who decided that wars should occur so that they could reap vast profits on war loans, enrich themselves by the sale of arms, and at the same time kill upon battlefields the most vigorous elements of the working class who posed a threat to their continued domination. By this means the Kingdom of Shylock was sustained.

The tendency to depict abstract social relationships in terms of human types and motives was a productive source of symbols. Populist rhetoric, in its spoken, written and pictorial forms, abounded with them. Those most commonly invoked were the crafty Shylock, the slothful John Bull or Fat, the maniacal militarist, the sturdy worker, the yeoman farmer, the distressed war widow, and Prometheus chained. They all served to reinforce the stark distinction between the industrious and the indolent, the virtuous and the venal.

This reflected the populist conception of classes under modern capitalism, where the great struggle had finally been reduced to one between the people and the predators, the masses and the Money Power. That position had arisen from a process of accumulation in which rival capitalists had engaged in ruthless competition for increasingly concentrated wealth. Because of its control over the 'life blood of industry', the Money Power had emerged victorious. Lesser capitalists were reduced to a dependent status where they became mere playthings or instruments of its ambition. As a result of this process two hostile classes had arisen—a small plutocracy opposed by a vast democratic majority. The problems of social transformation were thus greatly simplified. All that was necessary was to eliminate the plutocratic clique.

Although it was an easy matter to identify the enemy, it was much more difficult to abolish him. To do so required that the people should be mobilized and, through some tangible expression of their collective will, assail the citadel of Mammon. In the populist imagination the labour movement, with its unions and its party, was the most appropriate instrument of social transformation. Although it had emerged out of a working-class mobilization, the Labor Party was not simply an instrument of narrow class interest. It gave institutional expression to the aspirations of all true democratic nationalists. It was the people's party, their voice and their weapon. It would defend them against their enemies and raise them to a higher level of existence. Even its methods of doing so would be exemplary. There would be no need for the violent upheavals so common among the brutalized masses of the Old World. By moral force, rational persuasion, and collective, democratic action, the Labor Party would capture the institutions of the State and turn them into benevolent agencies dedicated to the people's welfare.

Where existing institutions were unequal to the task, Labor would create new ones. The Commonwealth Bank was such a case. It was a tangible assertion of the belief that a nation's finances could be conducted efficiently without the usurious exactions of the Money Power. It was also a weapon to defeat Shylock, because its competitive advantage would squeeze the financial dictators out of national life. By that means the very basis of Mammon's overlordship—interest—would be undercut, and the whole Kingdom of Shylock would inevitably crumble. This would be followed gradually, but with equal inevitability, by the elimination of poverty, hunger, crime and all the social evils that had attended the reign of Mammon. In the populist imagination, if not in reality, that was the bank's purpose.

It was abundantly clear that the Money Power had no intention to happily acquiesce in its own demise. By its very nature it was an aggressive and cunning foe whose attacks on the people, their institutions and leaders had to be resisted. This was demonstrated in the events of 1930–32, when the people's bank, captured by the Money Power in 1924, was turned against a Labor Government in its efforts to protect the people from the ravages of economic depression. Cowered by the relentless hostility of the forces surrounding Australian finance and seduced to treachery by the

Bank of England's emissary, that Government had collapsed in abject surrender. Only in New South Wales did the people have a resolute and incorruptible leader. The charismatic figure of Jack Lang embodied all the symbolism of a heroic populist struggle against the Money Power and its minions. When all others had betrayed them, he stood firm. He was the personification of their stubborn, fighting spirit. With 'Man versus Money' proudly emblazoned on his battle flag, this 'saviour of the people', this 'great commoner' would defend them to the bitter end. As such he provided a sharp focus for their discontent, but the logic of his populist ideology led them to suppose that the defeat of a small plutocratic élite would remove the cause of their distress. All the complexities of the capitalist mobilization that confronted them were thus reduced to this one gladiatorial contest. Lang was their only remaining weapon. The fragility of that strategy was revealed in his summary dismissal by an imperial governor and the subsequent collapse of organized resistance. In 1947 the Chifley Government committed a similar error. This same populist heritage had convinced them that they were only attacking the Money Power when they tried to nationalize the banks. They too encountered a full-blooded capitalist mobilization that they had not predicted. Even then they were not entirely sure what had hit them.

As we observed at the beginning of this book, populism is not an isolated phenomenon. It occurs within wider processes. In this study we have seen how Labor's populist inclinations became more pronounced during periods of crisis and class mobilization, in war and depression. They arose in that context, not as an independent body of ideology, but as an expression of the contradictions inherent in a movement that harnessed its radical impulses to a reformist program in a hostile system of social relationships.

Three examples should be sufficient to draw out this point. In its formative years the labour movement built a sense of collective identity from the conjunction of three contradictory ideas; class, nation and race. As we have seen, the tension between those ideas was resolved in the form of a racist national populism. Second, the conflict between the notions of social classes and the people gave rise to a theory that identified capitalism as a set of predatory monopolies resolutely hostile to a fundamentally co-operative populace. According to that theory, the process of class conflict was finally reduced to a heroic struggle between ruthless plutocrats and the champions of the people. The third contradiction was contained in the belief that it was possible to transform capitalism into a people's democracy through the institutional framework of the capitalist state. This encouraged misleading assumptions about the nature of power in such a system, so that capitalist mobilizations were explained in terms of malicious conspiracy and base treachery.

Although Labor's preoccupation with these ideas about the Money Power pointed to the importance of finance in a capitalist system, the ultimate sterility of their analysis only served to keep them captive within it. As the popular radical interpretations of 11 November 1975 showed, that tradition did not end in 1950. Moreover, it would be an act of Whiggish folly to suppose that the contradictions that gave rise to populist ideology in the labour movement between 1890 and 1950 have finally been resolved.

Notes

INTRODUCTION

[1] See Richard Hofstadter, *The Age of Reform from Bryan to F.D.R.;* Franco Venturi, *Roots of Revolution: A History of the Populist and Socialist Movements in Nineteenth Century Russia;* Gino Germani, *Authoritarianism, Fascism, and National Populism.*

[2] Ghita Ionescu and Ernest Gellner (eds), *Populism: Its Meaning and National Characteristics.*

[3] Germani, op. cit., chapter 2. He argues from a functionalist position. See also Torcuato Di Tella, 'Populism and Reform in Latin America', in Claudio Veliz (ed.), *Obstacles to Change in Latin America.*

[4] Ernesto Laclau, *Politics and Ideology in Marxist Theory,* chapter 4, 'Towards a Theory of Populism'. He argues from within the Althusserian school of Marxist structuralism.

[5] Hofstadter, op. cit., chapter 1. See too Hofstadter, 'North America', in Ionescu and Gellner, op. cit.; John D. Hicks, *The Populist Revolt: A History of the Farmers' Alliance and People's Party,* chapter 3, 'The Grievances'.

[6] Isaiah Berlin, *Russian Thinkers,* chapter on 'Russian Populism'. This originally appeared as the introduction to Venturi, op. cit. For more recent discussion, see Andrzej Walicki, 'Russia', in Ionescu and Gellner, op. cit.; Margaret Canovan, *Populism,* chapter 2. For a discussion of the ideology that surfaced at the 1905 congresses of the All-Russian Peasant Union, see Teodor Shanin, 'The Peasant Dream: Russia 1905–7', in Raphael Samuel and Gareth Stedman Jones (eds), *Culture, Ideology and Politics.*

[7] See Hofstadter, op. cit., chapter 2.

[8] N. G. Chernyshevsky, *What is to be done? Tales about new people*; Edward Bellamy, *Looking Backward, 2000–1887*; Ignatius Donnelly, *Caesar's Column: A story of the twentieth century*; Hofstadter, op. cit.;

Berlin, op. cit.; E. J. Hobsbawn, *Primitive Rebels*, especially pp. 57–65.

9 For a discussion of anti-Semitism in American populism see Hofstadter, op. cit., pp. 72–81.

10 Referring to 'the idle holders of idle capital' who favoured the gold standard, William Jennings Bryan told the 1896 Democratic Convention: 'You shall not press down upon the brow of labor this crown of thorns, you shall not crucify mankind upon a cross of gold'. For the text of this famous speech see George Brown Tindall (ed.), *A Populist Reader*, pp. 203–11.

11 See *Hummer*, 19 October, 7 November 1891, 3 September 1892; Melbourne *Worker*, 30 June 1894, 26 January, 29 June 1895; Brisbane *Worker*, 3 March 1894.

12 Robin Gollan, 'The Australian Impact', in Sylvia E. Bowman (ed.), *Edward Bellamy Abroad*; Robin Gollan, *The Commonwealth Bank*, pp. 47–53.

13 Brisbane *Worker*, 1 March 1890. For a discussion of Lane's attitude to Bellamy's teachings see Robin Gollan, *Radical and Working Class Politics*, pp. 123–4; G. Hannan, 'William Lane—Mateship and Utopia', in Murphy, Joyce and Hughes (eds), *Prelude to Power*, pp. 181–6. See also E. H. Lane, *Dawn to Dusk*, p. 12, and *Hummer*, 16 January 1892.

14 William Lane, *The Workingman's Paradise: An Australian Labour Novel*, p. ii.

15 *Albany Observer*, 15 July 1890, reprinted in Brian Kiernan (ed.), *Portable Australian Authors: Henry Lawson*, p. 81

16 *Bulletin*, 1 February 1890. *Hummer*, 6 February 1892. Gollan, 'The Australian Impact', pp. 128.9. *Tocsin*, 2 December 1897. The reviewer went on to remark: 'Marx had thundered it out in Sanscrit (or something as unintelligible to the masses) before him'. For a full account of New Australia see Gavin Souter, *A Peculiar People.* For a personal memoir by one who went, see Mary Gilmore, 'Colonia Cosme', in Higham and Wilding (eds), *Australians Abroad.*

17 See Gollan, *The Commonwealth Bank*, pp. 51–2. The *Bulletin* also treated *Caesar's Column* as a book of considerable contemporary relevance. On 6 January 1894 the Brisbane *Worker* published an enthusiastic review of Donnelly's *The Golden Bottle* and began to serialize it the following week. For a humorous perspective on popular debate about the respective merits of Bellamy, Donnelly and Henry George see Henry Lawson's 'A Day on a Selection' in Kiernan, op. cit., pp. 86–91.

18 For a selection of the literature available to self-improving workers during the 1890s see Brisbane *Worker*, 1 April 1890, 3 October 1891, 8 August 1896; *Hummer*, 6 February 1891; *Tocsin*, 24 March 1898, 6 April 1899.

19 See R. W. Connell and T. H. Irving, *Class Structure in Australian History*, chapter 4; Terry Irving, 'Socialism, working class mobilization and the origins of the Labor Party' in Bruce O'Meagher (ed.), *The Socialist Objective: Labor and Socialism*; Gollan, *Radical and Working Class Politics*, chapters 6, 7 and 8; Bede Nairn, *Civilising Capitalism*.

20 See Tom Collins [Joseph Furphy], *Such is Life*; W. K. Hancock, *Australia*, p. 63; Gollan, op. cit., pp. 113–15; Lawson, 'A Neglected History', in Kiernan, op. cit., pp. 75–6.

21 For Lawson's 'The New Religion' see Kiernan, op. cit., p. 82. The *Boomerang* article appeared on 6 April 1889. On 9 March 1889 it urged readers to 'stand by White Queensland' because coloured labour 'degrades and demoralises the labour which must be the backbone of our national greatness and true prosperity and for this we will not have it at any price'. For differing views on this variety of racism see: Verity Burgmann, 'Capital and Labour', and Ray Markey, 'Populist Politics', both in Ann Curthoys and Andrew Markus (eds), *Who Are Our Enemies?*; Andrew Markus, *Fear and Hatred*, chapter 11; Humphrey McQueen, *A New Britannia*, chapter 2.

22 See, for example, Ned, the hero of Lane's *Workingman's Paradise*, who exemplifies the virtues of manly courage and honest simplicity.

CHAPTER 1

1 For a contemporary account of unemployment in Melbourne during this period see a series of articles in the *Age* entitled 'Among the Workless', which began on 22 June 1892.

2 For contemporary assessments of the bank crashes see A. G. V. Peel, *The Australian Crisis of 1893*, and George Gibbs, *The Imperial State Paper on 'The Australian Crisis of 1893'*; T. A. Coghlan, *Labour and Industry in Australia*, vol. 3, considers it in a wider context. For more recent interpretations see E. A. Boehm, *Prosperity and Depression in Australia, 1887–1897*; Geoffrey Blainey, *Gold and Paper*; S. J. Butlin, *Australia and New Zealand Bank*; Robin Gollan, *The Commonwealth Bank of Australia*; R. F. Holder, *Bank of New South Wales: A History*. The most reliable economic statistics for the period are available in N. G. Butlin, *Private Capital Formation in Australia, Estimates 1861–1900*.

[3] See Michael Cannon, *The Land Boomers*; D. B. Waterson, 'Thomas McIlwraith. A Colonial Entrepreneur', in Murphy and Joyce (eds), *Queensland Political Portraits.*

[4] Black's comments are in *New South Wales Parliamentary Debates* [*NSWPD*], vol. 65, 27 April 1893, p. 6637. He repeated the sentiments in even stronger terms on 23 November. See ibid., vol. 68, pp. 1359–60. McKinnon's views are expressed in ibid., p. 1357, and Schey's, ibid., pp. 1361 and 1431–2.

[5] See, for example, speeches by the following Labor members in *Victorian Parliamentary Debates* [*VPD*], vol. 72, 17 August 1893: Dr Moloney, p. 1020; Trenwith, p. 1024; Bromley, p. 1039.

[6] *Commonweal*, 27 May 1893.

[7] *Queensland Parliamentary Debates* [*QPD*], vol. 70, 22 June 1893, pp. 98–115.

[8] Brisbane *Worker*, 14 December 1895. The paper persisted in its campaign against McIlwraith and his friends long after his resignation. Allegations, rhetorical swipes and even allegorical stories about him and the bank appeared regularly in the *Worker*'s pages until the end of the century. See, for example, William Henry Pann's story, 'How They Started the Great Gone Bung Bank', in the issue of 16 December 1899. The whole affair had by then assumed the proportions of a saga in Labor folklore.

[9] Ibid., 24 February 1894.

[10] For McPherson's evidence see 'Progress Report of the Select Committee of the Legislative Council on the Unemployed Problem', *Proceedings of the Parliament of South Australia*, 1894, part 2, paper no. 110, p. 9. For examples of Labor platforms see: reports of the Intercolonial Trades Union Congresses, nos 1–7, 1879–1891; the policy of the New South Wales Trades and Labour Council in the *Australian Workman*, 27 December 1890; and the platform of the United Labor Party of Victoria in the Melbourne *Worker*, 30 June 1894. For the programmes of the more radical groups see: 'Manifesto of the Australian Socialist League to the People of Australia', in *Australian Workman*, 13 October 1894; Sydney *Socialist*, 13 August 1898; and the report of the General Council of the Australian Labour Federation in Brisbane *Worker*, 1 September 1890.

[11] For a short summary of George's theory see Robin Gollan, *Radical and Working Class Politics*, pp. 120–1. For a discussion of his influence in the Australian colonies see Craufurd D. W. Goodwin, *Economic Enquiry in Australia*, pp. 110–22. On labour literature see *Hummer*, 9 January 1892. The comment by W. G. Spence at a public meeting

that 'he found the country full of Henry George followers' was greeted with cheers. See *Shearers' Record*, March 1890.

[12] C. von Hagen, *The Banking Crisis and General Depression*. See also *Beacon*, 1 June 1893.

[13] Gollan, *Radical and Working Class Politics*, pp. 33–49.

[14] *Hard Cash*, 10 July 1893. It was edited by Arthur Desmond. According to J. T. Lang (*The Great Bust!*, p. 10), it was published by the Active Service Brigade, who frequented McNamara's Bookshop in Sydney. He claims that Desmond was fined £2 for placing a 'Gone Bung' sign on a suspended bank, and that W. H. McNamara was charged with criminal libel as a result of an article published in the magazine. The Melbourne *Worker* of 10 March 1894 reported that McNamara and S. A. Rosa had been gaoled for some months for selling *Hard Cash*.

[15] Sydney *Worker*, 23 February 1895.

[16] *QPD*, Vol. 70, 18 July 1893, p. 222. See also p. 206 for the same sentiments.

[17] *New Order*, 8 September 1894.

[18] *Tocsin*, 10 February 1898.

[19] Melbourne *Worker*, 10 March 1894. In the same year Henry Lawson altered a line in the last stanza of his 'Freedom on the Wallaby' from 'We'll make the tyrants feel the sting' to:

> We'll make the bankers feel the sting
> Of those that they would throttle.
> They needn't say the fault is ours
> If blood should stain the wattle.

See Colin Roderick (ed.), *Henry Lawson: Collected Verse*, vol. 1, pp. 123–4.

[20] See, for example, Melbourne *Worker*, 5 May, 2 June 1894, 26 January 1895.

[21] Melbourne *Worker*, 26 January 1895.

[22] Ibid., 16 September 1893.

[23] See H. V. Evatt, *Australian Labour Leader*, pp. 124–30.

[24] D. J. Murphy, 'Queensland', in D. J. Murphy (ed.), *Labor in Politics*, p. 166. Brisbane *Worker*, 20 January 1900.

[25] *Tocsin*, 22 June, 2 November 1899, 18 January, 8 February 1900, 12 March 1903.

CHAPTER 2

1 For a detailed discussion of monetary affairs in the early colonial period see S. J. Butlin, *The Foundations of the Australian Monetary System, 1788–1851*. For an examination of the debates in Australia about the role of the state in banking and currency see Goodwin, op. cit., pp. 134–94. For further discussion see Gollan, *The Commonwealth Bank of Australia*, chapters 1 and 4.

2 For the reports of the various inquiries see: 'Final Report from the Select Committee on Post Office Savings Bank—National Bank', New South Wales, *Votes and Proceedings of the Legislative Assembly*, session 1892–3, vol. II, p. 1389; 'Final Report of the Select Committee of the Legislative Council on the Unemployed Problem', *Proceedings of the Parliament of South Australia*, 1894, part 2, paper no. 110A, p. 5; 'Report of Royal Commission appointed to consider the desirability of establishing a State Bank and Royal Mint', ibid., 1889, vol. 2, paper no. 27, p. v; and 'Report of the Royal Commission on State Banking', Victoria, *Papers Presented to Parliament*, Legislative Assembly, vol. IV, session 1895–6, p. vi. For a brief summary of the process between Royal Commission Report and the State Bank Act Amendment Bill in Victoria, see Gollan, op. cit., pp. 60–7.

3 On Queensland, see Brisbane *Worker*, 1 September 1890. For New South Wales see R. N. Ebbels (ed.), *The Australian Labor Movement, 1850–1907*, pp. 212, 217, and Sydney *Worker*, 5 February 1898. The Victorian view is in Melbourne *Worker*, 30 June 1894, and *Commonweal*, 17 June 1893. On South Australia and Tasmania see W. G. Spence, *Australia's Awakening*, pp. 402, 405. The Congress resolution is reported in the Sydney *Worker*, 27 January 1894.

4 Zouabi (pseud.), *The Banking System: Australia's Incubus, an Immediate Remedy*, Brisbane, 1894.

5 Flürscheim's proposal appeared in *Tocsin*, 24 March 1898 and 17 August 1899. See also his article, 'A Perfect Money and its Effects', *New Zealand Illustrated Magazine*, August 1901, pp. 835–40.

6 See Moreton Frewen, 'The Crime in America that Impoverishes Australia', *Review of Reviews*, 20 March 1895, pp. 288–90. For a general discussion of bimetallism's influence in Australia see Goodwin, op. cit., pp. 197–209.

7 See *Flame*, July 1907, for the manifesto of the Socialist Federation of Australia. See also *People*, the paper of the Australian Socialist League, for similar views.

8 Geoffrey Sawer, *The Australian Constitution*, p. 49.

[9] Australian Labor Party, *Australian Labor Conference, Official Report*, Sydney, 1902, pp. 9, 13.

[10] J. M. Scott, *The Circulating Sovereign*. For discussion of its influence in New South Wales see Gollan, op. cit., p. 80.

[11] Australian Labor Party, *Official Report of the Fourth Commonwealth Political Labour Conference*, Brisbane, 1908.

[12] *Argus*, 21 March 1910.

[13] Ibid., 30 March 1910.

[14] See Gollan, op. cit., chapter 6.

[15] *Labor Call*, 21, 28 September, 19, 26 October 1911.

[16] Sydney *Worker*, 7 September 1911. In similar vein, E. J. Brady, writing as 'Scrutator' for *Labor Call*, assailed the 'Financial Spielers; Mortgage Mongers; and Blackmailing Boodlers' of Australian finance in a seemingly endless series of articles. See 7 September, 12, 19 October, 2, 9, 16, 23, 30 November, 7, 14, 28 December 1911.

[17] O'Malley's claims to have been the 'father of the Commonwealth Bank', although an interesting story, are beyond the scope of this study. His several versions are examined by Kim Beazley, 'The Labor Party and the Origins of the Commonwealth Bank', *Australian Journal of Politics and History*, vol. IX, no. 1, May 1963. They are discussed further by Gollan, op. cit., pp. 96–100. For Fisher's second reading speech see *Commonwealth Parliamentary Debates* [*CPD*], vol. 62, pp. 2644–62.

[18] Gollan, op. cit., pp. 101–8. L. F. Giblin, *The Growth of a Central Bank*, p. 3.

[19] *Labor Call*, 9 November, 14 December 1911; Sydney *Worker*, 30 November 1911, 17 October 1912, 9 April, 21 May 1914.

CHAPTER 3

[1] Both speeches were reported in the *Argus*, 1 August 1914. For a short survey of initial reactions see Ian Turner, '1914–19' in F. K. Crowley (ed.), *A New History of Australia*, pp. 312–15. For early responses within the labour movement see Ian Turner, *Industrial Labour and Politics*, pp. 68–71, and D. J. Murphy (ed.), *Labor in Politics*.

[2] See Turner, op. cit., p. 70, and G. Hewitt, The Victorian Socialist Party, p. 175.

[3] See Turner, op. cit., p. 69.

[4] For a brief sketch of Anstey's career see Ian Turner's entry on him in Bede Nairn and Geoffrey Serle (eds), *Australian Dictionary of Biography*, vol. 7, pp. 79–81.

[5] On the British radicals, see Clive Trebilcock, 'Radicalism and the Armament Trust', in A. J. A. Morris (ed.), *Edwardian Radicalism, 1900–1914*, pp. 180–201.

[6] Labor Call, 29 October 1914.

[7] Ibid., 5 November 1914.

[8] Ibid., 15 April 1915.

[9] Frank Anstey, *The Kingdom of Shylock*, 1917, p. vi. See also *Money Power*, pp. 9.10.

[10] *The Kingdom of Shylock*, p. 2. Emphasis in original.

[11] *Money Power*, pp. 15–18.

[12] Ibid., pp. 19–21.

[13] *The Kingdom of Shylock*, p. 2.

[14] Ibid., p. 5.

[15] Ibid., p. vii.

[16] Turner, op. cit., pp. 71–81.

[17] On the Ryan Government's action see D. J. Murphy, 'Queensland', op. cit., p. 187. For Finlayson's remarks see *CPD*, vol. 77, p. 3674, and the Brisbane *Worker*, 17 June 1915. McDougall's comments are in *Labor Call*, 1 February 1917. Political Labor Council of Victoria, *Annual Conference*, Melbourne, 21–24 April 1916, p. 23.

[18] This view was argued in its most explicit form by 'R.J.C.' in the *Australian Worker*, 18 April 1918. Fragments of it appeared in ibid., 20 January, 10, 17 February 1916; and *Labor Call*, 24 June, 22 July 1920, 27 January, 28 April 1921. Despite the Marxist overtones of the term 'surplus value', it appears that the idea owed more to a highly selective interpretation of J. A. Hobson's concept of 'surplus'. For a discussion of that see Michael Bleaney, *Underconsumption Theories*, pp. 158–63.

[19] All-Australian Trade Union Congress, *Manifesto of the National Executive of the Congress*, Melbourne, May 1916. See also Turner, op. cit., pp. 98–101; *Labor Call*, 4 May 1916; Melbourne *Socialist*, 19 May 1916.

[20] *CPD*, vol. 80, pp. 8741–2. For similar views see *Labor Call*, 26 October 1916; Brisbane *Daily Standard*, 29 October 1917. For a discussion of

Labor's attitude on race in the 1890s see Andrew Markus, *Fear and Hatred*, chapter 11.

[21] Dan Coward, 'Crime and Punishment', in Iremonger, Merritt and Osborne (eds), *Strikes*, pp. 51–80, and Turner, op. cit., chapter 6.

[22] Ernest Scott, *Australia During the War*, p. 412; Turner, op. cit., pp. 163–6.

[23] *Australian Worker*, 15 November 1917

[24] *QPD*, vol. 128, p. 3147. For an example of how Labor had marshalled its arguments by the second referendum see '20 Points Against Conscription', in Adelaide *Daily Herald*, 18 December 1917.

[25] Walter Kendall, *The Revolutionary Movement in Britain, 1900–21*, p. 188.

[26] Frank Anstey, *Red Europe*, p. 192.

[27] Turner, op. cit., chapter 8; Australian Labor Party, State of Victoria, *Annual Conference*, 18–21 April 1919, p. 33.

[28] Australian Labor Party, *Official Report of the Eighth Commonwealth Conference*, Sydney, June 1919, p. 69.

CHAPTER 4

[1] For a discussion of the crisis see S. J. Butlin, *Australia and New Zealand Bank*, pp. 366–7; Geoffrey Blainey, *Gold and Paper*, pp. 312–13; and Turner, op. cit., pp. 210–11.

[2] For a detailed account of this issue see Bernie Schedvin, 'E. G. Theodore and the London Pastoral Lobby', *Politics*, vol. v, no. 1, May 1970. See also: Irwin Young, *Theodore: His Life and Times*, chapter 6; D. J. Murphy, 'Edward Granville Theodore', in Murphy and Joyce (eds), *Queensland Political Portraits*, pp. 314–19. The delegation comprised: Sir Robert Philp, former Premier and a founder of Burns, Philp; Sir Alfred Cowley, former Speaker of the Legislative Assembly and Chairman of Directors of the Bank of Queensland; and John Walsh, solicitor and Executive Member of the National Union of Queensland.

[3] Brisbane *Worker*, 26 August 1920.

[4] Ibid., 30 September 1920.

[5] Bernie Schedvin, op. cit., pp. 36–40. Scullin's motion was recalled in *Labor Call* on 10 November 1921. For a gloating statement from Theodore after he had appeared to win the second of the three rounds in his bout with British Money Power, see ibid., 16 February 1922.

[6] For the suggestion that London Jewish financiers were behind the whole business, see Brisbane *Worker*, 17 January 1924. For the claim that British financiers were partially responsible for Queensland Labor's nationalism, see ibid., 13 March 1924.

[7] Australian Labor Party, *Official Report of the Eighth Commonwealth Conference*, Sydney, 18 June 1919, p. 68.

[8] Patrick Weller and Beverley Lloyd (eds), *Federal Executive Minutes, 1915–1955*, p. 55.

[9] All-Australian Trades Union Conference, Melbourne, 20–25 June 1921, *Official Report*, p. 32.

[10] Australian Labor Party, *Official Report of Proceedings of the Ninth Commonwealth Conference*, Brisbane, October 1921. For commentary on this issue see: Turner, op. cit., pp. 210–26; L. F. Crisp, *The Australian Federal Labour Party, 1901–1951*, pp. 277–82; and D. W. Rawson, *Labor in Vain?*, pp. 67–70.

[11] *Labor Call*, 26 October 1922.

[12] See, for example, ibid., 24 February, 3 November 1921, 24 August, 16 November 1922, 22 October 1925, 4 November 1926. See also *Australian Worker*, 14 July, 18 August, 22 December 1921.

[13] L. F. Giblin, *The Growth of a Central Bank*, pp. 14–18. For Page's second reading speech on the Bill see *CPD*, vol. 106, pp. 1264–92.

[14] Ibid., vol. 107. Charlton's speech begins on p. 1513, Makin's on p. 1729 and Anstey's on p. 1939. The following year Anstey wrote a pamphlet, *Money Power Strangles Australia*, in which he argued that the 1924 Act was the culmination of a whole series of offensives against the bank.

[15] *Labor Call*, 14 June 1923; *Westralian Worker*, 13 June 1924; Brisbane *Worker*, 27 March 1924; *Labor Daily*, almost any issue during May–June 1924; *Australian Worker*, 18 June, 16, 30 July, 29 October 1924.

[16] *Labor Call*, 3 September 1925; *Australian Worker*, 23 September 1925.

[17] *Labor Call*, 28 April 1921, 9 February, 23 November 1922. *Australian Worker*, 19 March, 23 April 1924, 3 June, 5 August, 25 December 1925, 8 December 1926, 10 August, 5 October 1927, 4 January 1928.

CHAPTER 5

[1] *Westralian Worker*, 18 July 1930.

2 For the most comprehensive account of this process see C. B. Schedvin, *Australia and the Great Depression*, chapter 6. See too, David Clark, 'A Closed Book? The Debate on Causes', in Judy Mackinolty (ed.), *The Wasted Years? Australia's Great Depression.*

3 A forerunner of the Niemeyer mission reported this concern in 1929. See 'Report of the British Economic Mission', *Commonwealth Parliamentary Papers* [*CPP*], 1929, vol. II, pp. 1231–72. On 2 December 1929 Professor Edwin Cannan wrote to Professor Theodore Gregory on the subject of Australia's slide off the gold standard, asking 'Is anything being done in influential quarters to stop the Australians from making currency fools of themselves?' See Sir Theodore Gregory papers, British Library of Political and Economic Science, Miscellaneous Collection 460.

4 Despite the objections of some radical members, Cabinet reappointed him on 4 August 1930. See Cabinet Minutes, Australian Archives, A3264. Scullin's main concern was that dumping Gibson would endanger Australia's delicate negotiations in London. See John Robertson, *J. H. Scullin*, p. 260.

5 See Schedvin, op. cit., pp. 132–5, 180–1.

6 Hopkins to Fergusson, 13 June 1930, Treasury Files, Public Record Office, London, T160/807/F11935/1.

7 *CPD*, vol. 126, p. 4844. Although, on 5 June, 'the consensus of Cabinet was that the proposed visit of N. be welcomed', the matter had not been raised in Caucus, Parliament or before the public prior to the announcement.

8 See *Report of the All-Australian Trade Union Congress*, Melbourne, February 1930; Australian Labor Party, *Official Report of Proceedings of the Twelfth Commonwealth Conference*, Canberra, May 1930; Weller (ed.), *Caucus Minutes*, vol. 2, p. 371.

9 Schedvin, op. cit., pp. 172–6.

10 Ibid., pp. 174–5. They were referred to a select committee, which finally reported in December 1930, approving the principle of a central bank but taking exception to a number of provisions in the Bills. They were eventually abandoned late in 1931.

11 *NSWPD*, vol. 122. p. 4534.

12 There are entries on Niemeyer, Gregory and Kershaw in *Who's Who, 1969*, and a substantial obituary for Niemeyer in *The Times*, 8 February 1971.

13 For a general survey of the Niemeyer mission see W. F. Mandle, *Going*

it Alone: Australia's National Identity in the Twentieth Century, chapter 4. The full text of his statement is reprinted in E. O. G. Shann and D. B. Copland (eds), *The Crisis in Australian Finance, 1929–1931: Documents on Budgetary and Economic Policy*, pp. 18–29. Some of his private opinions can be seen in Peter Love, 'Niemeyer's Australian Diary and other English records of his mission', *Historical Studies*, vol. 20, no. 79, pp. 267–77.

[14] *Labor Daily*, 22 August 1930. On 4 September 1930 the Adelaide *Advertiser* reported: 'Before the NSW ALP–Union Conference last week which recommended credit expansion and "repudiation", Anstey had "a long and private" conversation with Garden who later drafted and steered the resolution urging that action must be taken by the movement to stand up to Niemeyer, as a Cabinet majority will not'.

[15] Lang opened his campaign on 22 September. For a representative sample of his speeches see *Labor Daily*, 23 September–3 October 1930.

[16] *Sydney Morning Herald*, 29 October 1930. For an account of the mission's itinerary see Mandle, op. cit., and Love, op. cit. Niemeyer's claim that he was not a representative of British bondholders was strictly true. It was not until the mid-1930s that he became a member of the Council of Foreign Bondholders.

[17] *CPD*, vol. 127, p. 383.

[18] In a letter in 1935 Niemeyer stated categorically that he was not Jewish or of Jewish descent. A. J. T. Williams, Secretary of the Bank of England, to Peter Love, 20 December 1982.

CHAPTER 6

[1] The most reliable account of economic policy in this period remains C. B. Schedvin, *Australia and the Great Depression*. The most detailed studies of political developments are found in John Robertson, *J. H. Scullin*, and Peter Cook, The Scullin Government, 1929–1932.

[2] The economic indicators are in Schedvin, op. cit., pp. 210–11. The rates for trade union unemployment are in L. J. Louis and Ian Turner (eds), *The Depression of the 1930's*, p. 89. For a specific study of unemployment see Ray Broomhill, *Unemployed Workers: A Social History of the Great Depression in Adelaide*.

[3] Australasian Council of Trade Unions, *Minutes of Conference of Key Unions*, Melbourne, 9 September 1930. For a detailed discussion of the State Conference deliberations see L. J. Louis, *Trade Unions and the Depression*, pp. 52–5.

4 Weller and Lloyd (eds), *Federal Executive Minutes*, pp. 151–2. See also, *Labor Daily*, 16 October 1930; *Labor Call*, 23 October 1930.

5 For the Caucus debates see Weller (ed.), *Caucus Minutes*, vol. 2, pp. 389–418. For a discussion of the Irvine–Theodore relationship see Bruce McFarlane, *Professor Irvine's Economics in Australian Labour History, 1913–1933*. On Theodore's ambitions see Cook, op. cit., p. 262. Scullin's cablegram is reprinted in Shann and Copland (eds), *The Crisis in Australian Finance, 1929 to 1931*, p. 63.

6 Harvey's record of his interview with Scullin at the Savoy Hotel on 3 December 1930 is in Treasury files, Public Record Office, London, T160/396/F11935/02.

7 Quoted in Schedvin, op. cit., p. 195.

8 Weller, op. cit., pp. 416–18. Schedvin, op. cit., p. 227, doubts the extent to which the burden of sacrifice would have been equally shared.

9 Both the Lang and Theodore plans, as presented at the Conference, are in *CPP*, 1929-1931, vol. II, pp. 108–14, 121. For an economic analysis of the Lang Plan see David Clark, 'Was Lang Right?', in Heather Radi and Peter Spearritt (eds), *Jack Lang*, pp. 138–59. Cooksey's observations can be found in his review of Lang's *The Great Bust!*, in *Labour History*, no. 6, May 1964, pp. 64–6. Lang's *Labor Daily* articles appeared on 3, 4, 5, 6 February 1931.

10 For the theoretical ancestry of the two plans see McFarlane, op. cit., and Clark, op. cit. For a critical analysis of that school of thought see Michael Bleaney, *Underconsumption Theories.*

11 Schedvin, op. cit., pp. 230–2.

12 Australasian Council of Trade Unions, *Minutes of Special Congress*, Sydney Trades Hall, 16–22 February 1931.

13 For the two NSW Executive declarations see *Labor Daily*, 14 February 1931; *Sydney Morning Herald*, 21 February 1931. The Federal Executive decision is recorded in Weller and Lloyd (eds), *Federal Executive Minutes*, pp. 156–9.

14 *Labor Daily*, 24 February, 2 March 1931.

15 For the Caucus deliberations see Weller, op. cit., pp. 418–22. The NSW Conference resolution is reported in *Labor Daily*, 16 March 1931. The Federal Conference reply is in Australian Labor Party, *Official Report of Proceedings of the Special Federal Conference*, Sydney, 27 March 1931, pp. 15–16.

16 Schedvin, op. cit., pp. 233–4.

17 Theodore's second reading speech is in *CPD*, vol. 128, pp. 300–19. The correspondence between Theodore and Gibson is quoted in Schedvin, op. cit., p. 242. Gibson's evidence to the Senate is in *CPD*, vol. 129, pp. 1615–32.

18 For the advertisements see *Labor Daily*, 4 April 1931. For a detailed account see Kenneth Polden, 'The Collapse of the Government Savings Bank of New South Wales, 1931' in *Australian Economic History Review*, vol. XII, no. 1, March 1972, and Schedvin, op. cit., p. 235. O'Halloran was a former Secretary of the NSW Parliamentary Labor Party. His comments are in *Labor Daily*, 23 April 1931.

19 The history of the Old Guard has been exhaustively researched by Andrew Moore, 'Send Lawyers, Guns and Money', A Study of Conservative Para-military Organisations in New South Wales, 1930–32, Background and Sequel, 1917–1952. On the New Guard see Keith Amos, *The New Guard Movement, 1931–1935*. The suggestion by Dalton, the British Trade Commissioner, is in Treasury files, Public Record Office, London, T160/396/F11935/02. The same file contains Kershaw's comment that Dalton's suggestion was neither necessary nor desirable. It also contains an assessment of the situation in June 1931 by Hore-Ruthven, Governor of South Australia. On the Emergency Committee see Sir A. Grenfell Price, 'The Emergency Committee of South Australia and the Origin of the Premiers' Plan, 1931–2' in *South Australiana*, vol. 17, no. 1, March 1978.

20 For a detailed discussion of the Premiers' Plan see Schedvin, op. cit., chapters 10 and 11; Robertson, op. cit., chapter 21; and Cook, op. cit., chapter 7. Davidson's prediction is quoted in Schedvin, op. cit., p. 247.

21 The ministerial expression of regret is recorded in Cabinet Minutes, op. cit. The Caucus debate is in Weller, op. cit., pp. 431–2. Holloway resigned on 12 June, Culley on 24 June. For Holloway's reflections on this see chapter 13 of his memoirs, 'From Labor Council to Privy Council', National Library of Australia, MS 2098.

22 For details of each State Executive's resolution see Cook, op. cit., pp. 390–1. The Federal Executive ruling is in Weller and Lloyd, op. cit., p. 166. For the Conference decision see Australian Labor Party, *Special Federal Conference*, Melbourne, 27 August 1931, p. 6.

23 *CPD*, vol. 132, p. 1906.

24 *Labor Call*, 3 December 1931.

25 Theodore's radio talk is reported in the *Age*, 3 December 1931. McKenna's comment is in ibid., 4 December 1931; Anstey's in ibid., 7 December 1931.

[26] Theodore's definition of Lang Laborites is in ibid., 17 December 1931. For Lang Labor election propaganda see *Labor Daily*, 4–19 December 1931.

[27] See John Manning Ward, 'The Dismissal', in Radi and Spearritt, op. cit.

[28] The attendance of 'huge and enthusiastic' crowds had been a feature of the three main campaigns that Lang fought between October 1930 and June 1932. On 19 October 1930 he told an estimated 100 000 people in the Sydney Domain: 'Australians have earned the reputation of being a nation of fighters. In this election the whole of Australian idealism is being challenged by Sir Otto Niemeyer and the London financial interests'. See *Labor Daily*, 20 October 1930. In December 1931 he preached a similar message to another large crowd in the Domain. Ibid., 14 December 1931, says it was 150 000 but the *Age*, 12 December 1931, and the *Sydney Morning Herald*, 14 December 1931, put it at 80 000. For a stimulating discussion of the psychological and ideological wellsprings of Lang's career see Miriam Dixson, *Greater than Lenin?* For the first of several self-justifying books see J. T. Lang, *Why I Fight.*

[29] *Labor Daily*, 17 June 1932.

[30] With the exception of Tasmania, which remained staunchly conservative, popular opinion turned against all governments in this period. Conservative coalitions replaced Labor governments in Victoria in May 1932 and South Australia in April 1933; Labor regained office in Queensland in June 1932 and Western Australia in April 1933.

CHAPTER 7

[1] The economic statistics are in C. B. Schedvin, *Australia and the Great Depression*, p. 44, and Sheridan, *Mindful Militants*, p. 106.

[2] Douglas's major works include: *Economic Democracy*; *Credit Power and Democracy*; *These Present Discontents and the Labour Party and Social Credit*; *Social Credit*; *The Monopoly of Credit*; and *The New and the Old Economics*. For a detailed discussion of the social and economic doctrines of Douglas Social Credit see C. B. Macpherson, *Democracy in Alberta: Social Credit and the Party System.* For an analysis of the theory's influence in Australia see Baiba Berzins, The Social Credit Movement in Australia to 1940. For some examples of Australian criticism of the theory in the 1930s see F. J. Docker, *Douglas Delusions: a critical examination of the Douglas Social Credit Proposals*, and 'Report of the Royal Commission appointed to inquire

into the Monetary and Banking Systems at present in operation in Australia . . .', pp. 171–87. For a short discussion of the A + B theorem and an explanation of its basic fallacy in double counting see Bleaney, *Underconsumption Theories*, pp. 204–6.

3 Macpherson, op. cit., p. 111.

4 Douglas, *The Monopoly of Credit*, pp. 83–4.

5 For an exhaustive bibliography of Douglas Credit literature in Australia see Berzins, op. cit. 'By far the strongest force . . .' is quoted in Clark, 'Was Lang Right?', p. 155.

6 The Following account relies substantially upon Berzins, op. cit.

7 *Manifesto issued by the Douglas Credit Party of Australia*, Sydney, 1934. The party won 4.69 per cent of the total valid vote in the 1934 Federal election. The State by State breakdown of this figure is a good indicator of its regional support: New South Wales 4.72 per cent; Victoria 2.39 per cent; Queensland 4.61 per cent; South Australia 8.6 per cent; Western Australia 6.4 per cent; and Tasmania 11.58 per cent. See Hughes and Graham, *A Handbook of Australian Government and Politics, 1890–1964*, pp. 351–6.

8 Australian Labor Party, *Official Report of Proceedings of the 14th Commonwealth Conference*, Adelaide, July 1936, p. 5.

9 Keith Sinclair, *Walter Nash*, pp. 105–7, and Macpherson, op. cit., chapter 6.

10 *Labor Call*, 23 August 1934.

CHAPTER 8

1 See Weller (ed.), *Caucus Minutes*, vol. 3, p. 61. For a summary of the election campaign see Geoffrey Sawer, *Australian Federal Politics and Law, 1929–1949*, pp. 71–3. For the announcement by Lyons see *CPD*, vol. 147, p. 506. For a wider discussion of the Commission see Giblin, *The Growth of a Central Bank*, pp. 212–37.

2 *CPD*, vol. 146, pp. 1057–75.

3 Giblin, op. cit., p. 212; L. F. Crisp, *Ben Chifley*, p. 167; *CPD*, vol. 147, p. 630.

4 See *Labor Call*, 31 October 1935; *Westralian Worker*, 1 November 1935; Brisbane *Worker*, 31 December 1935; *Australian Worker*, 18 March 1936.

5 Tasmania, 'Monetary System: Report of Select Committee, with Minutes of Proceedings', *Journals and Printed papers of the Parliament*

of Tasmania, 1935, paper no. 25, p. 2. It was presented on 29 October.

[6] Caucus began the process of tidying up its monetary policy on 16 October 1935 when it agreed to establish a subcommittee to 'investigate the whole question of Defence, Immigration, National Insurance and Monetary Reform'. This was followed, on 21 May 1936, by the motion from Ward and Scullin. The report was presented on 24 July 1936 and adopted the following day. See Weller, op. cit., pp. 115, 138–42.

[7] Australian Labor Party, *Federal Conference Agenda Paper*, Adelaide, 27 July 1936, pp. 5–7, and Australian Labor Party, *Official Report of Proceedings of the 14th Commonwealth Conference*, Adelaide, July 1936.

[8] Crisp, *Ben Chifley*, p. 170, suggests that Caucus began its review of banking policy with the intention of making a submission. Weller and Lloyd, *Federal Executive Minutes*, p. 200, claim the Federal Executive decided at its only meeting in 1936 that 'there was no point in presenting evidence to the Royal Commission on Banking because of the personnel on the Commission'.

[9] See 'Report of the Royal Commission appointed to inquire into the Monetary and Banking Systems at present in operation in Australia . . .', *CPP*, session 1937, vol. 5. The recommendations are summarized on pp. 275–81.

[10] Chifley's minority report is on pp. 262–8.

[11] See: S. J. Butlin, 'The Banking Commission's Report', *Australian Quarterly*, vol. IX, no. 3, September 1937; *Labor Call*, 29 July 1937; *Australian Worker*, 28 July, 4, 18 August, 22 September 1937; Brisbane *Worker*, 20 July 1937; *Westralian Worker*, 23, 30 July, 6 August 1937; *Workers' Weekly Herald*, 1 October 1937.

[12] In May 1938 Holloway rather forlornly asked Page whether there was to be a discussion of the report. The Treasurer answered, in effect, 'If business permits'. See *CPD*, vol. 155, p. 1543.

[13] John Maynard Keynes, *The General Theory of Employment, Interest and Money*. See especially chapter 24, 'Concluding Notes on the Social Philosophy towards which the General Theory might lead'. On the underconsumptionists see pp. 324–7 and 364–71. See also Crisp, op. cit., p. 169, and H. C. Coombs, *Trial Balance*, pp. 3–6.

[14] Australian Labor Party, *Official Report of Proceedings of Special Federal Conferences*, Melbourne, 1942 and 1943, pp. 26–7. See also Jim Hagan, *The History of the ACTU*, pp. 186–7.

[15] For the most extensive account of post-war planning see S. J. Butlin and C. B. Schedvin, *War Economy, 1942–1945.* For a blow-by-blow description of how the White Paper was developed see Selwyn Cornish, 'Full Employment in Australia: The Genesis of White Paper'. For an insider's account see Coombs, op. cit., pp. 48–55.

[16] Ministerial comments by Ashley, Holloway, Keane, Lazzarini and Scully are in Prime Minister's Department, Australian Archives, CP 131/1 item 45/637. Ward promised to comment but appears not to have done so. He made his views abundantly clear during debate on ratification of the Bretton Woods Agreement. Beasley's observations are in CP 131/1 item 45/642. Departmental Officers' notes on 'Comments Received from ministers' are in CP 131/1 item 45/637. Lazzarini offered his own version in the pamphlet, *The 'How' in Post-War Planning.* For an example of how Keynesian language was translated, compare discussion of the 'multiplier' in chapter 10 of *The General Theory* with paragraph 22 of the White Paper on 'Full Employment in Australia', *CPP*, 1945–46, vol. 4, p. 1197.

[17] *CPD*, vol. 182, pp. 2237–40.

CHAPTER 9

[1] See Butlin and Schedvin, *War Economy*, pp. 661–7.

[2] Chifley told delegates to the 1945 ALP Federal Conference that he would not weary them with details about the IMF. He was true to his word. See Australian Labor Party, *Official Report of Proceedings of the 17th Commonwealth Triennial Conference*, Melbourne, November 1945, p. 44.

[3] The quote is from Keynes, *The General Theory,* p. 383. As early as 18 November 1944 the Hobart *Voice*, whose Social Credit leanings made it hypersensitive to such matters, had warned: 'Sir Robert Gibson, who forced the Premiers' Plan on Australia in 1931, was a gold idolator. So are the members of the Bank Board today, and the Australian representatives at Bretton Woods'.

[4] For a detailed account of Chifley's campaign see Crisp, *Ben Chifley,* chapter 14, and Weller and Lloyd, *Federal Executive Minutes,* pp. 323–5, 330–1. For the newspaper articles see *Westralian Worker,* 17, 24 January, 14 March 1947; *Australian Worker*, 15, 22 January 1947; and *Labor Call*, 9, 16 January 1947.

[5] The text of the broadcast was reprinted in the *Westralian Worker*, 10 May 1946. For a broad sample of Ward's publicity against Bretton Woods see E. J. Ward papers, National Library of Australia, MS 2396, series 15.

[6] For O'Flaherty's comments see *Australian Worker*, 6 March 1946; Cameron's, ibid., 4 December 1946, 15 January, 5 February 1947; Calwell's, ibid., 4 December 1946; Hodsdon's, *Westralian Worker*, 5 April 1946; and Lang's, *Century*, 21, 28 February, 7, 14 March 1947. The pamphlet was entitled *Bretton Woods*. The Melbourne THC Executive resolution is in *Labor Call*, 20 February 1947. On 30 January 1947 the same paper reported E. J. Trait's 'Labor Hour' talk in which he suggested that Bretton Woods was a guarantee of another depression. There were similar divisions in the New Zealand Labour Party. See Sinclair, *Walter Nash*, pp. 245–6.

[7] Nash was reported in the *Westralian Worker*, 10 January 1947; Crean in *Labor Call*, 30 January 1947.

[8] Crisp, op. cit., chapter 14; Weller, *Caucus Minutes*, vol. 3, pp. 412–13; *Age*, 7 March 1947.

[9] *Australian Worker*, 15, 22 January 1947.

[10] *CPD*, vol. 190, p. 1003. Chifley replied directly to Ward in the *Westralian Worker*, 14 March 1947, stating that international financiers would have no place in the IMF. But such accusations were commonly made in many countries. The World Bank was concerned by this general suspicion and so published a pamphlet that identified its senior staff. See *Who's Who in the International Bank for Reconstruction and Development*.

[11] *CPD*, vol. 190, pp. 936–9.

[12] For the House of Representatives vote see ibid., p. 1004. Those who spoke against it were Doris Blackburn, Archie Cameron, W. G. Turnbull, Lang, and G. J. Rankin. For the Senate debate see ibid., pp. 1059–84.

CHAPTER 10

[1] Giblin, *The Growth of a Central Bank*, pp. 341–4; Butlin and Schedvin, *War Economy*, pp. 612–13. For Chifley's speech see *CPD*, vol. 181, pp. 546–58. He did not refer to the Commission's recommendation that the board be retained. Instead, he chose to quote paragraph 543, which suggested that, had the bank acted differently in 1931–32, the effects of the depression would have been less harsh.

[2] *CPD*, vol. 182, pp. 2202–11.

[3] Australian Council of Trade Unions, *Minutes of ACTU Congress*, 1945, tenth session, p. 5. Australian Labor Party, *Official Report . . .*, pp. 22, 27.

[4] Detailed accounts of the events leading up to the famous '42 words' of 16 August 1947 can be found in A. L. May, *The Battle for the Banks*, chapters 1 and 2; Crisp, *Chifley*, chapter 20; and Blainey, *Gold and Paper*, chapter 22.

[5] It is not known whether the banks intended to mount a further challenge to sections 18–22. Crisp, op. cit., p. 325, says that the possibility of their doing so weighed heavily in Chifley's judgement of the situation. Blainey, op. cit., p. 364, claims that 'they were in fact convinced that no other section of the legislation could be thrown out as unconstitutional'.

[6] Cabinet Minutes, Australian Archives, A2703. It is ironic that the three ministers who were absent on that momentous occasion were Calwell, Dedman and Ward. See Crisp, op. cit., pp. 326–7, and Coombs, *Trial Balance*, pp. 115–16.

[7] See May, op. cit., pp. 14–16.

[8] *Australian Worker*, 20 August 1947. The reference to Great Britain concerned the nationalization of the Bank of England in February 1946. In 1945 the New Zealand Labour government had nationalized the Bank of New Zealand.

[9] 18 October 1947. Between then and the 1949 election it was increasingly clear that it had, in effect, become an anti-Labour paper.

[10] The NSW resolution is in the *Australian Worker*, 27 August 1947. The Melbourne THC view is in *Labor Call*, 28 August 1947. For the ACTU position see *Congress Report*, 3rd session, p. 2. See also Weller and Lloyd, *Federal Executive Minutes*, p. 354; *Westralian Worker*, 12 December 1947; Australian Labor Party, State of Victoria, *Report of 1948 Conference Decisions*, p. 3.

[11] *Labor Call* kept a running tally of public expressions by prominent Labor people. See, for example, 21 and 28 August 1947. See also May, op. cit., p. 16; and *Century*, 22 August 1947, for Lang's comments.

[12] Chifley's speech is in *CPD*, vol. 193, p. 14; James's, ibid., p. 35; and Calwell's, ibid., p. 59.

[13] The various speeches are located as follows: Chifley, ibid., vol. 194, p. 799; Ward, p. 1293; Williams, p. 1354; Langtry, p. 1442; Calwell, p. 1475; Dedman, p. 1406–7; and Lamp, vol. 195, p. 2449.

[14] *Australian Worker*, 17 September 1947.

[15] *CPD*, vol. 194, pp. 1279–91. The following account of the campaign relies substantially upon May, op. cit., in matters of detail. The general interpretation follows that offered by R. W. Connell and T. H. Irving,

'Yes Virginia, there is a ruling class', in Mayer and Nelson (eds), *Australian Politics: A Fourth Reader*, pp. 84–7. See also Crisp, op. cit., chapter 20, and Coombs, op. cit., chapter 4.

[16] See Denis Murphy, *Ken Laidlaw*, chapter 5.

[17] For an account of the legal challenges to the 1945 and 1947 Acts see David Marr, *Barwick*, chapter 7, and Geoffrey Sawer, *Australian Federal Politics and Law, 1929–1949*, pp. 212–14.

[18] See Robin Gollan, *Revolutionaries and Reformists*, chapter 6.

[19] See article by Sharkey in the *Communist Review*, September 1948, quoted in Gollan, op. cit., pp. 232–3.

Bibliography

This contains only those works referred to in the notes. A more extensive list of sources can be found in the master's thesis on which this book is based. Copies are available in the Borchardt Library, La Trobe University, and the National Library.

OFFICIAL PUBLICATIONS

1. Government

Australia, *Commonwealth Parliamentary Debates.*

——, 'Report of the British Economic Mission', *Commonwealth Parliamentary Papers*, 1929, vol. II.

——, 'Report of the Royal Commission appointed to inquire into the Monetary and Banking Systems at present in operation in Australia. . .', *Commonwealth Parliamentary Papers*, session 1937, vol. 5.

Dibbs, George. *The Imperial State Paper on 'The Australian Crisis of 1893'.* Sydney, Charles Potter, Government Printer, 1894.

New South Wales, 'Final Report from the Select Committee on Post Office Savings Bank - National Bank', *Votes and Proceedings of the Legislative Assembly*, session 1892–3, vol. II.

——, *Parliamentary Debates.*

Peel, A.G.V. *The Australian Crisis of 1893.* London, Her Majesty's Stationery Office, 1893.

Queensland, *Parliamentary Debates.*

South Australia, 'Final Report of the Select Committee of the Legislative Council on the Unemployed Problem', *Proceedings of the Parliament of South Australia*, 1894, part 2, paper no. 110A.

——, 'Progress Report of the Select Committee of the Legislative Council on the Unemployed Problem', *Proceedings of the Parliament of South Australia*, 1894, part 2, paper no. 110.

——, 'Report of Royal Commission appointed to consider the desirability of establishing a State Bank and Royal Mint', *Proceedings of the Parliament of South Australia*, 1889, vol. 2, paper no. 27.

Tasmania, 'Monetary System: Report of Select Committee, with Minutes of Proceedings', *Journal and Printed Papers of the Parliament of Tasmania*, 1935, paper no. 25.

Victoria, *Parliamentary Debates.*

——, 'Report of the Royal Commission on State Banking', *Papers Presented to Parliament*, Legislative Assembly, vol. IV, session 1895–6.

2. Labour Movement

All-Australian Trades Union Conference, *Official Report*, Melbourne, 20–25 June 1921.

All-Australian Trade Union Congress, *Manifesto of the National Executive of the Congress*, Melbourne, May 1916.

Australasian Council of Trade Unions, *Minutes of Conference of Key Unions*, Melbourne, 9 September 1930.

——, *Minutes of Special Congress*, Sydney, 16–22 February 1931.

——, *Report of the All-Australian Trade Union Congress*, Melbourne, February 1930.

Australian Council of Trade Unions, *Congress Report*, 1947.

——, *Minutes of ACTU Congress*, 1945.

Australian Labor Party, *Australian Labor Conference, Official Report*, Sydney, 1902.

——, *Federal Conference Agenda Paper*, Adelaide, 27 July 1936.

——, *Official Report of Proceedings of the 14th Commonwealth Conference*, Adelaide, July 1936.

——, *Official Report of Proceedings of the 17th Commonwealth Triennial Conference*, Melbourne, November 1945.

——, *Official Report of Proceedings of Special Federal Conferences*, Melbourne, 1942 and 1943.

——, *Official Report of Proceedings of the Special Federal Conference*, Sydney, 27 March 1931.

——, *Official Report of the Eighth Commonwealth Conference*, Sydney, June 1919.

——, *Official Report of the Fourth Commonwealth Political Labour Conference*, Brisbane, 1908.

——, *Official Report of Proceedings of the Ninth Commonwealth Conference*, Brisbane, October 1921.

——, *Official Report of Proceedings of the Twelfth Commonwealth Conference*, Canberra, May 1930.

——, *Special Federal Conference*, Melbourne, 27 August 1931.

——, State of Victoria, *Annual Conference*, Melbourne, 18–21 April 1919.

——, *Report of 1948 Conference Decisions*, Melbourne, 1948.

Political Labor Council of Victoria, *Annual Conference*, Melbourne, 21–24 April 1916.

NEWSPAPERS AND PERIODICALS

Advertiser, Adelaide
Age, Melbourne
Argus, Melbourne
Australian Worker, Sydney
Australian Workman, Sydney
Beacon, Melbourne
Bulletin, Sydney
Century, Sydney
Commonweal and Worker's Advocate, Melbourne
Daily Herald, Adelaide
Daily Standard, Brisbane
Flame, Broken Hill
Hard Cash, Sydney
Herald, Melbourne
Hummer, Wagga Wagga
Labor Call, Melbourne
Labor Daily, Sydney
New Order, Sydney
People, Sydney
Shearer's and General Labourer's Record, Melbourne
Socialist, Melbourne
Socialist, Sydney
Sydney Morning Herald, Sydney
Tocsin, Melbourne
Voice, Hobart
Westralian Worker, Perth
Worker, Brisbane
Worker, Melbourne
Worker, Sydney
Workers' Weekly Herald, Adelaide

BOOKS, ARTICLES AND PAMPHLETS

Amos, Keith. *The New Guard Movement, 1931–1935*. Melbourne, Melbourne University Press, 1976.

Anstey, Frank. *The Kingdom of Shylock* (revised edition). Melbourne, Labor Call Print, 1917.

——. *Money Power*. Melbourne, Fraser and Jenkinson, 1921.

——. *Money Power Strangles Australia*. Perth, Westralian Worker, n.d. [1925]

——. *Monopoly and Democracy: The Land Question of Victoria*. Melbourne, Labor Call Print, 1906.

——. *Red Europe*. Melbourne, Fraser and Jenkinson, 1919.

Australian Railways Union. *Bretton Woods*. Sydney, the union, 1947.

Beazley, Kim. 'The Labor Party and the Origins of the Commonwealth Bank', *Australian Journal of Politics and History*, vol. IX, no. 1, May 1963.

Bellamy, Edward. *Looking Backward, 2000–1887*. New York, Signet, 1960 (originally published 1888).

Berlin, Isaiah. *Russian Thinkers*. Harmondsworth, Penguin, 1979.

Blainey, Geoffrey. *Gold and Paper: A History of the National Bank of Australasia Limited*. Melbourne, Georgian House, 1958.

Bleaney, Michael. *Underconsumption Theories: A History and Critical Analysis*. London, Lawrence and Wishart, 1976.

Boehm, E. A. *Prosperity and Depression in Australia, 1887–1897*. London, Oxford University Press, 1971.

Broomhill, Ray. *Unemployed Workers: A Social History of the Great Depression in Adelaide*. St Lucia, University of Queensland Press, 1978.

Burgmann, Verity. 'Capital and Labour', in Ann Curthoys and Andrew Markus (eds). *Who Are Our Enemies? Racism and the Working Class in Australia*. Sydney, Hale and Iremonger in association with the Australian Society for the Study of Labour History, 1978.

Butlin, N. G. *Private Capital Formation in Australia: Estimates, 1861–1900*. Canberra, Australian National University Press, 1955.

Butlin, S. J. *Australia and New Zealand Bank: The Bank of Australasia and the Union Bank of Australia Limited*, 1828–1951. Melbourne, Longmans, 1961.

——. 'The Banking Commission's Report', *Australian Quarterly*, vol. IX, no. 3, September 1937.

——. *The Foundations of the Australian Monetary System, 1788–1851*. Sydney, Sydney University Press, 1968.

—— and Schedvin, C. B. *War Economy, 1942–1945*. Canberra, Australian War Memorial, 1977.

Cannon, Michael. *The Land Boomers*. Melbourne, Melbourne University Press, 1966.

Canovan, Margaret. *Populism*. London, Junction Books, 1981.

Chernyshevsky, N. G. *What is to be Done? Tales About New People*. New York, Vintage Books, 1961 (originally published 1863).

Clark, David, 'A Closed Book? The Debate on Causes', in Judy Mackinolty (ed.). *The Wasted Years? Australia's Great Depression*. Sydney, George Allen and Unwin, 1981.

——. 'Was Lang Right?', in Heather Radi and Peter Spearritt (eds). *Jack Lang*. Sydney, Hale and Iremonger, 1977.

Coghlan, T. A. *Labour and Industry in Australia from the First Settlement in 1788 to the Establishment of the Commonwealth in 1901*. Vol. 3, London, Oxford University Press, 1918.

Collins, Tom (pseud.) [Joseph Furphy]. *Such is Life*. Melbourne, Lloyd O'Neil, 1970 (originally published 1903).

Connell, R. W. and Irving, T. H. *Class Structure in Australian History.* Melbourne, Longman and Cheshire, 1980.

——. 'Yes Virginia, there is a Ruling Class', in Henry Mayer and Helen Nelson (eds). *Australian Politics: A Fourth Reader.* Melbourne, Cheshire, 1976.

Cooksey, Robert. Review of J. T. Lang, *The Great Bust*, in *Labour History*, no. 6, May 1964.

Coombs, H. C. *Trial Balance.* Melbourne, Macmillan, 1981.

Coward, Dan. 'Crime and Punishment', in John Iremonger, John Merritt and Graeme Osborne (eds). *Strikes: Studies in Twentieth Century Australian Social History.* Sydney, Angus and Robertson in association with the Australian Society for the Study of Labour History, 1973.

Crisp, L. F. *Ben Chifley; a Political Biography.* Melbourne, Longmans, 1960.

——. *The Australian Federal Labour Party, 1901–1951.* London, Longmans, 1955.

Di Tella, Torcuato. 'Populism and Reform in Latin America', in Claudio Veliz (ed.). *Obstacles to Change in Latin America.* London, Oxford University Press, 1965.

Dixson, Miriam. *Greater Than Lenin? Lang and Labor, 1916–1932.* Melbourne, Melbourne Politics Monographs, 1977.

Docker, F. J. *Douglas Delusions: A Critical Examination of the Douglas Social Credit Proposals.* Sydney, Angus and Robertson, 1933.

Donnelly, Ignatius (pseud.) [Edmund Boisgilbert]. *Caesar's Column: A Story of the Twentieth Century.* London, Sampson, Low, Marston, n.d. (originally published 1891).

Douglas, C. H. *The Monopoly of Credit.* London, Chapman and Hall, 1931.

Douglas Credit Party of Australia. *Manifesto Issued by the Douglas Credit Party of Australia.* Sydney, 1934.

Ebbels, R. N. *The Australian Labor Movement, 1850–1907.* Sydney, Australasian Book Society, 1960.

Evatt, H. V. *Australian Labour Leader: The Story of W. A. Holman and the Labour Movement.* Sydney, Angus and Robertson, 1940.

Flürscheim, Michael. 'A Perfect Money and its Effects', *New Zealand Illustrated Magazine*, August 1901.

Frewen, Moreton. 'The Crime in America that Impoverishes Australia', *Review of Reviews*, 20 March 1895.

Germani, Gino. *Authoritarianism, Facism, and National Populism.* New Brunswick, Transaction Books, 1978.

Giblin, L. F. *The Growth of a Central Bank: the Development of the Commonwealth Bank of Australia, 1924–1945.* Melbourne, Melbourne University Press, 1951.

Gilmore, Mary. 'Colonia Cosme', in Charles Higham and Michael Wilding (eds). *Australians Abroad.* Melbourne, Cheshire, 1967.

Gollan, Robin. 'The Australian Impact', in Sylvia E. Bowman (ed.). *Edward Bellamy Abroad.* New York, Twayne, 1962.

——. *The Commonwealth Bank of Australia: Origins and Early History.* Canberra, Australian National University Press, 1968.

——. *Radical and Working Class Politics: A Study of Eastern Australia, 1850–1910.* Melbourne, Melbourne University Press in association with the Australian National University, 1960.

——. *Revolutionaries and Reformists: Communism and the Australian Labour Movement, 1920–1955.* Canberra, Australian National University Press, 1975.

Gombrich, E. H. *Meditations on a Hobby Horse and other essays on the theory of art.* London, Phaidon, 1978, chapter 'The Cartoonist's Armoury'.

Goodwin, Craufurd D. W. *Economic Enquiry in Australia.* Durham, Duke University Press, 1966.

Hagan, Jim. *The History of the A.C.T.U.* Melbourne, Longman Cheshire, 1981.

Hagen, C. von. *The Banking Crisis and General Depression.* Newtown, the author, 1893.

Hancock, W. K. *Australia.* London, Benn, 1930.

Hannan, G. 'William Lane—Mateship and Utopia', in D. J. Murphy, R. B. Joyce and C. A. Hughes (eds). *Prelude to Power: The Rise of the Labor Party in Queensland, 1885–1915.* Brisbane, Jacaranda, 1970.

Hicks, John D. *The Populist Revolt: A History of the Farmers' Alliance and the People's Party.* Minneapolis, University of Minnesota Press, 1931.

Hobsbawm, E. J. *Primitive Rebels: Studies in Archaic Forms of Social Movement in the 19th and 20th Centuries.* Manchester, Manchester University Press, 1959.

Hobson, J. A. *The Evolution of Modern Capitalism: A Study of Machine Production.* London, Walter Scott Publishing Co., 1916 (originally published 1894).

Hofstadter, Richard. *The Age of Reform: From Bryan to F.D.R.* New York, Vintage Books, 1955.

Holder, R. F. *Bank of New South Wales: A History.* 2 vols, Sydney, Angus and Robertson, 1970.

Hughes, Colin A. and Graham, B. D. *A Handbook of Australian Government and Politics, 1890–1964.* Canberra, Australian National University Press, 1968.

International Bank for Reconstruction and Development, *Who's Who in the International Bank for Reconstruction and Development.* Washington, the bank, 1947.

Ionescu, Ghita and Gellner, Ernest (eds). *Populism: Its Meaning and National Characteristics.* London, Weidenfeld and Nicolson, 1969.

Irving, Terry. 'Socialism, Working Class Mobilization and the Origins of the Labor Party', in Bruce O'Meagher (ed.). *The Socialist Objective: Labor and Socialism.* Sydney, Hale and Iremonger, 1983.

Kendall, Walter. *The Revolutionary Movement in Britain, 1900–21: The Origins of British Communism.* London, Weidenfeld and Nicolson, 1969.

Keynes, John Maynard. *The General Theory of Employment, Interest and Money.* London, Macmillan, 1936.

Kiernan, Brian (ed.). *Portable Australian Authors: Henry Lawson.* St Lucia, University of Queensland Press, 1976.

Laclau, Ernesto. *Politics and Ideology in Marxist Theory: Capitalism, Fascism, Populism.* London, Verso, 1979.

Lane, E. H. *Dawn to Dusk: Reminiscences of a Rebel.* Brisbane, William Brooks, 1939.

Lane, William. *The Workingman's Paradise: An Australian Labour Novel.* Brisbane, The Worker, 1892.

Lang, J. T. *The Great Bust! The Depression of the Thirties.* Sydney, Angus and Robertson, 1962.

——. *Why I Fight.* Sydney, Labor Daily, 1934.

Lazzarini, H. *The 'How' in Post-War Planning.* Westmead, n.d.

Louis, L. J. *Trade Unions and the Depression: A Study of Victoria, 1930–1932.* Canberra, Australian National University Press, 1968.

—— and Turner, Ian. *The Depression of the 1930's*, Melbourne, Cassell, 1968.

Love, Peter. 'Niemeyer's Australian Diary and Other English Records of His Mission'. *Historical Studies*, October 1982.

McFarlane, Bruce. *Professor Irvine's Economics in Australian Labour History, 1913–1933.* Canberra, Australian Society for the Study of Labour History, 1966.

Macpherson, C. B. *Democracy in Alberta: Social Credit and the Party System.* Toronto, University of Toronto Press, 1962.

McQueen, Humphrey. *A New Britannia. An argument concerning the social origins of Australian radicalism and nationalism.* Ringwood, Penguin, 1970.

Mandle, W. F. *Going it Alone: Australia's National Identity in the Twentieth Century.* Ringwood, Allen Lane, 1978.

Markey, Ray. 'Populist Politics', in Ann Curthoys and Andrew Markus (eds). *Who Are Our Enemies? Racism and the Working Class in Australia.* Sydney, Hale and Iremonger in association with the Australian Society for the Study of Labour History, 1978.

Markus, Andrew. *Fear and Hatred: Purifying Australia and California, 1850–1901.* Sydney, Hale and Iremonger, 1979.

Marr, David. *Barwick.* Sydney, George Allen and Unwin, 1980.

May, A. L. *The Battle for the Banks.* Sydney, Sydney University Press, 1968.

Murphy, Denis. *Ken Laidlaw, A White Collar Union Leader*. Brisbane, Australian Bank Employees' Union, Queensland Division, 1979.

Murphy, D. J. (ed.) *Labor in Politics: The State Labor Parties in Australia, 1880–1920*. St Lucia, University of Queensland Press, 1975.

Nairn, Bede. *Civilising Capitalism: The Labor Movement in New South Wales, 1870–1900*. Canberra, Australian National University Press, 1973.

Polden, Kenneth. 'The Collapse of the Government Savings Bank of New South Wales, 1931', *Australian Economic History Review*, vol. XII, no. 1, March 1972.

Price, Sir A. Grenfell. 'The Emergency Committee of South Australia and the Origin of the Premiers' Plan, 1931–2', *South Australiana*, vol. 17, no. 1, March 1978.

Rawson, D. W. *Labor in Vain? A Survey of the Australian Labor Party*. Melbourne, Longmans, 1966.

Robertson, John. *J. H. Scullin: A Political Biography*. Nedlands, University of Western Australia Press, 1974.

Roderick, Colin (ed.). *Henry Lawson: Collected Verse, vol. 1, 1885–1900*. Sydney, Angus and Robertson, 1967.

Sawer, Geoffrey. *Australian Federal Politics and Law, 1929–1949*. Melbourne, Melbourne University Press, 1963.

——. *The Australian Constitution*. Canberra, Australian Government Publishing Service, 1977.

Schedvin, Bernie. 'E. G. Theodore and the London Pastoral Lobby', *Politics*, vol. V, no. 1, May 1970.

Schedvin, C. B. *Australia and the Great Depression: A Study of Economic Development and Policy in the 1920s and 1930s*. Sydney, Sydney University Press, 1970.

Scott, Ernest. *Australia During the War*. Vol. XI of C. E. W. Bean (ed.). *Official History of Australia in the War of 1914–18*. Sydney, Angus and Robertson, 1939.

Scott, J. M. *The Circulating Sovereign*. Sydney, the author, 1903.

Shanin, Teodor. 'The Peasant Dream: Russia 1905–7', in Raphael Samuel and Gareth Stedman Jones (eds). *Culture, Ideology and Politics: Essays for Eric Hobsbawm*. London, Routledge and Kegan Paul, 1983.

Shann, E. O. G. and Copland, D. B. (eds). *The Crisis in Australian Finance, 1929–1931: Documents on Budgetary and Economic Policy*. Sydney, Angus and Robertson, 1931.

Sheridan, T. *Mindful Militants: The Amalgamated Engineering Union in Australia, 1920–72*. Melbourne, Cambridge University Press, 1975.

Sinclair, Keith. *Walter Nash*. Auckland, Auckland University Press, 1976.

Souter, Gavin. *A Peculiar People: The Australians in Paraguay*. Sydney, Angus and Robertson, 1968.

Spence, W. G. *Australia's Awakening: Thirty Years in the Life of an Australian Agitator*. Sydney, The Worker Trustees, 1909.

Tindall, George Brown (ed.). *A Populist Reader: Selections from the Works of American Populist Leaders*. New York, Harper, 1966.

Trebilcock, Clive. 'Radicalism and the Armament Trust', in A. J. A. Morris (ed.). *Edwardian Radicalism, 1900–1914: Some Aspects of British Radicalism*. London, Routledge and Kegan Paul, 1974.

Turner, Ian. 'Frank Anstey', in Bede Nairn and Geoffrey Serle (eds). *Australian Dictionary of Biography*. Vol. 7, Melbourne, Melbourne University Press, 1979.

——. *Industrial Labour and Politics: The Labour Movement in Eastern Australia, 1900–1921*. Canberra, Australian National University Press, 1965.

——. '1914–1919', in F. K. Crowley (ed.). *A New History of Australia*. Melbourne, William Heinemann, 1974.

Venturi, Franco. *Roots of Revolution: A History of the Populist and Socialist Movements in Nineteenth Century Russia*. New York, Knopf, 1964.

Ward, John Manning. 'The Dismissal', in Heather Radi and Peter Spearritt (eds). *Jack Lang*. Sydney, Hale and Iremonger, 1977.

Waterson, D. B. 'Thomas McIlwraith: A Colonial Entrepreneur', in D. J. Murphy and R. B. Joyce (eds). *Queensland Political Portraits, 1859–1952*. St Lucia, University of Queensland Press, 1978.

Weller, Patrick (ed.). *Caucus Minutes, 1901–1949: Minutes of the Meetings of the Federal Parliamentary Labor Party*. 3 vols, Melbourne, Melbourne University Press, 1975.

—— and Lloyd, Beverley (eds). *Federal Executive Minutes, 1915–1955: Minutes of the Meetings of the Federal Executive of the Australian Labor Party*. Melbourne, Melbourne University Press, 1978.

Young, Irwin. *Theodore: His Life and Times*. Sydney, Alpha Books, 1971.

Zouabi (pseud. ?). *The Banking System: Australia's Incubus, an Immediate Remedy*. Brisbane, the author, 1894.

UNPUBLISHED MATERIAL

1. Manuscripts

Australia, Cabinet Minutes of the Scullin Government, Australian Archives, A 3264.

Australia, Prime Minister's Department, Papers relating to White Paper on Full Employment, Australian Archives, CP 131/1 items 45/637 and 642.

Cornish, Selwyn. Full Employment in Australia: The Genesis of a White Paper. Paper presented to the Post-War Reconstruction Conference, Australian National University, 1981.

Gregory, Sir Theodore. Papers. British Library of Political and Economic Science, Miscellaneous Collection 460.

Holloway, E. J. From Labour Council to Privy Council. National Library of Australia, MS 2098.

United Kingdom, Treasury Files, Public Record Office, London, T160/396/F11935/02, T160/807/F11935/1.

Ward, E. J. Papers. National Library of Australia, MS 2396.

2. Theses

Cook, Peter. The Scullin Government, 1929–1932. PhD, Australian National University, 1970.

Hewitt, G. The Victorian Socialist Party. MA, La Trobe University, 1974.

Love, Peter. Labor and the Money Power, 1890–1950: A Study of Australian Labor Populism. MA, La Trobe University, 1980.

Moore, Andrew. 'Send Lawyers, Guns and Money': A Study of Conservative Para-military Organizations in New South Wales, 1930–32; Background and Sequel, 1917–1952. PhD, La Trobe University, 1982.

Index

www.ingramcontent.com/pod-product-compliance
Lightning Source LLC
LaVergne TN
LVHW050619100826
845148LV00011B/1649

* 9 7 8 1 5 9 7 4 0 6 5 4 3 *